Translation, Adaptation and Transformation

Continuum Advances in Translation

Series Editor:
Jeremy Munday, Centre for Translation Studies, University of Leeds

Published in association with the International Association for Translation and Intercultural Studies (IATIS), Continuum Studies in Translation aims to present a series of books focused around central issues in translation and interpreting. Using case studies drawn from a wide range of different countries and languages, each book presents a comprehensive examination of current areas of research within translation studies written by academics at the forefront of the field. The thought-provoking books in this series are aimed at advanced students and researchers of translation studies.

Cognitive Explorations of Translation: Eyes, Keys, Taps
Edited by Sharon O'Brien
Media Translation
Edited by Judith Inggs and Libby Meintjes
Translation as Intervention
Edited by Jeremy Munday
Translation Studies in Africa: Central Issues in Interpreting and Literary and Translation: Theory and Practice in Dialogue
Edited by Rebecca Hyde Parker, Karla L. Guadarrama García, and Antoinette Fawcett
Translator and Interpreter Training: Issues, Methods, and Debates
Edited by John Kearns

Translation, Adaptation and Transformation

Laurence Raw

Continuum Advances in Translation Studies

BLOOMSBURY
NEW DELHI • LONDON • OXFORD • NEW YORK • SYDNEY

BLOOMSBURY INDIA
Bloomsbury Publishing India Pvt. Ltd
Second Floor, LSC Building No. 4, DDA Complex, Pocket C–6&7,
Vasant Kunj, New Delhi 110070

BLOOMSBURY, BLOOMSBURY ACADEMIC INDIA and the Diana logo are trademarks of Bloomsbury Publishing Plc

First published in India 2024

This edition published with permission from Bloomsbury Publishing Plc,
50 Bedford Square, London, WC1B3DP, UK

British Library Cataloguing-in-Publication Data
A catalogue record for this book is available from the British Library

Library of Congress Cataloging-in-Publication Data

ISBN: 978-93-54359-95-8

Typeset by Newgen Imaging Systems Pvt Ltd, Chennai, India
Printed at Manipal Technologies Limited, Manipal
To find out more about our authors and books
visit www.bloomsbury.com and sign up for our newsletters

Contents

Series Editor's Preface vii

Preface viii

Acknowledgements x

Notes on Contributors xi

Introduction: Identifying Common Ground 1
Laurence Raw

Chapter 1: Adaptation and Appropriation: Is there a Limit? 21
Hugo Vandal-Sirois and Georges L. Bastin

Chapter 2: Translation and Adaptation – Two Sides of an Ideological Coin 42
Katja Krebs

Chapter 3: The Authenticity in 'Adaptation': A Theoretical Perspective from Translation Studies 54
Cynthia S. K. Tsui

Chapter 4: Translation and Rewriting: Don't Translators 'Adapt' When They 'Translate'? 61
João Azenha and Marcelo Moreira

Chapter 5: Adapting, Translating and Transforming: Cultural Mediation in Ping Chong's *Deshima* and *Pojagi* 81
Tanfer Emin Tunç

Chapter 6: The Transadaptation of Shakespeare's Christian Dimension in China's Theatre – To Translate, or Not to Translate? 99
Jenny Wong

Chapter 7: 'Tradaptation' *Dans le Sens Québécois*: A Word for the Future 112
Susan Knutson

Chapter 8: *Waltz with Bashir* as a Case of Multidimensional Translation 123
Ayelet Kohn and Rachel Weissbrod

Chapter 9: The Paradoxes of Textual Fidelity: Translation and Intertitles in Victor Sjöström's Silent Film Adaptation of Henrik Ibsen's *Terje Vigen* 145
Eirik Frisvold Hanssen and Anna Sofia Rossholm

Chapter 10: Les Liaisons Dangeureuses à l'Anglais: Examining Traces of 'European-ness' in *Cruel Intentions*, *Dangerous Liaisons* and *Valmont* 162
Sarah Artt

Chapter 11: Turnips or Sweet Potatoes . . . ? 171
Kate Eaton

Chapter 12: The Mind's Ear: Imagination, Emotions and Ideas in the Intersemiotic Transposition of Housman's Poetry to Song 188
Mike Ingham

Chapter 13: Cultural Adaptation and Translation: Some Thoughts about Chinese Students Studying in a British University 210
Ruth Cherrington

Index 219

Series Editor's Preface

The aim of this new series is to provide an outlet for advanced research in the broad interdisciplinary field of translation studies. Consisting of monographs and edited themed collections of the latest work, it should be of particular interest to academics and postgraduate students researching in translation studies and related fields, and also to advanced students studying translation and interpreting modules.

Translation studies has enjoyed huge international growth over recent decades in tandem with the expansion in both the practice of translation globally and in related academic programs. The understanding of the concept of translation itself has broadened to include not only interlingual but also various forms of intralingual translation. Specialized branches or subdisciplines have developed for the study of interpreting, audiovisual translation, and sign language, among others. Translation studies has also come to embrace a wide range of types of intercultural encounter and transfer, interfacing with disciplines as varied as applied linguistics, comparative literature, computational linguistics, creative writing, cultural studies, gender studies, philosophy, postcolonial studies, sociology, and so on. Each provides a different and valid perspective on translation, and each has its place in this series.

This is an exciting time for translation studies, and the new Continuum Advances in Translation Studies series promises to be an important new plank in the development of the discipline. As General Editor, I look forward to overseeing the publication of important new work that will provide insights into all aspects of the field.

Jeremy Munday
General Editor
University of Leeds, UK

Preface

Piotr Kuhiwczak

The terms adaptation and translation have many contextual meanings. In a cultural and literary context, adaptation signals the change of medium through which meaning is communicated. In a wider social context the term acquires even more meanings and generates a wider range of associations. To be able to adapt means to be able to survive or navigate in uncharted territory without losing an intrinsic sense of identity. Walter Benjamin's essay *The Task of the Translator* sees translation as a strategy that allows texts to survive and adapt to a new cultural milieu. Paradoxically, the essay (which was written in 1923) has survived because of its multiple translations and disagreements among scholars about the possible interpretations of what Benjamin intended to communicate. So the history of the essay's reception serves as the best illustration for Benjamin's thesis about the adaptive power of translation.

Interest in *The Task of the Translator* was not the case of an accidental revival of a forgotten intellectual work. The essay was rediscovered at a particular historical juncture when translation began to be viewed as something more than simple decoding and recoding of printed text. It would be pointless to argue what came first – the rediscovery of Benjamin's essay or the rise of interest in translation as a cultural phenomenon. Let's agree that the two 'discoveries' were interconnected and took place sometime in the late 1970s and the early 1980s. In countries with a long history of multilingual communication, translation was viewed as a significant cultural and social phenomenon, but in the English-speaking countries this was not the case. It was a combination of genius, clever planning and pure coincidence that in the early 1980s Warwick University established a research centre devoted to what is commonly called now translation studies. At that time the term was completely new, and many viewed it if not with hostility, then at least with considerable suspicion. The uniqueness of the centre rested in its interdisciplinary nature because it attracted scholars from related but distinct disciplines. They put aside many differences in the name of intellectual curiosity and set out to adapt to what this unusual combination of subjects could produce. The cocktail of subjects included comparative literature, cultural studies, applied linguistics, history, media studies, literary theory and postcolonial studies and at some point politics and sociology. Despite a good dose of scepticism surrounding the centre, the experiment survived and expanded. Publications began to proliferate, conferences were attended by scholars from all corners of the world and postgraduate students were willing to spend several years at Warwick to be supervised by staff at what was then known as the Centre for Translation and Comparative Cultural Studies (CTCCS).

The unexpected and rapid closure of the centre in 2009 had the impact of a Pacific tsunami; nevertheless the spirit of the place has produced a legacy that no academic manager will be able to control. CTCCS produced graduates who went off to set up similar academic outfits all over the world. They have developed what they learned at Warwick and adapted this new knowledge to their local circumstances. With time, translation studies, and to a lesser extent adaptation studies, has been transformed into a significant branch of the humanities. What the students took away with them from Warwick was a conviction that culture – in all senses of the term – was about change, survival and adaptation; translation was a major force that made the survival possible. At a time when the humanities are under a major managerial onslaught, the story of CTCCS injects some optimism. This volume is itself a testimony to the work of the centre over a quarter of a century.

Acknowledgements

The inspiration for this anthology came from two sources. The first came from a colleague in my old department at Başkent University, whose perpetual questioning as to the academic validity of analysing adapted texts prompted me to investigate the issue further. The second came on a cold yet clear afternoon in the English Midlands, when I was discussing the relationship between translation and adaptation with my old friend Joanne Collie of the University of Warwick. Out of such discussions came the idea to put together this collection, in which scholars from translation and adaptation studies could contribute their ideas. Originally Joanne was to have co-edited this anthology, but had to withdraw at the last moment due to other commitments. Nonetheless this anthology would not have come about without her invaluable support.

I would like to thank Jeremy Munday, Director of the Centre for Translation Studies at the University of Leeds, and General Editor of the Continuum Studies in Translation series, for supporting this project as well as offering invaluable advice and suggestions. I'd also like to thank Gurdeep Mattu of Continuum for green-lighting the project, and Colleen Coalter for her editorial guidance.

Inevitably, with a project of this nature, I have relied on the generous support of referees from a variety of disciplines. In alphabetical order, I'd like to pay tribute to: Veronica Alfano, John Burton, Dirk Delabastita, Pedro de Senna, Ken Garner, Edwin Gentzler, Richard J. Hand, Lucia Krämer, Hyuneson Lee, Thomas Leitch, Kara McKechnie, John Milton, Márta Minier, Frank Su, Lawrence Venuti, James M. Welsh and Camilla Werner.

Last, but not, least, I'd like to pay tribute to the Centre for Translation and Comparative Cultural Studies at the University of Warwick. Sadly the Centre ceased to exist in 2009, the victim of a change in university policy. However its legacy lingers on in successive generations of academics and learners who worked and studied there. They include: Ruth Cherrington and Cynthia S. K. Tsui (both of whom contributed interesting pieces), Joanne Collie, David Dabydeen, John Gilmore and former Directors Lynne Long and Piotr Kuhiwczak (who kindly contributed the preface). This anthology is for you all.

Notes on Contributors

Sarah Artt is Lecturer in English and Film at Edinburgh Napier University, United Kingdom. She holds degrees from Brock, McGill, and Queen Margaret Universities. Her research interests include adaptation and transnational cinema, with the occasional foray into popular television. Her teaching interests centre around science fiction literature and cinema, contemporary Hollywood cinema, women's writing and filmmaking, and narrative structure in literature and film. Her previous publications have dealt with cult cinema as well as classic screen adaptations, and have appeared in edited collections with Palgrave and in the *Journal for Adaptation in Film and Performance.*

João Azenha is Professor of Translation Theory at the German Institute of the Department of Modern Languages of the University of São Paulo, Brazil. As a researcher, he works with Translation Theories in the German Romanticism and Translation for Children and Young People. Among his publications in these fields are: *The Translator as a Creative Genius: Robert Schumann* (John Benjamins, 2004) and *Dependencies, Asymmetries and Challenges in Translating for Children and Young People in Brazil* (EDUFBA, 2008). As a translator from the German of books for children and the youth he has published the series *Der Kleine Vampir* (The small vampire), by Angela Sommer-Bodenburg, *Wo Warst du, Robert (*Where have you been, Robert?), by Hans-Magnus Enzensberger, and *Sophies Welt* (Sophie's World), by Jostein Gaarder, among others.

Georges L. Bastin, Ph.D. in Translation Studies from the Université de Paris III, is full professor in the Département de linguistique et de traduction at the Université de Montréal, Canada and Head of the Département de littératures et de langues modernes. He is the author of *Traducir o adaptar?*, of two entries of the *Routledge Encyclopaedia of Translation Studies,* and has published in *Meta, TTR, The Translator, La Linguistique, The Interpreter's Newsletter,* and other journals. He heads the Research Group on Translation History in Latin America (www.histal.umontreal.ca) and edited two *Meta* special issues on translation history (vol. 49, no. 3 and vol. 50, no. 3). He co-edited

Charting the Future of Translation History (University of Ottawa Press, 2006). Since 2009, he has been *Meta* chief editor.

Ruth L. Cherrington trained as a sociologist (B.Sc. Sociology, Bath; M.Sc. Sociology, London School of Economics; Ph.D., University of London, – School of Oriental and African Studies), and taught at a number of Universities in the United Kingdom and overseas, including China and Eastern/Central Europe. She conducted research into teaching and learning methods in adult education. Publications include two books on Chinese educated youth/young intellectuals and a number of other China related issues. She has been Senior Teaching Fellow, University of Warwick in the Centre for Translation and Comparative Cultural Studies (from 2001 to 2010), with specializations in the teaching and research of Cultural and Media Studies.

Kate Eaton originally worked as an actor in theatre, television, and radio. She is currently a freelance theatre translator and has an M.A. in Literary Translation from the University of East Anglia. The plays of Virgilio Piñera and the collaborative process of translation for performance are the twin strands of her practice-led Ph.D. research at Queen Mary, University of London, which she is on the point of completing. Apart from translating ten of Piñera's plays to date as well as several of his poems, critical essays, and short stories she has also translated Cuban ballet dancer Carlos Acosta's autobiography *No Way Home* (Harper Collins: 2007).

Eirik Frisvold Hanssen is Associate Professor of film studies at the Norwegian University of Science and Technology (NTNU) in Trondheim. His Ph.D. dissertation, Early Discourses on Color and Cinema: Origins, Functions, Meanings (Stockholm University, 2006), is a historical and theoretical study on technological, cultural, and aesthetic aspects of colour in cinema between 1909 and 1935. He has written on film technology and aesthetics, fashion, visual culture, intermediality, and Scandinavian television history, and published in journals such as *Film History* and *Journal of Art History*. He has also worked at the Ingmar Bergman Archive in Stockholm.

Mike Ingham has been teaching English Studies as Associate Professor in the English Department at Lingnan University since 1999. Mike directs English drama in Hong Kong and student productions as part of the university's liberal arts mission. His current work focuses on intermediality studies between poetry and art song forms. His more recent monograph and article publications include *City Voices – An Anthology of Hong Kong*

Writing in English (H.K.U. Press, 2003), *Staging Fictions – The Prose Fiction Stage Adaptation as Social Allegory* (Edwin Mellen Press: 2004), *Hong Kong – A Cultural and Literary History* in the *City of the Imagination* series (Signal Books U.K./H.K.University Press, 2007), and 'Subject–Verb Inversion and Iambic Rhythm in Shakespeare's Dramatic Verse' in *Stylistics and Shakespeare* (London: Continuum Books, 2011).

Susan Knutson is Professor of English and Director of English Studies at Université Sainte-Anne, Nova Scotia's only francophone university, located in the rural heartland of old Acadie. Since completing her doctorate in comparative Canadian literature in 1989, she has contributed to feminist literary poetics in Canada and has published articles and one book on leading Canadian and Québécois feminist writers, Daphne Marlat and Nicole Brossard. Other research passions include Canadian Shakespeare, Acadian theatre, and the works of George Elliott Clarke and Tibor Egervari.

Ayelet Kohn is Senior Lecturer in the Department of Photographic Communication at Hadassah Academic College, Jerusalem, Israel. Her main area of research is the mutual relations existing between images and written texts in their sociological contexts. Her recent publications focused on political graffiti, talkbacks, and short documentary reportages. She has published in *Visual Communication*, *Multicultural Education*, *Emergencies: Journal for the Study of Media and Composite Cultures*, and more.

Katja Krebs is Lecturer in the Department of Drama: Theatre, Film, and TV, University of Bristol, United Kingdom. Her research interests lie with translation for the stage, translation and censorship, as well as the construction of national histories of theatre and performance. She is one of the founding co-editors of the *Journal of Adaptation in Film and Performance* and has published widely on translation for performance. Her recent monograph (*Cultural Dissemination and Translational Communities: German Drama in English Translation, 1900 –1914*, St. Jerome Publishing) investigates translation of German Drama and performance practices at the turn of the twentieth century.

Piotr Kuhiwczak, Director of the Centre for Translation and Comparative Cultural Studies at the University of Warwick between 1997 and 2007, is the editor of two books and author of numerous articles on translation studies and comparative literature. He is at present working at the British Red Cross Refugee Services in Leicester, United Kingdom. He has a special interest in immigration law and the psychological effects of forced emigration.

Marcelo Moreira obtained a Bachelor's degree in Portuguese and German languages at the University of Sao Paulo, and studied further with scholarship at the University of Duisburg-Essen (short-term course) and at the University of Leipzig (academic interchange), both in Germany. During his graduation, he was engaged in a research project commissioned by the Brazilian Culture Ministry focusing on the translation of folk literature for children and young people. He is currently pursuing a Master's in Translation Theory with emphasis on the German Functionalist Approach.

Laurence Raw teaches in the Department of English at Başkent University, Ankara, Turkey. A leading figure in adaptation studies, he has published two volumes, *Adapting Henry James to the Screen* (2006) and *Adapting Nathaniel Hawthorne to the Screen* (2008). He has co-edited three collections of articles on adaptation: *The Theme of Cultural Adaptation* (2009) (with Tanfer Emin Tunç and Gülriz Büken), *The Pedagogy of Adaptation*, and *Redefining Adaptation Studies* (both 2010) (with Dennis Cutchins and James M. Welsh). In 2011 he published *Exploring Turkish Cultures*, a volume of essays focusing on how concepts such as 'adaptation', 'translation', and 'Westernization' have been reinterpreted in the Republic of Turkey from 1923 onwards.

Anna Sofia Rossholm is Assistant Professor in Cinema Studies at Linnaeus University in Växjö, Sweden. Rossholm's research combines a film historical interest with media theoretical perspectives and cultural theory. Her dissertation *Reproducing Languages, Translating Bodies: Approaches to Speech, Translation, and Cultural Identity in Early European Sound Film* (Stockholm University, 2006) is a historical and media theoretical study and speech representation and translation in early European sound film. Her current research examines Ingmar Bergman's manuscripts and media versions from a perspective of genetic criticism.

Cynthia S. K. Tsui teaches translation at the School of Chinese, University of Hong Kong, China. She obtained her Ph.D. at the University of Warwick, United Kingdon. Her research focuses on independence in the concept of 'translation', which is a cutting-edge invention in the theories of translation studies. Dr. Tsui is keen on promoting 'translation' as a new thinking method. This applies to East–West comparative studies in literature and multimedia, cultural and interdisciplinary research, and issues in globalization. Another aspect of her scholarship is to bring Hong Kong culture and Chinese/Asian perspectives to the international platform of translation studies.

Tanfer Emin Tunç is Assistant Professor in the Department of American Culture and Literature at Hacettepe University, Ankara, Turkey. She received her B.A., M.A., and Ph.D. in American History and an Advanced Graduate Certificate in Women's Studies from the State University of New York at Stony Brook. She specializes in U.S. women's history and literature; the history of medicine, sexuality and reproduction, and American social and cultural history (with an emphasis on transnational/ethnic studies). She is the author of over seventy book chapters, reference book entries, book reviews, and journal articles. Her six books include *Positioning the New: Chinese–American Literature and the Changing Image of the American Literary Canon* (co-edited with Elisabetta Marino, Cambridge Scholars Publishing, 2010) and *The Transnational Turn in American Studies: Turkey and the United States* (co-edited with Bahar Gursel, forthcoming, Peter Lang Publishing, 2012).

Hugo Vandal-Sirois is a certified translator working in the field of advertising and marketing. He adapted many campaigns (Web, print, TV, and radio spots) for major clients worldwide to the French market of Québec. He writes and gives lectures about the challenges of adapting advertising and promotional communications, and is currently pursuing a Ph.D. in Translation Studies at Université de Montréal, where he teaches writing techniques and adaptation at the Département de Linguistique et Traduction.

Rachel Weissbrod is Senior Lecturer in the Department of Translation and Interpreting Studies at Bar Ilan University, Israel. Her areas of research include theory of translation, literary translation into Hebrew, translation for the media, and the interrelation between translation and other forms of transfer. She has published in *Target, The Translator, Meta, Babel, Linguistica Antverpiensia, Jostrans, Translation Studies,* and more. Her book *Not by Word Alone: Fundamental Issues in Translation* (in Hebrew) was published by The Open University of Israel in 2007.

Jenny Wong is Assistant Professor in the Division of Humanities and Social Sciences at Beijing Normal University, – Hong Kong Baptist University, and United International College. She teaches translation and applied ethics. Prior to joining U.I.C,, she taught commercial translation at the Chinese University of Hong Kong and media translation at the Open University of Hong Kong. Her vast experience in business writing and translating gained at various multi-national and local conglomerates enabled her to deliver lectures that combine theory and practical experience. Her research interests in the study of Bible and English literature grew out of her postgraduate degrees: M.A. in Translating and Interpreting (Newcastle, United Kingdom), M.A. in Christian Studies (C.U.H.K.) and Ph.D. in literature, theology and the arts (candidate, Glasgow, United Kingdom). She is the founder of S.E.L.B.L. www.selbl.org, a non-profit organization based in Hong Kong that promotes the English Bible abroad.

Introduction

Identifying Common Ground

Laurence Raw

At present the relationship between translation and adaptation studies seems to be an uneasy one. This was certainly not the case two decades ago, when Susan Bassnett confidently declared that 'Much time and ink has been wasted attempting to differentiate between translations, versions, adaptations and the establishment of a hierarchy of 'correctness' [. . .] all texts are translations of translations of translations' (Bassnett 1991: 78–9). Since then adaptation studies has emerged as a fully fledged discipline with its own corpus of theoretical texts (e.g., Robert Stam's *Literature through Film* (2005) or Linda Hutcheon's *A Theory of Adaptation* (2006)), and its own journals (*Adaptation* 2008–; *Journal of Adaptation in Film and Performance* 2007–). Bassnett's views have been questioned by the adaptation studies critic Mark O'Thomas, who argues that adaptations differ from translations in the sense that they 'take place across media rather than cultures – literature into film, diary extract into stage play, etc.' (O'Thomas 2010: 48).

Some translation studies scholars have treated such developments sceptically. Hendrik van Gorp argued, somewhat contradictorily, in a 1985 article (reprinted in 2004) that while no clear-cut distinction could be drawn between adaptation and translation, adaptations should not be thought of as genuine translations, even if they 'represent a primary text with a comparable form and volume' (Van Gorp 2004: 66). Despite their undoubted links, Van Gorp suggests that ever since Romantic hermeneutics emerged during the nineteenth century, the concept of adaptation has 'gradually acquired more negative connotations', when compared to translation. While translation creates the 'ideal image' of a source text, an adaptation potentially subverts that image (66). Three years later Lawrence Venuti criticized Stam's *Literature through Film* on the grounds that he invoked 'a dominant critical orthodoxy based on a political position (broadly democratic, although capable of further speculation [. . .] that the [adaptation] critic applies as a standard on the assumption that the film should somehow inscribe that and only that ideology' (Venuti 2007: 28). Venuti proposed that adaptation studies should learn from translation studies' example: rather than drawing on a predetermined methodology, translation studies concentrates on 'the recontextualizing process [. . .] the creation of another network of intertwining relations by and within the translation, a receiving intertext [. . .] [as well as] another context of reception whereby the translation is mediated by promotion and marketing strategies' (Venuti 2007: 30).

This representation of adaptation studies as a subaltern discipline to translation studies should be looked at in evolutionary terms. Two decades ago Bassnett and André Lefevere claimed that 'we no longer talk about translation in terms of what a translator 'should' or 'should not' do. That kind of learning has its place in the language learning classroom, where translation has a very precise, narrowly defined pedagogical role' (Bassnett and Lefevere 1990: xviii). I will return to Bassnett's comment on language learning later on; at this point, however, we should note her firm conviction that translation studies would continue its intellectual and theoretical progress well into the twenty-first century, helping educators and students alike to acquire 'a greater awareness of the world in which we live' (Bassnett and Lefevere ix). Edwin Gentzler quotes her claim that translation studies was so theoretically advanced by the early 1990s that perhaps older disciplines such as comparative literature needed to be redefined 'as a subcategory of translation studies' (Gentzler 1993: 196). Within fifteen years, however, the evolution of translation studies had been challenged by the nascent discipline of adaptation studies. Van Gorp and Venuti both respond by portraying adaptation studies as translation studies' poor relation, particularly in the way it foregrounds value-judgments rather than deconstructing the ways in which texts are consumed in different contexts.

In contrast the translation studies scholar John Milton constructs translation and adaptation as fundamentally different processes, using the work of the Brazilian translator Monteiro Lobato to prove his point. In his translations of Western classics, published during the mid-twentieth century, Lobato 'was struggling to give value to his own language, the Portuguese of Brazil, dominated at the time by the norms of Portugal'. He created adaptations of works such as Barrie's *Peter Pan*, incorporating newly written interpolations expressing 'his secular liberalism, his hatred of the traditional dominant oligarchies, and his belief in the need for greater economic freedom'. Lobato offers paratextual comments on the tales: near the end of *D. Quixote des Crianças* (Lobato's version of the Cervantes classic) the child Pedrinho asks whether his grandmother Dona Benta is telling the whole story or just parts. Dona Benta replies that only mature people should attempt to read the whole work and that only what entertains children's imagination should be included in the tales. Lobato believes that: '"literary" qualities had no place in works for children, whose imaginations should be stimulated by fluent, easy language' (Milton 2006: 494). Milton describes Lobato's work not as a 'resistant translation' (invoking Venuti's term), but as a text that both translates and adapts Western sources, localizing them and altering their thematic emphases. Here translation is understood as the process of recreating the text in Brazilian Portuguese, while adaptation injects contemporary 'Brazilian reality' into the finished product. In another article Milton confirms adaptation studies' subaltern status, as he recommends that it should draw upon translation studies' theoretical insights – for example, André Lefevere's concept of 'refraction', as a way of understanding the many ways in which a source text is transformed into 'translations, summaries [and] critiques' (Milton 2009a: 58).[1]

In what follows I propose a framework for translation and adaptation studies that eschews value judgments but rather views both disciplines as fundamentally different yet interrelated processes. Following Maria Tymoczko's recommendation, I propose an extension of the intellectual field that will 'expand the conception of translation [and adaptation], moving it beyond dominant, parochial, and stereotypical thinking about [. . .] processes and products'. By focusing on transformative processes such as transfer and re-presentation, I view translation and adaptation studies within a more all-inclusive framework that recognizes the demands of 'a globalizing world demanding flexibility and respect for differences in cultural traditions' (132). Using examples drawn from my own context in the Republic of Turkey, as well as other territories, I begin by showing that the perceived distinctions – whether methodological or descriptive – between translation and adaptation, as well as the ways in which they are represented, are culturally as well as historically determined. I subsequently propose that adaptation studies in particular needs to expand its field of vision by examining the relationship between psychology, psychoanalysis, and adaptation as put forth by Piaget and Freud (among others). This is an important move; like their counterparts in translation studies, adaptation studies scholars should acknowledge the post-positivist view of knowledge that problematizes notions of 'objectivity' and 'fidelity', and emphasizes the significance of perspective. I conclude by suggesting that this post-positivist view should inspire new approaches to research, teaching, *and* learning in translation studies and adaptation studies, with the emphasis placed on interdisciplinary negotiation. This issue is of particular personal significance: I write as an adaptation studies specialist concerned to explore new intellectual avenues in a context where greater collaboration between colleagues of different disciplines might ensure the continued survival of the humanities in secondary and higher education at a time when resource – both financial and material – are rapidly shrinking.

The belief that ideas of translation and adaptation are culturally constructed is a familiar one, but requires further elaboration. The idea of translation became dominant during the Middle Ages, when it was used to describe a process of carrying across cultures (originally used to refer to the physical transfer of relics), linked to the Latin words *translatio* or *transferre*. The European words *translation*, *traduction* or *traducción* emerged as a consequence of growing demands for the *Bible* to be translated into the vernacular. The religious associations of the translation process were extended: the word became associated with the Word of God in Vulgate versions of the *Bible*, as well as personified in Jesus. Adaptation, on the other hand, only really became significant in Western cultures with the development of copyright laws, which gave authors the power to preserve the integrity of their work, protecting it from alteration, distortion, or mutilation. They appeared in Britain from 1838 onwards, and later codified in the Berne Convention for the Protection of Literary and Artistic Works (1928). Katja Krebs's piece 'Translation and Adaptation – Two Sides of an Ideological Coin', included in this anthology, argues that until the creation of such laws there was little recognizable distinction between 'original' and 'adapted' texts: texts could be reshaped at will for a variety of purposes (especially in the theatre).

These histories have proved particularly influential in shaping current views of translation and adaptation in the West. As well as being a much older form of textual transformation, translation requires its practitioners to be conversant with more than one foreign language; adapters, on the other hand, can be monolingual, performing an 'intralingual' or 'intersemiotic' translation (Jakobson 1959). If adapters want to improve themselves, they should learn from translators, who have been working with texts for thousands of years. The distinctions between translation and adaptation have proved particularly influential in defining textual transformations: for instance, Thornton Wilder's well-known play *The Matchmaker* (1954) is based on a translation of Johann Nestroy's German play *Einen Jux Will er Sich Machen* (1842), which is itself a translation of John Oxenford's 1835 one-act farce *A Day Well Spent*. However Jerry Herman and Michael Stewart's musical *Hello, Dolly* (1964) is an adaptation of *The Matchmaker*. Christopher Hampton's renderings of Ibsen's *A Doll's House* (1973) and

An Enemy of the People (1998) are both adaptations, in the sense that they are based on Michael Meyer's English translations of Ibsen's Norwegian text, as Hampton did not read Norwegian. Sometimes directors have deliberately challenged Western concepts of translation and adaptation to make a specific political point. The French-Canadian theatre director Michel Garneau coined the term 'tradaptation',[2] to describe the ways in which canonical texts were invested with new meanings in an attempt to force the target culture to confront itself through exposure to the rewritten source text. His version of *Macbeth* (1978) was rewritten in Québécois as part of an overall initiative designed to protect and promote the language in opposition to standard French – that is, *français de France* – that dominated most existing translations (Brisset 1988: 193–257). Tradaptation involves processes of translation and adaptation that defy distinction between the two practices: Garneau created hybrid texts that expressed Québec's 'double colonization' by French language purists and English language speakers. The translation studies scholar Denis Salter comments that the tradaptation technique is 'close to being oxymoronic, as it discloses the kind of prodigious doubling to which the translator's identity [. . .] is necessarily subjected', as he seeks to preserve the Québécois heritage of the past and assert cultural autonomy in the present (Salter 1993: 63). This issue is explored further from a translation studies perspective in Susan Knutson's 'Tradaptation dans le sens Québécois: A Word for the Future' in this collection. However the significance of the term (both for Garneau and his non-Québécois audiences and readers) stems from a shared assumption – predominant in Western cultures – that adaptation and translation are fundamentally different processes. If that were not the case, there would be no need to establish a Bhabaesque 'Third Space' combining the two together.

Both translation and adaptation studies have developed models of textual transformation that have proved highly effective in promoting Western interests in different contexts. One such model is the notion of translation as transfer referred to above, in which 'transfer is figured in terms of transporting material objects or leading sentient beings (such as captives or slaves in one direction or soldiers and missionaries in the other) across a cultural and linguistic boundary' (Tymoczko 2007: 6).[3] Into that category of 'missionaries' we might add language teachers and/or experts. An early instance of this process at work can be found in the writings of St. Jerome where he observes that: 'like some conqueror [Hilary the Confessor] marched the original text, a captive, into his native language' (Robinson 1997: 26). Note the metaphor here that portrays Hilary as a military figure participating in a linguistic conquest. The same process underpinned government policy in the early years of the Turkish Republic after its creation in 1923, when Mustafa Kemal Atatürk marched Western-formulated ideas into the fortress of a new national culture. He created a Translation Bureau with the specific purpose of commissioning translations of a series of 'Western classics', to be distributed to schools and higher education institutions, as well as drawing on the expertise of European experts (particularly refugees from Nazi Germany such as Erich Auerbach). This policy used Westernization as a means of furthering national interests, as translators made use of the Turkish language (newly purged of Ottoman, Persian, and other neologisms) and created neologisms borrowed from Western languages, primarily French. Atatürk was determined to suppress the country's Ottoman past and reinvent it as a forward-looking, dynamic state that could compete on a cultural and artistic footing with its western European allies.[4]

Despite their differences (as understood in the West), adaptation studies have also drawn upon this translation as transfer model. Thomas Leitch constructs a typology of ten textual strategies, ranging from celebration (a resistance to change any words of a source text) to colonization (introducing new material in the target text that does not exist in the source text), and encompassing parody, pastiche, and imitation. He cites Baz Luhrmann's *Romeo + Juliet* (1996) as a film incorporating all these strategies in an 'intertextual bricolage [. . .] that resist[s] reduction [. . . .] There is no normative model for adaptation' (Leitch 2007: 125–6). This last claim is in fact untrue: Leitch's primary concern is to evaluate the effectiveness of the transfer of themes, plots, and characters (neatly summed up as 'what has been gained and lost') between Luhrmann's adaptation and Shakespeare's 'original' text.

However, the representation of adaptation and/or translation is often very different in non-Western contexts. My use of the term 'representation' is deliberate, as a way of summing up a form of transformation that involves issues of gender, race, politics, and cross-cultural transfer. To understand the process of representation is fundamental in 'knowing how to construct, read, and deconstruct translation [or translated] products [and terminology]' (Tymockzo 2007: 115). The translation studies scholar Şehnaz Tahir Gürçağlar has studied the works of Selâmi Munir Yurdatap and Kemal Tahir, two translators who worked on the publishing margins in the post-1945 Republic of Turkey (Gürçağlar 2008). Unlike their counterparts in the government-sponsored Translation Bureau, they were not concerned with introducing Western-inspired ideas; rather they produced texts that appropriated well-known fictional figures (e.g., Sherlock Holmes) and resituated them in local situations, while showing a marked indifference toward the authorial provenance of their sources. Tahir created new versions of Mickey Spillane's Mike Hammer novels set in İstanbul, all of which appeared under a range of pseudonyms ('F. M. İkinci' being one of them). Neither he nor Yurdatap placed any importance on 'originality'; they were more concerned to write for a rapidly expanding market of locally published texts, often issued in serial or magazine formats. Yurdatap's version of *Dracula* fitted 'the narrative structure of Turkish folk-tales which have an emphasis on action over dramatic or lyric features and focus on fantastic elements' (Gürçağlar 208: 211). Using Milton's formulation referred to above, we might describe such texts as 'adaptations', in the sense that (like Monteiro Labato) both Yurdatap and Tahir wrote for the 'enterprising citizens' of their country. Or we could follow the adaptation scholar Julie Sanders' example by describing them as 'appropriations', in the sense that they are ideologically rather than artistically driven (Sanders 2006: 27). At the time Yurdatap's and Tahir's works were first published, however, they were neither described as translations, adaptations, nor appropriations, but '*romanlar* [novels]' – a genre generously assigned by the publishers to short stories and novellas as well as larger works (Gürçağlar 2008: 248). In fact there is no equivalent in Turkish for 'adaptation' or 'appropriation'; depending on the context, the words *çevirmek* (to translate) and *hazırlamak* (meaning to prepare verbally, either for spoken or written delivery) are generally employed.[5] To 'adapt' translates either as *alışmak* (to get used to), *alıştırmak* (to get accustomed to), or *uyum sağlamak* (to suit a new purpose, as in the phrase 'Adapting our native cuisine to the available food resource of a new country'). As André Lefevere remarked over two decades ago, this untranslatability is less to do with the lack of syntactic or morphosyntatic equivalents, and more to do with the absence of poetological equivalents: 'Language is not the problem. Ideology and poetics are, as are cultural elements that are not immediately clear, or seen as completely 'misplaced' in what would be the target culture version of the text to be translated' (Lefevere 1990: 26). In Turkish terms, to *translate* a text means drawing on Western-inspired notions of transfer; to render a source text comprehensible to members of the target culture. To *adapt* a text, on the other hand, offers the chance to expand the possibilities of Turkish languages and cultures – for example, by coining new terms or developing new characterizations in the target language (Gambier 2009: 187). Yurdatap and Tahir wrote 'indigenous books' (Gürçağlar's term) designed to prove the effectiveness of Kemal Atatürk's language reforms, and hence maintain support for the Turkish nation. Understanding such processes of representation should help us realize the futility of imposing pre-established categories of translation and/or adaptation on non-Western material. In spite of the thoroughness of her research, Gürçağlar invokes Gideon Toury's concept of pseudotranslations[6] to describe Yurdatap's and Tahir's books (244–6), while minimizing the fact that both authors wrote for a context-specific purpose, at a time when the Turkish nation was freeing itself from its Ottoman past.

Our understanding of the translation and/or adaptation process is not only culturally determined; it is informed by the creators' relationship to their texts. In *The Interpretation of Dreams* (translated into English in 1913), Freud writes: 'when the work of interpretation [including translation] is completed we perceive that a dream is the fulfillment of a wish' (Freud 1913: 154). But since the wish often conceals hidden thoughts and feelings, the work of the dreamer consists of hiding the true expression of that wish by means of symbols and other obfuscations, so as to render it more acceptable. The dreamer becomes the censor of the wish to such an extent that the opposite meaning is conveyed: hot is cold, pleasure is pain, joy is sorrow, and so on. The dreamer understands the cause and effect of this censorship process, but can do little about it; it is the psychoanalyst's task to puncture the emotional façade the dreamer has created through censorship and reveal the true meaning underneath. However this becomes more complicated, as another element of the individual unconscious fears the exposure of hidden desires, and works hard to sustain that façade. As a result the dream is drastically distorted, as in *Oedipus Rex.* In a later essay 'The Loss of Reality in Neurosis and Psychosis', Freud develops his ideas: neurosis and psychosis are the product of constructing an emotional façade: 'in neurosis a piece of reality is avoided by a sort of flight, whereas in psychosis it is remodeled' (Freud 1924: 185).

Translators are also dreamers who occasionally construct a similar façade – for example, by refusing to have their names printed on the frontispiece to their work, in the belief that they are serving the cause of indigenous writing. This was often the case, for example, with translators of popular fiction in the Turkish Republic during the mid-twentieth century, whose books 'would have been received as works written originally in Turkish' (Gürçağlar 2008: 125). Other translators (e.g., those scholars commissioned by the Translation Bureau to render Western classics into Turkish) place themselves in the service of the source text by claiming that their sole responsibility is to make an author's work accessible to members of the target culture. The notion of fidelity can be treated as another façade, as translators and adapters confine themselves to keeping to the spirit and the letter of 'the original text'. The only way translators can understand the significance of their dreams (as expressed through their work) is to trust in their 'somatic feel' for the source text; for the sense of words and phrases and their meaning. They should question the way things look on a page and not worry about keeping close to what the source text's author wants to say; instead they should concentrate on what the author *implies*, even if that means going against what he or she holds most sacred. They should look beneath the source-text's surface to discover what they think is its basic meaning. By such methods the translator can create 'an imaginative construction' of the source text that the translator – and no one else – believes truly represents the whole (Robinson 1991: 156). They articulate their dreams, and at the same time intervene, subvert, divert, and even entertain. They are transformed from 'neutral, impersonal, transferring devices' into creative individuals in their own right, drawing on their personal experiences – emotions, motivations, attitudes, associations – and showing how such experiences can contribute to the societies they inhabit' (Robinson 1991: 260).

To some translation critics employing a Freudian approach, adaptation is still perceived as an inferior process. The translation scholar Willis Barnstone claimed in 1993 that while Dryden, Cavafy, and Umberto Eco based some of their works on earlier texts, they were happy to make their borrowings visible on the grounds they could 'not tolerate adaptation's thefts' (129). On this view adaptation is explicitly identified with plagiarism and hence unworthy of a so-called great author. However psychiatrists such as Jean Piaget thought that adaptation had as much potential for creativity as translation – especially for growing children. In his model of development, as set forth in seminal texts such as *The Origin of Intelligence in the Child* (first published in English in 1953), Piaget argued that children enrich their understanding of things by acting and reflecting on the effects of their own previous knowledge; that is, they *adapt* to a new environment, and as a consequence learn to organize their knowledge in increasingly complex structures. By reflecting on that knowledge, children develop a sophisticated awareness of the 'rules' that govern social and personal interactions – for example, understanding the distinctions between right and wrong. Piaget characterized adaptation as 'an equilibrium between assimilation and accommodation' – in other words, a process of incorporating all the given data of experience within a framework (accommodation), and restructuring that data in one's own terms (assimilation). Adaptation 'consists of putting an assimilatory mechanism and a complementary accommodation into progressive equilibrium'

(Piaget 1997: 7). Piaget describes the adaptive process as a series of reactions: the first of these involves a gradual understanding of the differences between accommodation and assimilation; the second involves utilizing that knowledge in understanding things; while the third 'marks the beginning of experimental behaviour [. . .] the discovery of new means through active experimentation' (Piaget 1997: 330). Piaget refers to 'the development of representations' – where the term 'representation' is the outcome of the accommodation and assimilation processes. This development only becomes meaningful if accompanied by invention or mental combination (353). On this view adaptation is viewed as a process of representation similar to that described earlier on, where children look at the world around them and invest it with their own social meanings. Piaget not only gives importance to individuals, while emphasizing the importance of difference: every child should have the freedom to construct their own world-view. He stated in a 1979 interview that: 'education [. . .] for me and no one else [. . .] means making creators [. . .] You have to make inventors, innovators – not conformists' (Bringuier 1979: 132).

In *Ego Psychology and the Problem of Adaptation* (first published in German in 1939 and in English nineteen years later), Heinz Hartmann uses Freud to make a similar point. The ego and the id come from a common matrix: obliged to define the boundaries between them, they create a zone of conflict that finds its expression in 'defense methods' (e.g., constructing an emotional façade so as to dilute the content of a dream). Although adaptation has a lot in common with defence, it is a function of a different order. Hartmann characterizes the defence mechanism as a process of 'fitting together', set against adaptation, yet inextricable from it. For individuals to learn to adapt, they must also learn to 'fit together'; to emphasize defence mechanisms to consolidate their adaptive discoveries (Hartmann 1986: 40). Hartmann identifies adaptation as something free of conflict or repression – the main means by which humans define themselves in relation to their environment. Piaget's and Hartmann's theories confirm the notion that adapters are as creative as translators, both of them employing the kind of transformative processes that are fundamental to human growth and development.

The links between translation and Freudian psychoanalysis have been explored to show how the unconscious appears indispensable to the translation process; how the process of translation of a work of art involves the psyche's four poles (the wish and its superego, the ego and its reality); and how an impersonal translation – in other words, a translation where the authors have not employed their creative faculties – has no unconscious (Abraham 1995: 130). By contrast the bulk of adaptation theory to date has used psychoanalysis to explain the *outcomes* of a text, rather than looking at the transformation *process*. The adaptation scholar Robert Stam describes *Robinson Crusoe* (in his view an adaptation of a mimetic novel based on real life) as 'a family romance, that is, the mechanism by which the childish imagination conjures up mythic 'solutions' to the crises emerging from the Oedipal situation' (Stam 2005: 68). I recommend instead a concentration on the *process* of textual transformation in the light of Freud's, Piaget's, and Hartmann's insights. By such means we can set aside predetermined value judgments – for example, that there exists something called 'an original text', or that a translation is automatically superior to an adaptation (in Western European terms) as it involves a second language. Such beliefs inhibit rather than develop the creative impulse; in Freudian terms, they force authors to conceal rather than express their true responses to a source text. In Piagetian terms, they no longer have the chance for 'active experimentation'. More importantly, the emphasis on adaptation and translation as creative processes should encourage scholars in both disciplines to set aside their value judgments and work toward creating some common intellectual ground instead.

While this suggestion might work in western European contexts, it might prove problematic elsewhere. From the mid-1950s to the late 1970s, the local film industry (collectively known as *Yeşilçam*, or Green Pine, named after a street in the film district of İstanbul) churned out up to two hundred films a year, the majority of them adaptations (in the Turkish sense) of popular stories both ancient and modern. The plots, characters, and situations seldom varied: boy-meets-girl, rich-versus-poor melodramas and comedies set in İstanbul, invariably containing sequences shot by the Bosphorus designed to reinforce belief in the Republic of Turkey's unique status in the world as the only nation to straddle two continents. This nationalistic tradition of filmmaking survives to this day in the seemingly endless stream of serials (or *diziler*) broadcast on state and private television stations. To criticize such material for its repetitiveness presupposes that a distinction exists between 'repetition' and 'creativity' – something that does not prevail in the Republic of Turkey. In a recent piece on the actor Ayhan Işık, I argued that his star-image was constructed in explicitly local terms, by rejecting a basic assumption of European socio-political thought – that human beings are ontologically singular, while gods and spirits are in the end social facts (Raw 2011: 258). Işık did not try to be 'original' – that is, leading a life that differed from his legions of adoring fans of both sexes – but constructed himself as an ordinary person following the path of virtue and subjecting oneself to God's will ('If we want to be with God or be his friend, we should try to possess some of His attributes', as the thirteenth-century mystic Mevlâna Celaleddin-i Rumi once observed (Türkmen 2002: 83)). Işık overcame all obstacles and defeated his adversaries of all shapes and sizes while frequently seeking divine assistance. Işık was a 'creative' person in the sense that he relied on the divine Creator – a point so significant that it was repeated in film after film. On this view it is quite acceptable for creative artists not to strive for 'originality' (as understood in western European terms), but to repeat themselves, so long as what they say continues to attract audience or reader interest.[7] This formulation challenges Piaget's belief that individuals should strive for innovation at the expense of conformism.

Bearing such differences in mind, we might wonder whether it is practical to formulate a transcultural framework for looking at adaptation and translation. In a recent piece the translation scholar Dirk Delabastita suggests that radical distinctions should be drawn between three levels of reality: the *status* of discursive phenomena (encompassing translations and adaptations), which he defines as 'what they are claimed to be or believed to be in a given cultural community'; their *origin* ('the real history of their genesis, as revealed by a diachronically oriented reconstruction'); and their *features* ('as revealed by a synchronic analysis, possibly involving comparisons') (Delabastita 2008: 235). This model allows for alternative conceptions of language, translation, and adaptation in non-Western contexts, as well as inviting a considerable degree of methodological flexibility. Delabastita quotes his fellow translation scholar Theo Hermans, who emphasizes the futility of 'fixing stable units for comparison [. . .] of excluding interpretation, of studying translation in a vacuum'. Delabastita does not propose stable units, but offers instead 'a conceptual tool to make such a discussion [of how translation works in the real world] more effective', by envisaging 'all kinds of possible relationships between various kinds of 'translation' and various kinds of "non-translation.'" With this 'three-dimensional view of the full range of virtual possibilities, we should be in a better position to look at discursive realities and the normative constraints behind them and to appreciate fully the choices [. . .] made [. . .] for certain reasons and certain effects' (Delabastita 2008: 243). By means of his *status/origin/features* scheme we can discover how the distinction between translation and adaptation prevails (or does not prevail) in different situations. Most importantly Delabastita rejects the idea of discipline-specificity; his 'open model of translation' does away with 'ontological definitions ('is this a translation') or territorial disputes ('does this problem come under the remit of Translation Studies?') [.. . .] The scheme's radically open and relativistic view of translation ends up questioning the existence of Translation Studies as an autonomous discipline' (Delabastita 2008: 245).

However, I am not certain that territorial disputes can be so readily dispensed with. It is highly likely that some colleagues in adaptation studies might view Delabastita's intervention as another attempt to subsume their research under the overall rubric of translation studies. Perhaps the best that we can hope for is that scholars of different disciplines – not only adaptation and translation studies but also others in the humanities and social sciences – might negotiate with one another on how acts of translation and adaptation are employed in a range of metaphorical senses. Delabastita cites two seminars, one held in Philadelphia in 2006, the other at Boğaziçi University, İstanbul, a year later, as examples of this process of 'negotiating differences', where scholars from different disciplines assembled to discuss different interpretations of the term 'translation' and its relationship to interdisciplinarity (Delabastita 2008: 238).

In an attempt to negotiate such differences, whether disciplinary or cultural, I suggest that we go back to Freud's and Piaget's view of translation and adaptation as basic processes by which every individual learns to come to terms with the world around them. This provides the common base from which we can analyse the different status, origins, and features of discursive phenomena (to use Delabastita's suggestive framework). More significantly, however, I believe that scholars in translation and adaptation studies have to concentrate more on *what is being learned* in their discipline by educators and students alike. The American educational theorist Tim Riordan explains why: 'The point of education, after all, is the learning that students [and faculty] do [. . . .] to ensure that students [learners] develop the understanding and abilities they need in order to respond to and shape the world in which they live' (Riordan 1994: 3). In other words, we should consider how we might help students and faculty *adapt* or *translate* to their environments, both inside and outside the academy. Any scholarly activity should also assist the learning process. In my own specialist area of using adaptation in an English department in a Turkish institution, for instance, I need to ask how adaptation studies can help students come to terms with Western cultural products, as well as discovering more about the contexts in which they live and work. At the same time I should consider how the study of a variety of authorities – including Piaget as well as more discipline-specific interventions by the adaptation scholars Leitch and Stam – could contribute to the learning process. I explored some of these issues in a recent article, by showing how Leitch's concept of 'active literacy' – understood as the ability to engage with texts 'critically and productively' – could be acquired through practical and collaborative exercises such as representing *Romeo and Juliet*. I asked students to participate in precisely the same kind of activity practiced by adapters and translators of Shakespeare's play into Turkish (Raw 2009: 234–6). Inspired by Piaget, I treated adaptation studies as a way of approaching the world, as well as helping students to develop the kind of transferable skills – negotiation, teamwork, and presentation (all of which involve forms of adaptation) – that would help them in the world of work. My scholarship and research was determined by these objectives.

By approaching one's discipline as a framework for learning, as well as research, we can address some important issues. In what ways can adaptation or translation studies prove significant for educators and their students? As we consider the shifting nature of these disciplines, what are the abilities and qualities of each that will be most helpful to our students' future careers? How can we adapt or translate our scholarly insights, so as to make them meaningful to our students? Are there other modes of discourse that will help students to better understand our disciplines? Other questions relate to the process of helping students use their experience of the discipline to reflect on their own lives. What kinds of experiences – readings, seminars, or practical activities – will engage students in using and understanding the discipline? How can educators organize their syllabi so that students are *using* as well as *participating* in acts of transformation (adaptation as well as translation)? How can we help students forge connections between their disciplines and their own lives? And how can we determine whether students *respond to* as well as *understand* the ideas they are discussing?

These questions are hardly exhaustive, and have limits of their own. For example, they are posed in a way that could imply a narrow focus on individual disciplines, while neglecting the interdisciplinary character of most learning. Earlier on I quoted Susan Bassnett and André Lefevere, who believed that translation in language learning had a very precise pedagogical role (Bassnett and Lefevere 1990: xviii). I suggest that we need to look beyond these rather reductive judgments and look closely at what the processes of adaptation and translation involve, how they differ in various situations, and how they function as vehicles for learning in all disciplines. Translation and adaptation are an essential means of determining how different disciplines view themselves and their future, both academically and pedagogically. Like Delabastita, I believe in the process of negotiating difference, but I think that this negotiation should take place in the context of learning *as well as* research, so as to better understand how adaptation and translation are fundamental to the process of constructing knowledge for learners and educators alike. Such an approach would render learning and research more meaningful; not only can we understand the essential concepts, issues, and objectives of our various disciplines, but we can acquire a greater awareness of how different disciplines relate to one another so that we can help students see that too.

The main purpose of this anthology consists of exploring some of the issues raised in this introduction. The thirteen contributions are divided into three main sections; in the first, some of the main theoretical debates surrounding translation and adaptation are discussed. The translation studies scholars Hugo Vandal-Sirois and Georges L. Bastin cite the example of adapting texts across cultures in the advertising industry as a way of showing how translation studies scholars might benefit from rethinking their beliefs about adaptation studies' subaltern status. Katja Krebs, co-editor of the *Journal of Adaptation in Film and Performance*, cites the example of theatrical productions (e.g., the National Theatre of Wales's *The Persians* (2010), based on Aeschylus), to show how elusive various descriptions of 'translation' and 'adaptation' actually are: 'Is this a performance of a 'translation' [. . .] Or is it an 'adaptation,' even though it labels itself a version?' Bearing this in mind, Krebs proposes that both translation and adaptation studies scholars might benefit from 'an equal and mutually beneficial exchange of ideas, which will, no doubt, strengthen our understanding of contemporary as well as historic constructions of culture'. Krebs's views are challenged by another translation studies scholar, Cynthia S. K. Tsui, who firmly believes that adaptation studies should benefit from 'the experience of translation studies, a discipline that provides practical directions and theoretical inspirations, that are highly relevant and useful in conceptualizing adaptation'. Her construction of adaptation studies as an emerging discipline, as compared to the more 'mature' translation studies, provides an interesting counterpoint to Sirois and Bastin's views. The first section of this anthology is rounded off with the translation studies scholars Joâo Azenha and Marcelo Moreira's contribution 'Translation and Rewriting: Don't Translators "Adapt" when they "Translate?"' Using a comparative case study of an excerpt from a 'retold story', *A Saga de Siegfried*, with a translation of the same piece from German into Brazilian Portuguese, they follow Krebs by suggesting that while translation and adaptation are different, it is often difficult to determine hard and fast distinctions between the two. Academics from different disciplines, as well as different cultures, view adaptation and translation in different ways.

The second section of the anthology underlines the importance of this point. For the cultural studies critic Tanfer Emin Tunç translation and adaptation are both defined as 'transformative processes which serve as cultural and epistemological bridges, especially between East and West'. She looks at the work of the contemporary Chinese American dramatist

Ping Chong, who uses translation and adaptation as a way of reconciling his identity struggle, as well as transforming different cultural traditions into staged works through *bricolage*. Like Krebs, Tunç believes that distinctions between translation and adaptation are insignificant, especially in the Western theatre. The translation studies scholar Jenny Wong's discussion of Zhang Qi Hong's revival of *The Merchant of Venice* (1981) in Beijing insists the two processes should be differentiated. The production used a 1954 translation by Fang Ping, which had removed all the Christian references and replaced them with localized references. Zhang's 'adaptation' (Wong's term) reshaped the text for early 1980s audiences by introducing Confucian terms and minimizing Shylock's Jewish identity. Both Fang's 'translation' and Zhang's 'adaptation' domesticated Shakespeare's text in an attempt to develop their respective audiences' knowledge of Western humanism. In spite of Wong's claims, there was no real distinction between the two transformative processes: Fang and Zang tried to establish a bridge between Western and Eastern cultures.

Continuing the Shakespearean theme, Susan Knutson's translation studies-inspired piece 'Tradaptation Dans le Sens *Québécois*', develops some of the ideas explored earlier on in this introduction. She looks at the idea of 'tradaptation' in Garneau's and Robert Lepage's Shakespearean productions. Tradaptation is not simply a blend of translation and adaptation; rather it is a form of writing 'that exists at a particular conjuncture of memory and intentionality with respect to the language(s) of the past and the future'. The practice of tradaptation has contributed to the survival of the local language, as well as enhancing the status of French in contemporary Québec. In contrast to Wong, Knutson argues that the domestication process was designed to foreground the concerns of a minority culture, rather than to provide a bridge between cultures.

The translation studies scholars Ayelet Kohn and Rachel Weissbrod move the discussion away from theatre into film. In their analysis of Ari Folman's animation *Waltz with Bashir* (2008), and the graphic novel based on it (2009), they draw on Freud's concept of 'translation' to show how the director and writers create parallel worlds of dream and hallucination, reflecting invisible processes in the minds of the characters. Kohn and Weissbrod move the discussion away from text-based issues to demonstrate that the processes of 'translation' (and 'adaptation') are characteristic of all individuals in all cultures, as they learn how to accommodate themselves to different situations.

Continuing the film theme – albeit from an adaptation studies perspective – Eirik Frissvold Hansen and Anna Sofia Rossholm's piece on Victor Sjöström's silent film *Terje Vigen* (1917) argues that while direct translation and adaptation between two different media (in this case, poem and film) is impossible, both source and target texts inform one another – for example, through fragmented, elliptical narration or the use of repetition. They challenge Jakobson's assertion that adaptation is simply an intralingual process of transformation, arguing instead that filmic transposition is a combination of translational *and* adaptive processes. By such means Sjöström negotiates and problematizes notions of 'fidelity' and 'originality'. The adaptation studies scholar Sarah Artt likewise rejects ideas of fidelity; in her analysis of three cinematic versions of Choderlos de Laclos' *Les Liaisons Dangereuses*, she shows how the source text lends itself to translational and adaptive techniques.

Turning once again to the theatre, the practising translator Kate Eaton offers an account of translating two works by the Cuban playwright Virgilio Piñera. Following Tunç, Eaton makes no distinction between translation and adaptation; while preparing a text for performance neither of them assume particular significance. Nor is fidelity of particular significance: Eaton is far more concerned with rendering the Cuban texts accessible to contemporary British audiences. As with Wong, she introduces a domesticating strategy – for example, by translating the Spanish word *boniato* (sweet potato) into 'turnip'. This word, she believes, has a comedic value in English (it forms one of the principal running jokes of the four *Blackadder* series on the BBC).

The final section of the anthology moves away from film and theatre studies to look at translation and adaptation in different areas. Mike Ingham's 'The Mind's Ear' looks at the ways in which A. E. Housman's collection *A Shropshire Lad* (1896) has been adapted by successive generations of composers, including George Butterworth, Ralph Vaughan Williams, and Ivor Gurney. This is a fascinating piece: in this process of transformation fidelity issues have little or no importance. Rather each composer transmutes Housman's source text into 'an emotionally and cognitively 'other' experience and expand[s] its semiotic frame of reference'. Ingham also argues that the distinction between adaptation and translation is not significant as composers search for the 'arch of meaning [that] [. . .] stretches over a whole song'. The concluding piece, Ruth Cherrington's 'Cultural Adaptation and Translation', moves the discussion away from textual issues into the ways in which individuals psychologically translate *and* adapt to the experience of different cultures. While focusing exclusively on the experience of Chinese students, Cherrington offers a way forward for academics and students in different disciplines to re-examine the implications of the translation and adaptation processes through negotiation.

I must stress that this anthology does not provide any definitive answers as to the relationship between translation and adaptation, and how (and whether) they can be distinguished. Instead I offer a variety of perspectives on the translation/adaptation issue, in the fervent hope that it might inspire the kind of interdisciplinary discussion about research, teaching, and learning that I believe is fundamental to the future of both disciplines.

Notes

1 See also Milton 1991 and Milton 2009b.

2 Yves Gambier has also used the term to investigate film adaptations from a translation studies perspective (Gambier 2004). See also Hanssen's and Rossholm's essay in this collection, even though they don't actively use the term *tradaptation.*

3 See also Cronin 2003.

4 See Gürçağlar 2008: 20–6.

5 Between 1923 and 1960 other words were used for the term to translate in the Turkish Republic. See Gürçağlar 2008: 126–8.

6 Defined by Toury as 'texts which have been presented as translation with no corresponding source texts in other languages ever having existed – hence no factual 'transfer operations' and translation relationships' (Toury 1995: 6)

7 This issue is also significant in much recent critical writing on remakes in Hollywood, Bollywood and elsewhere. For an accessible introduction to the topic, see Jess-Cooke 2009.

Bibliography

Abraham, Nicolas (1995). 'Psychoanalytic Aesthetics: Time, Rhythm, and the Unconscious', trans. Nicholas T. Rand, in *Rhythms: On the Work, Translation, and Psychoanalysis.* Stanford: Stanford University Press: pp. 107–30.

Barnstone, Willis (1993). *The Poetics of Translation: History, Theory, Practice.* New Haven and London: Yale University Press.

Bassnett, Susan (1991). *Translation Studies*, rev. edn. London and New York: Routledge.

Bassnett, Susan and Lefevere, André (1990). 'Preface'. In *Translation, History and Culture.* London and New York: Pinter Publishers.

Bringuier, Jean-Claude (1979). *Conversations with Piaget*, trans. Basia Miller Gulati. Chicago: University of Chicago Press.

Brisset, Annie (1988). *A Sociocritique of Translation: Theater and Alterity in Québec, 1969–1988*, trans. Rosalind Gill and Roger Gannon. Toronto: University of Toronto Press.

Cronin, Michael (2003). *Translation and Globalization.* London and New York: Routledge.

Delabastita, Dirk (2008). 'Status, Origin, Features: Translation and Beyond'. In *Beyond Descriptive Translation Studies: Investigations in Homage to Gideon Toury.* Anthony Pym, Miriam Shlesinger, and Daniel Simeoni (eds), pp. 233–46. Amsterdam and Philadelphia: John Benjamins.

Freud, Sigmund (1913). *The Interpretation of Dreams*, trans. James Strachey and Anna Freud. London: Hogarth Press.

— (1924). 'Reality in Neurosis and Psychosis', trans. James Strachey and Anna Freud, in *The Ego and the Id.* pp. 183–7. London: Hogarth Press.

Gambier, Yves (2004). 'Tradaptation Cinématographique'. In *Topics in Audiovisual Translation.* Pilar Orero (ed.), pp. 169–81. Amsterdam and Philadelphia: John Benjamins.

—(2009). 'Translation Terminology and Its Offshoots'. In *The Metalanguage of Translation.* Gambier and Luc van Doorslaer (eds), pp. 183–91. Amsterdam and Philadelphia: John Benjamins.

Gentzler, Edwin (1993). *Contemporary Translation Theories.* London and New York: Routledge.

Gürçağlar, Şehnaz Tahir (2008). *The Politics and Poetics of Translation in Turkey, 1923–1960.* Amsterdam and New York: Rodopi.

Hartmann, Heinz (1986). *Ego Psychology and the Problem of Adaptation*, trans. David Rapaport. New York: International Universities Press, Inc. (orig. edn 1958).

Jakobson, Roman (1959). 'On Linguistic Aspects of Translation'. Stanford University Translation Resources. http://www.stanford.edu/~eckert/PDF/jakobson.pdf (accessed July 30, 2011).

Jess-Cooke, Carolyn (2009). *Film Sequels.* Edinburgh: Edinburgh University Press.

Lefevere, André (1990). 'Translation: Its Genealogy in the West'. In Bassnett and Lefevere, pp. 14–29. *Translation, History and Culture.* London and New York: Pinter Publishers: pp. 14–29.

Leitch, Thomas (2007). *Film Adaptation and its Discontents: From Gone with the Wind to The Passion of the Christ.* Baltimore: The Johns Hopkins University Press.

Milton, John (2009a). 'Between the Cat and the Devil: Adaptation Studies and Translation Studies'. *Journal of Adaptation in Film and Performance* 2(1): 47–64.

(1991). 'Translating Classic Fiction for Mass Markets'. *The Translator* 7(1): 43–69.

— (2006). 'The Resistant Political Translations of Monteiro Lobato'. *Massachusetts Review* 47(3): 486–508.

— (2009b). 'Translation Studies and Adaptation Studies'. In *Translation Research Projects 2.* Anthony Pym and Alexander Perekrestenko (eds), pp. 51–8. Tarragona: Intercultural Studies Group.

O'Thomas, Mark (2010). 'Turning Japanese: Translation, Adaptation, and the Ethics of Trans-National Exchange'. In *Adaptation Studies: New Approaches.* Christa Albrecht-Crane and Dennis Cutchins (eds), pp. 46–61. Madison: Farleigh Dickinson University Press: pp. 46–61.

Piaget, Jean (1997). *The Origin of Intelligence in the Child*, trans. Margaret Cook. London and New York: Routledge (orig. edn 1953).

Raw, Laurence (2011). 'Ayhan Işık: Long Live the King'. In *Exploring Turkish Cultures*, pp. 250–60. Newcastle-upon-Tyne: Cambridge Scholars Publishing.

— (2009). 'Towards a Pedagogy for Teaching Adaptations'. *Journal of Adaptation in Film and Performance* 2(3): 223–37.

Riordan, Tim (1994). *Beyond the Debate: The Nature of Teaching.* Milwaukee, WI: Alverno College Institute.

Robinson, Douglas (1991). *The Translator's Turn*. Baltimore and London: The Johns Hopkins University Press.

— (1997). *Western Translation Theory from Herodotus to Nietzsche*. Manchester and Kinderbrook, New York: St. Jerome Publishing.

Salter, Denis (1993). 'Between Wor(l)ds: Lepage's Shakespeare Cycle'. *Theater* 24(3): 61–70.

Sanders, Julie (2006). *Adaptation and Appropriation*. London and New York: Routledge.

Stam, Robert (2005). *Literature through Film: Realism, Magic, and the Art of Adaptation*. Malden, MA, and Oxford: Blackwell Publishing Ltd.

Toury, Gideon (1995). *Descriptive Translation Studies and Beyond*. Amsterdam and Philadelphia: John Benjamins.

Türkmen, Erkan (2002). *The Essence of Rumi's* Masnevi *Including His Life and Works*. Ankara: Ministry of Culture.

Tymoczko, Maria (2007). *Enlarging Translation, Empowering Translations*. Manchester and Kinderbrook, NY: St. Jerome Publishing.

Van Gorp, Hendrik (1985) (2004). 'Translation and Comparable Transfer Operations', trans. Katheryn Bonnau-Bradbeer. In *Übersetzung, Translation, Traduction: An International Encyclopedia of Translation Studies*. Harald Kittel, Armin Paul Frank, Norbert Greimer, Theo Hermans, Werner Koller, José Lambert, and Fritz Paul (eds), Vol. 1, pp. 62–8. Berlin and New York: Walter de Gruyter.

Venuti, Lawrence (2007). 'Adaptation, Translation, Culture'. *Journal of Visual Culture* 6(1): 25–44.

Chapter 1

Adaptation and Appropriation: Is there a Limit?

Hugo Vandal-Sirois and Georges L. Bastin

Now that adaptation studies are currently thriving to become a discipline of their own that not only focuses on linguistic and cultural transfers, but also on a much broader spectrum of transpositions, it is important to step back and explore its presence in translation studies. After all, the idea of adapting any given text for a new specific audience has always been debated by quite a few theorists and practitioners, and eventually goes back to the old debate of domesticating versus foreignizing approaches. Yet, even the analysis of various aspects of genre adaptations such as the novelization of a movie, the transposition of a poem into a song, or the toning down of a certain narrative for younger readers finds echoes in many propositions published in translation studies papers.

The notion of adaptation itself was often discussed, supported or severely criticized in the field of translation studies. Regarded by some as a 'free' translation, even when the translational context demands it, adaptations are from time to time discarded or oversimplified. Still, in spite of the many accusations of being an abusive form of translation, or not a translation at all, adaptation is frequently listed among the possible valid solutions to various translational difficulties. Moreover, the idea that all translators do adaptations in their work, consciously or not, has already been around for a while. Lawrence Venuti, for instance, openly recognizes that any translation work implies a necessary domesticating task. This proposition denotes the importance of adaptation in the understanding of the process of creating efficient and accurate multilingual communications.

1.1 The Notion of Adaptation in Translation Studies (and Adaptation Studies)

One of the first acceptations of the notion of adaptation that comes to mind is certainly Vinay and Darbelnet's, who listed it as a simple translation procedure in their well-known *Comparative Stylistics of French and English* (1958, 1995 for the English translation). Here, adaptations are viewed as a 'situational equivalence' (Vinay and Darbelnet 1995: 39) conducted mostly to deal with cultural issues that might affect the target readers' reception or understanding of the source text. Vinay and Darbelnet illustrate the notion with the example of a French interpreter, who translated the English sport 'cricket' as 'Tour de France'. Although very basic, this example is a fine representation of a contextual situation that might justify such an initiative on the translator's behalf. An interesting addition of *Comparative Stylistics* to the matter is that the authors clearly mention that resorting to adaptation when translating might be disputable. Although this method is quickly described as the 'extreme limit of translation' (39), Vinay and Darbelnet clearly stress that a translator who systematically refuses to adapt will eventually produce a weakened target text. In other words, adaptation isn't necessarily a matter of treason or needless infidelity towards the original document or its author. The importance of adaptation is then underlined with the example of texts published by international organizations that often feel bland or inaccurate. That same point is still very relevant today in this era of mass communication and globalization, where organizations and corporations do not hesitate to send a single and unique message throughout the world. This situation is well illustrated by the examples taken from the fields of advertising and marketing that we will study later in this chapter.

Besides Vinay and Darbelnet's definition of adaptation as a procedure, another unavoidable contribution is provided by Julie Sanders' *Adaptation and Appropriation* (2006), which might very well be a classic in adaptation studies, alongside the breakthrough works of Robert Stam and Thomas Leitch. While Sanders seldom talks of translation itself in her book, she suggests a definition of adaptation that corresponds very conveniently to the process of translation: an 'attempt to make text 'relevant' or easily comprehensible to new audiences and readerships via the processes of proximation and updating' (Sanders 2006: 19). This notion originates from French literary theorist Gérard Genette. In the glossary of *Adaptation and Appropriation*, she defines this notion as '[. . .] an updating or the cultural relocation of a text to bring it into greater proximity to the cultural and temporal context of readers or audiences' (163). This represents precisely the motivation that pushes translators to take the initiative of distancing their work from more literal approaches in order to preserve the meaning, effect, or purpose of the original text, while ensuring the best reception possible of the translation among the target audience. Most professional translators face both cultural and linguistic obstacles in their work, and it would be erroneous to state that those who oppose the domesticating approach stick to word-for-word translations: an adaptation might well be an intrinsic part of a successful translation. This conclusion is in fact compatible with the clear distinction that Sanders draws between adaptation and appropriation: 'Adaptation signals a relationship with an informing source text or original. [. . .] Appropriation frequently affects a more decisive journey away from the informing source into a wholly new cultural product and domain (Sanders 2006: 26)'. Adaptation could be named *telos*, as suggested by Chesterman (2008): the personal goal of the translator. Examples taken from history will show how translators have often opted to adapt foreign texts to better serve their readers needs, but also decided to appropriate those texts to serve their own ideological commitments.

Adaptation seems to be part of the process of linguistic transfer of a document, created in one source culture and then aimed at another culture. In spite of the adjustments and modifications, often imposed by the language of the source text or deemed necessary by the translator, an adaptation still shares a very strong link to the source text. On this view, it is the notion of appropriation that could be accused of being an 'unfaithful' representation of the source text. And since appropriation is a conscious and creative undertaking that does not aim nor pretend to be a translation (although it shares most of its procedures), this whole matter of 'treason' and infidelity to the original seems resolved by this appropriation/adaptation distinction.

Another author who questions the systematic differentiation of 'adaptation' and 'translation' is Yves Gambier, who points out that there is an uncertainty in defining the notion of adaptation, and clarifying which line a translation has to cross to become an adaptation. In 'Adaptation: Une Ambiguïté à Interroger' (1992), he underlines this blurriness by noting that many translation procedures suggested by Vinay and Darbelnet other than 'adaptation', such as omission and condensation, are adaptations nonetheless. As he implies in this paper, it will be hard to find a satisfactory definition of adaptation if the very definition of translation itself is still an issue. Nevertheless, Gambier studies classic examples of translations that are commonly regarded as adaptations; this leads him to the conclusion that the labelling of any text produced by a translator as an adaptation is often a hasty personal judgment. Even if all source texts don't permit the translator to work with the same degree of 'freedom', an adaptation will occur at some point. Besides, a 'good' translation is frequently described as a text that 'feels' like an original. Yet, asking a translator to produce a text that would favour the target audience while avoiding any kind of linguistic, semiotic, or cultural adaptation would be unrealistic. This is precisely the ambiguity of adaptation Gambier refers to in the title of his paper.

Finally, our own reflections on the subject of adaptation are based on a personal translational experience: the creation of a Spanish version of Jean Delisle's *L'Analyse du Discours Comme Méthode de Traduction*. In order to produce a translation handbook that would be relevant, and above all, useful for our Spanish-speaking students (working from French to Spanish), it was obviously necessary to modify and adjust some of the content of the book that was originally intended for French-speaking students learning how to translate pragmatic texts from English. For instance, all the examples proposed by Delisle covered English-to-French translations, and by neglecting new examples in the Spanish version and just translating word-for-word would defeat the purpose of the book. On the contrary, our Spanish version aims to be a handbook equally 'formative' as the original. The purpose here is no doubt to form, and not to inform.

This experience inspired us to further study the notion of adaptation in the context of translation studies. After covering the earlier definitions of adaptation in the literature and reflecting upon the issues that came up during our translation project, we managed to formulate three hypotheses that would hopefully lead to a working definition of adaptation. These hypotheses, which are much more detailed in previous works (Bastin 1993, 1998), are that adaptations are 'recreations'; adaptations are necessary if not indispensable; and that it is possible to draw a line between the notions of adaptation and translation. Since all three notions appeared reasonably valid at the completion of our project, at the very least in the precise field of the translation of educational texts, we proposed our own definition: 'Adaptation is the process of creating a meaning that aims to restore a communicational balance that would be broken by the process of translation' (Bastin 1993: 477). We also noted that the most common factors that cause translators to resort to adaptation are cross-code breakdown, situational or cultural inadequacy, genre switching, and disruption of the communication process (Bastin 2008: 5). It is worth mentioning that the third factor refers to one of the main issues dealt with by Stam in his works on intertextuality and film adaptation (Stam 2004, 2005). In the Routledge *Encyclopedia of Translation Studies*, we further investigated the perceived distinction between adaptation and translation, and eventually suggested that adaptation may be viewed as 'a set of translative operations which results in a text that is not accepted as translation but is nevertheless recognized as representing a source text of about the same length' (Bastin 2008: 3). Translation processes meaning while adaptation favours communicative situation and thus functionality. Moreover, we found that adaptations can be tactical (when the translation faces a specific translational problem in a text, often of a linguistic or cultural nature), or strategic (when global modifications are needed to ensure the relevance and the usefulness of the translation, such as our version of Delisle's book). If the first kind of adaptation is optional and resorts to the text itself, the latter surely is needed for the translation to suit the expectations of the target culture. In other words, adaptations do not resort to the text itself, but to the communication situation (which, in our case study, was pedagogy). While these propositions were elaborated with metalanguage-filled academic texts in mind, we strongly feel that they might apply to a broader scope of translation domains. As for the questionable systematic distinction between translation and adaptation discussed by Gambier, our studies and practical work led us to believe that not only do these two notions share the same functions and objectives, but also that adaptation is essential to carry out the purpose of a message.

1.2 The Notion of Adaptation in Functionalism

In addition to underlining the cultural nature of adaptation that is clearly reflected in the various definitions we just surveyed, it is important to locate adaptation in the ever-growing field of translation theory. Although many theories that push the domesticating 'agenda' suit the notion of adaptation very well, the functionalist approach seems the most suitable to describe the reasons why a translator resorts to adapting a text. Since adaptations are motivated by keeping the source text applicable to the target culture, and ensuring the efficacy of a text for a specific group of readers, the translator should consider the purpose of the text that will be introduced in a different culture, the reason why the translation is requested, and the target readers of the translation. Mark Shuttleworth and Moira Cowie's definition of adaptation is also in the same vein: 'The term usually implies that considerable changes have been made in order to make the text more suitable for a specific audience (e.g., children) or for the particular purpose behind the translation' (Shuttleworth and Cowie 1997: 3). This last point about the purposeful nature of adaptations illustrates how well this translational practice comes within the scope of functionalist theories. Giuseppe Palumbo's definition of the functionalist approach, where translation is seen 'as an act of communication and a form of action involving not only linguistic but also social and cultural factors' (Palumbo 2009: 50), illustrates how convenient and valuable the technique of adaptation is for functionalist translators. Many elements related to the functionalist theory of translation are relevant to adaptations, from Hans Vermeer's *skopos* (Vermeer 1996) to Christiane Nord's loyalty (Nord 1997).[1]

1.3 Adaptation as a Part of the Translation Process

The four interpretations of the notion of adaptation and its role in the translation process surveyed at the beginning of this chapter contain similarities that can be combined in order to understand adaptation's 'ambiguity' in translation studies. First and foremost, as Gambier states at the beginning of his paper (Gambier 1992: 421), even a basic translation goes way beyond the word-by-word transfer process. These various definitions clearly emphasize the significance of adaptation's domesticating nature. Whether they are consciously carried out by a translator or not, successful adaptations allow (or even force) the target readers to discover the text in a way that suits its aim, ensures an optimal reception experience, or simply promotes the understanding of a specific message. Adaptations take place on the cultural or pragmatic levels at least as much as on the linguistic or textual level. Furthermore, the statement that every translator needs to adapt at some point or another seems to be a commonly held idea – something that is far from being just a creative whim. According to Vazquez-Ayora (1977), adaptations 'allow the adequacy of a content with the particular view of each language' (324, our translation). He then goes on: 'Except for the fields and the cases where it is necessary to keep the 'foreign element', every non-adaptation forces the reader to move him or herself into a strange and false reality' (330). In *Translation: An Interpretive Approach*, Jean Delisle writes: 'Creation, interpretation, re-creation, translation and adaptation are more closely related than one might think' (Delisle 1998: 63). And in *Berman, Étranger à Lui-même?*, Marc Charron brilliantly demonstrates that adaptation is, once again consciously or not, in the very nature of every translator. He studies the first pages of the French translation of Augusto Roa Bastos's *Yo el Supremo* done by Antoine Berman, a fierce opponent of the domesticating approach, and finds examples of each one of Berman's twelve deforming tendencies. Indeed, his translation includes among others clarifications, destructions of vernacular elements and expansions. Charron's paper indicates that there is a cross-cultural shift in most if not all translations, and that the gap between the foreignizing theories and the actual practice of translation appears to be almost unavoidable. Besides, we can also diverge from the field of translation studies to find definitions of the notion of adaptation that suit the ones we mentioned earlier. In our doctoral thesis for instance (Bastin 1998: 89), we already quoted Charles Darwin, for whom adaptation is the modification process whereby any living being adjusts itself, him, or herself and complies with the conditions imposed by their environment. Therefore, if adaptation is a matter of survival in biology, we can surely suggest it is a matter of communicational relevance in translation.

1.3.1 Localization versus internationalization

The notion of adaptation is at the heart of the localization/internalization dichotomy. In this era of globalization, where international corporations and organizations aim to promote the same product or idea to the widest range of potential targets possible, the need for efficient multilingual communication is constantly increasing. This is why the act of translation is more and more integrated to business plans and communication strategies at an early stage, instead of being the last-minute activity it has usually been in the past. Of course, both concepts of internationalization and localization raise important questions relevant to translation studies. Can a single idea be understood, interpreted, and remembered the same way in various cultures? Are any notions, realities, or philosophies understood in the same way by source and target readers? Can a translator ever ignore the target reader's cultural, social, and personal backgrounds? Have we reached a point where the inhabitants of this 'global village' think similarly and share the same ideals or needs? To answer these questions, we must not only consider the definitions of 'globalization' and 'localization' (since there seems to be a certain ambiguity about what they actually mean), but also adopt the point of view of those institutions whose activities include multilingual and multicultural communications. First of all, the Localization Industry Standards Association (LISA), an international non-profit organization helping corporations to communicate and do business globally, suggests two definitions of *localization*: (i) The process of modifying products or services to account for differences in distinct markets;[2] and (ii) The process of adapting software for a particular geographical region (locale).

Those two conceptions of the notion of localization seem very close to the various definitions of adaptation we studied earlier. The idea of changing the source text to ensure a better efficiency in the target culture, the domesticating nature of adaptation, and more precisely the constant focus on target readers and their environment are all evident. On the other hand, LISA defines *internationalization* as 'the process of generalizing a product so that it can handle multiple languages and cultural conventions without the need for re-design'.[3] In other words, whereas localization aims to create customized communications for various linguistic and cultural communities, internationalization aims to reproduce a unique reader experience (same content, same structure, same graphic presentation, and audiovisual elements, translations as close to the source text as possible, etc.) It is easy to recognize in these opposing strategies echoes of the adaptation/translation argument mentioned earlier. In her article about the translation of videogame advertising, Raquel De Pedro Ricoy sums up the dilemma multinational companies are facing of whether to choose a unique message that aims to reach the widest possible audience, or to 'adapt the message to specific locales, taking into account cultural differences and autochthonous peculiarities' (De Pedro Ricoy 2007: 262). The choice is not just up to the translator: other linguistic, cultural, and economic factors have to be borne in mind as well. Anthony Pym addresses the consequences of this: on the one hand, this reduction of responsibility on the translators' behalf allows them to focus on the translation itself, without being distracted or constrained by technical or business-oriented considerations. On the other hand, he notes that translators have a deep knowledge of the target culture, which can play a crucial role in the success of any given multilingual communication, and that 'they should be listened to at more than phrase level' (Pym 2010: 137). This trust in the translators' ability to facilitate the reception, or enhance the efficiency, of a given communication in a specific context is the cornerstone of most arguments in favour of localization and adaptation. In fact, many previous papers in translation studies analysed practical cases where the translators' creative input, not only from the linguistic, but also from the cultural content point of view, was deemed worthy or downright necessary. For instance, in *Voices in Translation*, the award-winning literary translator Margaret Jull Costa wrote about the role of creativity in the translation process of culturally specific elements such as food, puns, idioms, proverbs, as well as references of historical, geographical, or cultural nature (in short, of most elements of a text that might be considered untranslatable). She gave the example of the proverb '*o seguro morreu de velho*' quoted by the narrator in a Portuguese novel that is not only a narrative element, but also a pun referring to insurance and reinsurance. Since 'better safe than sorry', the English equivalent of the proverb, wasn't satisfactory on both the semantic and narrative levels, Jull Costa adapted the original proverb by creating a new and much more suitable one for the narrative context: 'slow but sure ensures a ripe old age'. She took great care to come up with an idea that had a strong 'proverbial ring', in order to render the phrase comprehensible to the target culture, a self-admitted domesticating strategy that seemed ideal in this case (Jull Costa 2007: 115).

As for the choice between internationalization and localization multinational organizations are facing, the motivation of the communication act itself seems to be the key element (functionalism once more) in choosing the best strategic and most relevant approach. Sometimes as important as the content, the aim and the target of such communications are crucial in the selection of the linguistic and semantic transfer strategies to be used. In a publication about commercial and institutional translation, Mathieu Guidère shows the importance of considering the target culture in order to avoid incoherence or inefficient translations, by giving the example of the website of the Canadian Embassy in Morocco (Guidère 2008: 69). Due to the bilingual status of Canada, it's natural that this website is in both French and English. Yet it's indeed surprising that absolutely no content has been translated into Arabic, not even the sections intended for Moroccan citizens. This case indicates how important the reflection process prior to undertaking the translation of such documents can be. In order to select a more suitable strategy, many factors should be considered by translators and their clients. First, from the business and operational standpoints, internationalization makes a lot of sense. Among other things, it allows economies of scale, is very compatible with the centralized structures such organizations tend to adopt, and if done well, favours the upholding of a strong, unique, and coherent brand image and corporate identity throughout the world. On the other hand, localization allows for more customized and in all likelihood more applicable target texts. With many kinds of source documents, the extra time, energy, and dollars invested in creating numerous local versions often result in a better overall reception in the target culture. Of course, this argument between domesticating and foreignizing approaches isn't new in translation studies, but the notions of localization and internationalization seem more sharply divided that ever before. For instance, just a quick glance at a translated website of a multinational corporation is enough to determine which multilingual communication strategy was used.

Finally, it is important to point out for the sake of clarity that nowadays many professional translators, translation agencies, and even advertising agencies frequently use the term 'localization' not to describe the act of customizing a product for a specific target culture, but simply as a generic buzzword referring to the process of adaptation itself. In these cases, the localization process is often promoted as a kind of target-oriented translation (or maybe as customized recreation). This common professional activity finds its echo in translation studies in André Lefevere's view of translations as a rewriting of the original text that reflects 'a certain ideology and a poetics and as such manipulate literature to function in a given society in a given way' (Lefevere 1992: xi). It also relates to what we called 'deliberate interventions' (Bastin 2007), conscious decisions that can be considered objective or subjective. Objective interventions, better known as 'shifts', are text-based and correspond to the necessary shifts translators usually resort to for the sake of language or culture adequacy. On the other hand, subjective interventions are dependent on historical or ideological factors, or because of the specific socio-cultural identity of the translator. These are 'deliberate', since nothing obliges the translator to behave that way; they depend on the translator's *telos*.

1.3.2 Adaptations in advertising and multilingual marketing

Until recently, the translation of advertising texts has been quite ignored by translation studies and yet, it provides a vast array of very interesting case studies about the influence of both source and target cultures on the translator's work, the constraints of translating a single message through different media, as well as the understanding of the notions of fidelity, equivalence, and adaptation. Furthermore, the analysis of translated advertising texts and multicultural marketing provides striking examples of the application of numerous major translation theories such as Toury's norms, the polysystem theory, the interpretive theory, and for obvious reasons, functionalism. To our knowledge, the first scientific publication entirely dedicated to the matter was a special issue of *Meta: Translators' Journal* published back in 1972, which addressed different practical matters related to the translation of advertisements. It is very interesting to note that adaptation was considered an obvious strategy by the authors; this view of adaptation as a natural choice for advertising still prevailed in subsequent publications and continues to this day – for example a special issue of *The Translator*, published in 2004, was titled *Key Debates in the Translation of Advertising Materials*. Numerous publications in translation studies spanning over more than three decades support adaptations in the case of multilingual advertising campaigns, from Roger Boivineau's *L'A.B.C. de l'Adaptation Publicitaire* (1972): 'It is rather a matter of reaching the goal of the original ad, and the way to achieve this goal might differ noticeably from the way followed by the copywriter' (Boivineau 1972: 15, our translation),[4] to the conclusion of Veronica Smith's article about the challenges of translating visual elements in advertisements: 'There are a number of factors which make the involvement of translators in the creation and adaptation of global advertisements desirable' (Smith 2008: 57). Many authors interested in the notion of culture in multilingual communication include advertising in their work (such as Marieke de Mooij, Beverly Adab, or Mathieu Guidère just to name a few). Advertising is one of the few fields of specialized translation where adaptation is free from the criticisms we highlighted earlier on. Due to the nature of the advertising text, this systematic use of adaptation and the high relevance of the functionalist approach are constantly discussed and promoted in the literature, as well as on numerous business websites of specialized translation agencies and marketing services companies.

It is crucial to briefly review the characteristics of the advertising text in order to understand why adaptation is so commonplace. First of all, advertising translators constantly face various practical challenges involving limited space or time frame, as well as untranslatable semantic correlations between text and image. In addition to these technical difficulties, there is always the matter of cultural, linguistic, and semantic differences, for example, the socio-cultural realities of a specific target market, the nature of the client's selling points and incentives, humour, and puns. But above all, it's the persuasive nature of the text itself that is behind this clear preference for domesticating translations. The purpose of an advertisement consists of broadening awareness of a cause, a company, or a product, and ultimately altering the opinions or behaviour of a specific demographic. To achieve this goal, the advertisement must not only reach its intended target, but also create the belief that the ad speaks directly to individual viewers. 'What's in it for me?' is truer than ever. This crucial process of identification by the target audience explains why foreignizing strategies are often dismissed at once, except for some very particular products such as imported luxury goods. In fact, any indication that the ad has been created in a distinct culture might jeopardize the viewer's ability and 'willingness' to feel concerned by the message and to comprehend its content. To successfully reach their target audience and efficiently get the key message across, the translator must go through a reflection phase that is in many ways similar to the creative process followed by the copywriters of the original version. This includes finding answers to questions such as: 'What do we need to say?', 'Who are we talking to?', 'Who is sending the message?', 'How and where will the target see the message?' But beyond these questions, the advertising translator must also consider the specific context of the demographic targeted by the translation. For instance, is the original ad featuring a product that is well known in the source culture, but new to the target culture? Is the product facing well-established local competitors in the target culture that do not exist in the source culture? Are the arguments and the incentives of the source ad as efficient in the target culture? To produce purposeful adaptations, according to functionalist concerns, advertising translators should be familiar with business and marketing strategies, as well as master the art of persuasive writing.

This tendency to adapt and to produce 'freer' translations than in many other fields is certainly linked to the highly domesticated nature of advertising, and by extension, to what the client actually expects from the translator: an advertisement that will impact the target culture. However, another point to consider is that the advertisements are requested by the clients and created on demand by marketing agencies, freelance copywriters, and art directors. Even the most creative brains adopt a functionalist approach and observe a set of concrete strategies. This is why the advertising translators feel that they have to be faithful towards the client (the product, the brand, the company) rather than the source text. The fact that advertising translators collaborate with copywriters, artistic directors, and graphic designers should not be overlooked. Being involved in such a collaborative environment has a strong influence on the creative decisions presented to the client (pragmatic, linguistic, cultural, strategic).

At this point, it's useful to refer to two case studies where typical translations are certainly possible, but would create a text that would be either dull or highly embarrassing for a client. We selected two simple and down-to-earth examples that actually happened in our professional experience as translators in an advertising agency. They give a good idea of common issues arising in this field of work. The adaptations are both from English

(Canadian and American, respectively) to Québec French; the first of these, which concerns translating humour, is an animated online ad from a major travel agency, in which a snowman is escaping a snow globe – a visual incentive for the viewer to take a break from the cold winter and go south. The short animation was topped by a headline saying 'give ice the slip', a common expression that refers both to the idea of getting away from a freezing winter, as well as to the visual elements of the advertisement. Obviously, translating an expression that doesn't have an exact French equivalent is unthinkable here, and suggesting a more generic sentence such as '*fuyez l'hiver*' ('Get away from winter') would be a significant loss. Therefore, we had to find a French headline that would carry the same polysemy, respect the constraints of the medium, and of course preserve the strong link to the image. We eventually came up with '*mettez l'hiver sur la glace*' (literally 'put winter on ice'), a funny way to say 'put winter on hold' that suited the visual elements perfectly. With this idea in mind, we produced a French version that was instantly understandable (which is particularly important for online advertisements), and as colloquial as the source text.

Even if these kinds of very specific adaptations are common, it is true that from time to time, translators must undertake much more extensive adaptations to sustain not the meaning but the function of a text. This is the case of our second example, which is a whole excerpt from an American brochure of a motorized recreational vehicle that stated that the engine remains efficient even in very warm weather such as 100°F (37.7°C). Those advertising translators, who are not only experts of the target language and culture, but who also have a deep knowledge of the habits, customs, and mentality of the potential customers they are writing for, should know that extreme heat isn't a big concern in Québec. Therefore, a literal translation of these brochures, no matter how well written, would be useless for the local Québec dealers and their customers, as well as being potentially damaging to the company's public image. Translators must then place themselves in the shoes of a copywriter and take the liberty of changing a portion of the source text's content ('Will the motor work in very cold temperatures?' or 'Is there some accessories that allow the vehicle to perform in snow?'). They also have to create a visual composition that would be more suitable (in this case, a boreal forest instead of desert and dry landscapes). This shows the importance of not only knowing the product and ideally experiencing it first-hand, but also mastering creative copywriting. In her article, De Pedro Ricoy gives examples of situations where the translator has to create new content. In one case, the original slogan was judged to be a little too sexist in some cultures (De Pedro Ricoy 2007: 270),[5] and in another, the reviews from specialized magazines unknown in the target culture were replaced by a compelling description of the game (271) that the translator wrote from scratch. In a globalized world, where the need for adapting advertising is constantly increasing, translators are often expected to be more involved in the whole communicative process as cultural and even creative consultants. This means taking part in briefings, strategic meetings and brainstorming sessions, suggesting modifications of textual content and visual presentation, and even being present during the casting and the recording of audiovisual productions. It is then interesting to note that, as Guidère remarks (2008), this preference for adaptations led to a shift of perception of the advertising translator's role, from linguistic expert to provider of more generalized communication services. The translator doesn't sign his work (at least publicly) and the reader cannot be misled as to authorship. Therefore, advertising translation is clearly a matter of adaptation, where a strong link to the source text is preserved, even though the gulf between both versions can turn out to be extremely wide.

1.3.3 Adaptations and appropriations in translation history

It is clear from the above discussion that two main kinds of strategies can be distinguished, namely *adaptations*, that we already addressed, and *appropriations*, where any link between the source and the target texts is voluntarily eluded. Of course, hybrid strategies can appear as what Stetting (1989) has called *transediting*, in the specific case of the pro-independence press in the nineteenth century, or *imitations* and *transcreations.*

Adaptations, as we said earlier, can be tactical or strategic. Since tactical adaptation can be considered as a commonplace translation procedure involving issues of textual fidelity, we will focus on strategic or global adaptations. A good example is certainly Manuel García de Sena's version of Thomas Paine's writings. Making a selection of extracts from various works by Thomas Paine, García de Sena published in Philadelphia the book *La Independencia de Costa Firme Justificada por Thomas Paine Treinta Años ha* (1811). García de Sena introduced explanations in his text in order to be sure that his readers understood the references to the North American political system described by Paine. He added paratexts of his own such as a dedication and various footnotes of the most aggressive style, designed to prompt his compatriots to rebel against the Spanish crown and build republics similar to the United States. He also exerted censorship on everything contrary to his Catholic beliefs, as well as aspects of the source text that were not directly applicable to the situation in Hispanic America.

Thus, this version is clearly an act of selective translation designed to suit the interests of his readers. Note that, by naming the original author in the very title of his book, Garcia de Sena does not appropriate Paine's texts.

As opposed to the translation of the first *Declaration of the Rights of Man* (1789) by Antonio Nariño in Bogota, which was quite a literal piece of translation, the translation of the second Declaration (1793) can be seen as an example of adaptation. It appeared in Venezuela in 1797 by Juan Bautista Picornell, who led the failed insurrection in Spain known as the San Blas Conspiracy (February 3, 1795) to overthrow the monarchy and establish a republican government. With his fellow conspirators, Picornell translated various revolutionary French documents, using a perlocutionary vocabulary designed to encourage his readers to take action. He does not present the text as a translation (nor does he put his name) but as an original document addressing Venezuelans. Therefore, he omits the Declaration's preamble beginning with the phrase: 'The French people . . . '

On the other hand, as Sanders observes, appropriations aim to create new products fully independent from their source. For instance, this can occur in obvious cases of plagiarism. A good example is that of Miguel José Sanz, a leading Venezuelan independence intellectual. All texts signed by him in the *Semanario de Caracas*, a pro-independence periodical during 1810–11, are in fact translations of Adam Ferguson's *Essay on the History of Civil Society* (1767). Falcón (1998) compared most of Sanz's writing in the *Semanario de Caracas* to Ferguson's *Essay* and there can be no doubt that they are literal translations, or *transeditions* of Ferguson's work. Sanz never mentions his sources, and quite a lot of Venezuelan historians have erroneously interpreted the ideological and political content of his writings as if they were his own. Plagiarism can also occur between two translations, as in Berman's translation of Schleiermacher, which is for the most part the French version of a Spanish translation by García Yebra of the same German text (Schleiermacher 2000). These examples of plagiarism are clear appropriations of the foreign text or of a previous translation by the translator.

Imitations constitute a different kind of appropriation. Although they might mention the source, they use procedures that change completely not only the 'reality' (as in adaptation) but above all the authorship of the text. Many examples of imitations can be seen in literature. Let us mention the famous imitations of European poets by Andrés Bello (1781–1865). Rafael Caldera summarizes this strategy as follows: '[Bello] makes his, in an original way, others' thinking and transports on the

American scene episodes that happened in completely foreign environments' (Caldera 1981: lxviii.)[6] In another kind of imitation, Bello transforms the source poem in order to express his own experiences. His translation of Victor Hugo's 'À Olympe' is used to express his sufferings in England while in exile. In the French text, Olympe finds supreme comfort in *love*, but this love becomes *honour* in Bello's imitation (Pagni 2004). Another example of appropriation in the same poem is the fact that for Bello, the emphasis is on peace while in Hugo's *Olympe*, enemies hope to fight a war. In another Victor Hugo's poem, 'La Prière pour Tous', Miguel Antonio Caro (1843-1909), stresses the interpolations by the translator, in particular by interrupting the religious and moral tone of the original and introducing verses charged with political and personal connotations (Caro 1982: 158).

Latin American literature reveals many more cases of appropriations by José Martí, Jorge Luis Borges, José María de Heredia (Bastin et al., 2004), and Monteiro Lobato (Milton 2002) among others. Hence,

> the concept and practice of appropriation may thus reconfigure the status of translation as the production of texts that are not simply consumed by the target language and culture but which, in turn, become creative and productive, stimulating reflections, theorizations and representations within the target cultural context. (Saglia 2002: 96)

An in-between adaptation and appropriation case is the Spanish version of the French Revolution song 'La Carmagnole', which appeared in La Guaira together with other 'subversive' texts in Spanish (among them the *Declaration of the Rights of Man*) gathered and printed by Juan Bautista Picornell in the French Antilles (Guadeloupe 1797). Several adaptations were introduced by the translator Manuel Cortés Campomanes, the so-called 'poet of the revolution': the joyful tone of the French text becomes very solemn in Spanish; the number of stanzas increases from thirteen to twenty-five; all cultural and historical French references are replaced by Spanish and American ones; and new concepts such as heroism, God, unity and Motherland appear. If it were not for one verse referring to the French revolutionaries, we might have assumed that it had been written to celebrate the rebellion of the Venezuelans against the Spaniards.

Transediting is the simultaneous interaction of both *translating* and *editing*, which implies tactical and strategic interventions such as expansion, deletion, summary, commentary and reformulation. Notorious examples can be found in a study of the *Gaceta de Caracas*, where this strategy is frequently used to serve the political interests of the journalists of this

Venezuelan pro-independence periodical (1808–22). Aura Navarro (2008) shows how translators add, suppress, paraphrase, summarize, and comment original texts from the English, North American or French press of that time. For instance, every time the source text refers to 'colonies' or 'Spanish provinces', the Gaceta speaks of 'America' or 'parts of South America'. There are various footnotes that make negative comments about words like 'insurgent', referring to revolutionaries or about actions taken by the Spanish government. In many cases, those translations are inserted in different parts of the articles, so that readers cannot distinguish between source and target texts, and in others, only the source text can lead the reader to acknowledge a translation. All are deliberate interventions motivated by the target journalists and their readers, and even though sources are often quoted, they still represent appropriations. The interest of studying deliberate interventions lies in the fact that the 'translation strategies go beyond the description level of analysis, since they help to explain the translator's behavior' (Gagnon 2006: 207).

Related to *transediting* is the process of *transcreation* put forward and used by Haroldo de Campos. According to de Campos (1983: 58), transcreation implies that the source and the target texts 'will be different in terms of language, but, as isomorphic bodies, they will be crystallized within the same system' since transcreation is, for de Campos, an act of transgressive appropriation and hybridism.

1.4 Conclusion

As Ladmiral (1994: 20) put it: 'adaptation refers less to a translation procedure than to the limits of translation [. . .] since the reality to which the source message refers does not exist for the target culture'.[7] Indeed, although some pretend that anything can be translated, translation has limits. Adaptations and appropriations as global strategies certainly go very often beyond the normal work of pragmatic translators, but nevertheless are commonly used by individuals in many translation settings. They are essential to translation studies and should not be seen any more as 'non-translations', 'treasons', or 'transgressions' of a source text. On the contrary, they represent the visibility that gives translators the same recognition as the author of the source text. Tejaswini Niranjana and Theo Hermans suggest that

> Translation is, of course, a rewriting of an original text. All rewritings, whatever their intention, reflect a certain ideology and a poetics and as

> such manipulate literature to function in a given society in a given way. Rewriting is manipulation, undertaken in the service of power, and in its positive aspect can help in the evolution of a literature and a society. Rewritings can introduce new concepts, new genres, new devices, and the history of translation is the history also of literary innovation, of the shaping power of one culture upon another. But rewriting can also repress innovation, distort and contain, and in an age of increasing manipulation of all kinds, the study of the manipulative processes of literature as exemplified by translation can help us towards a greater awareness of the world in which we live. (Niranjana 1992: 59)

> [T]ranslations appropriate, transform and relocate their source texts, adjusting them to new communicative situations and purposes. [. . .] The 'anterior text' to which a translation refers is never simply the source text, even though that is the claim which translations commonly make. It is a particular image of it [. . .]. And because the image is always slanted, coloured, pre-formed, never innocent, we can say that translation constructs and produces [. . .] its original. (Hermans 1999: 58–9)

Translation studies would greatly benefit from rethinking adaptation at hand, if only for the sake of the numerous authors who demonstrated its practical efficiency and necessity in the process of ensuring meaningful linguistic and cultural transfers.

Notes

1 Vermeer's *Skopos* theory advocates for translation as a purposeful activity and within this framework, Nord puts forward the need for the translator to be 'loyal' to both the source author and the target user.

2 LISA Globalization Glossary, available online at www.lisa.org (accessed April 4, 2011).

3 Quoted in Pym (2010).

4 'l s'agira plutôt d'atteindre le but recherché avec l'annonce originale, et la voie pour rejoindre ce but pourra s'écarter sensiblement de celle suivie par le concepteur'.

5 'Will'st thou save the girl, or play like one?', a line obviously aimed at the young male demographic.

6 'fait sienne, de manière originale, la pensée d'autrui et transportait sur la scène américaine les épisodes réalisés dans des environnements complètement étrangers'.

7 '. . . l'adaptation désigne moins un procédé de traduction qu'elle n'en indique les limites [. . .] la réalité à laquelle se réfère le message-source n'existe pas pour la culture-cible'.

Bibliography

Bastin, Georges L. (1993). 'La Notion d'Adaptation en Traduction'. *Meta: Translators' Journal* 38(3): 473–78.

— (1998). *Traducir o adaptar?* Caracas: Universidad Central de Venezuela, Consejo de Desarrollo Científico y Humanístico/Facultad de Humanidades y Educación.

— (2004). Á. Echeverri and Á. Campo 'La Traducción en América Latina: Propia y Apropiada'. In *Estudios* Vol. 24América Latina: Espacios de traducción, A. Pagni (dir.), pp. 69–94. Caracas: Universidad Simón Bolívar.

— (2007). 'Histoire, Traductions et Traductologie'. In *Quo Vadis Translatologie? Ein Halbes Jahrhundert Universitäre Ausbildung von Dolmetschern und Übersetzern in Leipzig,* ed. Gerd Wotjak. 35–44. Berlin: Frank & Timme GmbH.

— (2008). 'Adaptation'. In *The Routledge Encyclopedia of Translation Studies.* Mona Baker (ed.),pp: 3–6. London and New York: Routledge

Boivineau, Roger (1972). 'L'A.B.C. de l'Adaptation Publicitaire'. *Meta: Translators' Journal* 17(1): 5–28.

Caldera, Rafael (1982). 'Bello: El pedagogo, el Sociólogo, Conclusion'. In *Andrés Bello: Homenaje de la Universidad Central de Venezuela en el Bicentenario de su Natalicio.* 191–224. Caracas: Ediciones del Rectorado de la Universidad Central de Venezuela.

Caro, Miguel Antonio (1982). 'Caracteres de la Poesía de Bello'. In *Andrés Bello. Homenaje de la Universidad Central de Venezuela en el Bicentenario de su Natalicio.* 157–61. Caracas: Ediciones del Rectorado de la Universidad Central de Venezuela.

Charron, Marc (2001). 'Berman, Étranger à Lui-même'. *TTR* 14(2): 97–121.

Chesterman, Andrew (2008). 'Ethics of Renarration: Mona Baker is Interviewed by Andrew Chesterman'. *Cultus* 1(1): 10–33.

De Pedro Ricoy, Raquel (2007). 'Internationalization vs. Localization: The Translation of Videogame Advertising'. *Meta: Translators' Journal* 52(2): 260–75.

Delisle, Jean (1986). 'Dans les Coulisses de l'Adaptation Théâtrale'. *CIRCUIT* 12: 3–8.

— (1988). *Translation: an Interpretive Approach* (Translation of *L'Analyse du Discours Comme Méthode de Traduction* by Patricia Logan and Monica Creery). Ottawa: University of Ottawa Press.

Falcón, Fernando (1998). 'Adam Ferguson y el Pensamiento Ético y Político de Miguel José Sanz. Notas Para la Reinterpretación del Semanario de Caracas, 1810–1811'. *Politeia* 21: 44–50.

Gagnon, Chantal (2006). 'Ideologies in the History of Translation: A Case Study on Canadian Political Speeches'. In *Charting the Future of Translation History.* Georges L. Bastin and Paul F. Bandia (eds), 201–23. Ottawa: University of Ottawa Press.

Gambier, Yves (1992). 'Adaptation : une Ambiguïté à Interroger'. *Meta: Translators' Journal* 37(3): 421–5.

Guidère, Mathieu (2008). *La Communication ultilingue.* Bruxelles: De Boeck.

Hermans, Theo (1999). 'Translation and Normativity'. In *Translation and Norms.* Christina Schäffner (ed.), 50–71. Clevedon: Multilingual Matters.

Jull Costa, Margaret (2007). 'Mind the Gap: Translating the "Untranslatable"'. In *Voices in Translation*. Gunilla M. Anderman (ed.), 111–22. Clevedon: Multilingual Matters.

Ladmiral, Jean-René (1994). *Traduire: Théorèmes pour la Traduction*. Paris: Gallimard.

Lefevere, André (1992). *Translation, History, Culture*. London and New York: Routledge.

Leitch, Thomas (2007). *Film Adaptation and Its Discontents: from Gone with the Wind to The Passion of the Christ*. Baltimore: The Johns Hopkins University Press.

Milton, John (2002). *O Clube do Livro e a Traduçaõ*. Bauru: Editora da Universidade do Sagrado Coraçaõ (EDUSC).

— (2010). 'Adaptation', in *Handbook of Translation Studies*. Yves Gambier and Luc van Doorslaer (eds), Vol. 1. 3–6. Amsterdam/Philadelphia: John Benjamins.

Navarro, Aura (2008). 'La Traduction Dans la Gaceta de Caracas Pendant la Première Période Patriotique (1810–1812)'. Unpubl. M.A. thesis, Université de Montréal, Département de Linguistique et de Traduction.

Niranjana, Tejaswini (1992). *Siting Translation. History, Poststructuralism and the Colonial Context*. Berkeley: University of California Press.

Nord, Christiane (1997). *Translating as a Purposeful Activity: Functionalist Translation Theories Explained*. Manchester and Kinderhook, NY: St. Jerome Publishing.

Pagni, Andrea (2004). 'Olimpio en América del Sur. Usos hispanoamericanos del Romanticismo Francés'. Caracas, Universidad Simón Bolívar, ESTUDIOS 24: 117–32. www.histal.umontreal.ca/pdfs1/PagniOlimpioEnAmericaDelSur.PDF (accessed March 17, 2011).

Palumbo, Giuseppe (2009). *Key Terms in Translation Studies*. London and New York: Continuum International Publishing Group.

Pym, Anthony (2010). *Explaining Translation Theories*. London and New York: Routledge.

Saglia, Diego (2002). 'Translation and Cultural Appropriation: Dante, Paolo and Francesca in British Romanticism', *Quaderns* 7: 95–109.

Sanders, Julie (2006). *Adaptation and Appropriation*. London and New York: Routledge.

Schleiermacher, Friedrich (2000). *Sobre los Diferentes Métodos de Traducir*, trans. Valentín García Yebra. Madrid: Gredos.

Shuttleworth, Mark and Cowie, Moira (1997). *Dictionary of Translation Studies*. Manchester and Kinderhook, NY: St. Jerome Publishing.

Smith, Veronica (2008). 'Visual Persuasion: Issues in the Translation of the Visual in Advertising'. *Meta: Translators' Journal* 53(1): 44–61.

Stam, Robert (2005). *Literature Through Film: Realism, Magic, and the Art of Adaptation*. Oxford and Malden, MA: Blackwell Publishing.

Stam, Robert and Raengo, Alessandra (2004). *A Companion to Literature and Film*. Oxford and Malden, MA: Blackwell Publishing.

Stetting, Karen (1989). 'Transediting: A New Term for Coping with the Grey Area Between Editing and Translating'. In *Proceedings from the Fourth Nordic Conference for English Studies*. Graham Caie et al. (eds), 371–82. Copenhagen: University of Copenhagen.

Vàzquez-Ayora, Gerardo (1977). *Introducción a la Traductología*. Washington: Georgetown University Press.

Venuti, Lawrence (2007). 'Adaptation, Translation, Critique'. *Journal of Visual Culture* 6(1): 25–43.

Vermeer, Hans J. (1996). *A Skopos Theory of Translation (Some Arguments For and Against).* Heidelberg: TEXTconTEXT.

Vinay, Jean-Paul and Darbelnet, Jean (1995). *Comparative Stylistics of French and English,* trans. and Juan C. Sager and M.-J. Hamel (eds). Amsterdam and Philadelphia: John Benjamins.

Chapter 2

Translation and Adaptation – Two Sides of an Ideological Coin

Katja Krebs

Translation studies and adaptation studies have established themselves firmly as academic fields of enquiry in their own right. Translation studies, the older of the two in terms of the academy, has developed and continues to develop rigorous conceptual frameworks and perspectives within which the phenomena of such 'rewriting' (see, e.g., Lefevere 1985) can be analysed, and it has certainly emancipated itself from disciplines such as linguistics and comparative literature, which historically have subsumed the study of translation. In their important collection of essays *Constructing Cultures,* Bassnett and Lefevere go so far as to argue that: 'Translation Studies should be seen as the discipline within which comparative literature might be located, rather than the other way round' (Bassnett and Lefevere 1998: viii).

Adaptation studies too, is emerging from the shadows of English studies in particular, if a little later than translation studies. It is in the process of developing a diversity of approaches and perspectives, which is pivotal for its longevity and rigor as an academic discipline. While previous positions tended to be based upon the assumption that literature has an intrinsically higher value than other forms of (popular) culture such as cinema and television, current discourse is proving to be less prejudicial. Just as Robert Stam articulates the field's tendency to charge adaptation with parasitism (see Stam 2005), in his article 'Vampire Adaptation', Thomas Leitch subverts 'the hoariest clichés in the field' (Leitch 2011: 5) and employs a vampire analogy in order to challenge the frequent accusations of violation made against adaptation as process and product. Both translation studies and adaptation studies are interdisciplinary by their very nature; both discuss the phenomena of constructing cultures through acts of rewriting;

and both are concerned with the collaborative nature of such acts and the subsequent and necessary critique of notions of authorship.

It seems a curious state of affairs, then, that two distinct academic fields and discourses have developed that investigate such closely related acts of rewriting as adaptation and translation without engaging with each other's critical perspectives and methodologies. Both fields hold their own and quite separate set of conferences, have their own academic journals, and very rarely if at all exchange methodologies and conceptual insights. The *Journal of Adaptation in Film and Performance* tries to be the exception to the rule, by specifically inviting work that bridges the conceptual and institutional gulf (see, e.g., Hand and Krebs 2007, 2009, 2011). Yet so far, the vast majority of work submitted holds on to exactly those divisions and lines of separation and it seems almost impossible to break through these entrenched positions.

This phenomenon is not specific to the academy, but also very much present in popular Western discourse, where adaptation tends to be viewed as a creative version, rewriting of, or commentary on a source as opposed to translation that presumably offers sameness and strives for equivalence. Thus a binary is constructed around these two acts of (re)writing: creative freedom versus linguistic confinement, or piracy versus trustworthiness and faithfulness, depending on which side of the fence you are sitting on. Of course, this view 'betrays an ignorance of developments in translation studies over the past three decades' (Venuti 2007: 9), as well as in adaptation studies, both of which have gone beyond discussions of faithfulness and fidelity.[1]

According to Ritta Oittinen, 'within research of children's literature, translation is often found faithful to the original, while an adaptation is not', because it has 'changed' or 'altered'. In this way the word of the original is the authority that is not to be altered, not to be "misinterpreted"' (Oittinen 2000: 77). The faithfulness of a translation, in this line of thinking, should ideally lead to equivalence; apparently the aim and objective of all translation and its defining characteristic that renders it distinct from adaptation. Of course, as Theo Hermans has shown in *Conference of the Tongues,* equivalence cannot 'be extrapolated on the basis of textual comparison [. . .] Equivalence is proclaimed, not found' (Hermans 2007: 6). Once the sameness or equivalence of a translation has been proclaimed, and a translation authenticated, the text ceases to be a translation: 'Upon authentication, translated texts become authentic texts and must forget that they used to exist as translations' (Hermans 2007: 9–10). For Hermans, equivalence is not so much an 'inherent feature of relations between texts, equivalence is *declared*' (ibid.: 24). Equivalence is to all intents and purposes impossible because, as Frank (1998 cited in Krebs 2007: 70) argues, 'insurmountable differences' between cultures make it impossible for the translator to make exactly 'the same potential accessible to the target reader'. Not only does the notion of political, ideological, or linguistic equal value implied in the term 'equivalence', 'render it [the term] inappropriate' (Hermans 1999: 97; qtd. Krebs 2007: 70), but equivalence in translation is also a paradox: a translation that achieves equivalence (by declaration (see Hermans 2007)) ceases to be a translation. Yet equivalence seems decisive in the line of thought that claims that adaptation and translation are two different products and processes, bastard children (to allude to Manuela Perteghella's terminology; (2008), of very different backgrounds, distant cousins at best.

If, however, popular and to some extent scholarly notions of translation depend upon the paradox of equivalence, '[. . .] what', in Oittinen's words, 'is an adaptation? Is it a version, an imitation, an abridgement, or a copy? What is at issue – form or content? Who is the audience for the adaptation? Is an adaptation a deviant version of the images, words or pictures that came first? [. . .] In other words: can we really tell the difference between adapting and translating?' (Oittinen 2000: 77). Oittinen makes quite clear in her work on translation and children's literature that adaptation is to be understood as a form of domestication – in other words, transforming a text in line with the requirements of a target culture;[2] and thus a tool of translation. Using children's literature as an example, she refutes the idea expressed by several scholars that adapting as opposed to translating necessarily means 'denaturing' and 'pedagogizing' the source text.

In order to understand what an 'adaptation' is, perhaps we ought to begin by defining a 'translation'. If one views translation as offering 'sameness', or striving for equivalence, adaptation has to be defined as distinct from that. Rather than attempting to achieve equivalence, or in Hermans' words, 'equality in value and status' (Hermans 2007: 6), Julie Sanders proposes, in her influential work *Adaptation and Appropriation* (2006), that adaptations are 'reinterpretations of established texts in new generic contexts or [. . .] with relocations of [. . .] a source text's cultural and/or temporal setting, which may or may not involve a generic shift' (Sanders 2006: 19). However this definition does not seem especially helpful: in the work I have encountered in studies of translation in a theatrical context, where reinterpretation, relocation, and even generic shifts are commonplace, Sanders' definition of adaptation seems indistinguishable from translation.

Theatre seems a particularly useful point to continue this discussion. According to Sirkku Aaltonen: '[T]ranslation for the stage probably employs adaptation more frequently than does printed literature' (Aaltonen 2000: 75) because, as Gunilla Andermann observes when discussing the difference between a reader and a spectator, 'members of the audience are left to fend for themselves when, during the course of a performance, they are confronted with unfamiliar and often bewildering information' (Anderman 2005: 7). Both of these points are difficult to substantiate; for example, John Milton demonstrates the importance of adaptation as a technique of translation, focusing in particular on the Brazilian Clubo do Livro and their 'factory translations' of classics such as *Huckleberry Finn*, *Hard Times*, and *Gulliver's Travels* (Milton 2005: 52). Furthermore, the idea that printed literary translations include a copious amount of footnotes, explaining cultural, political, historical contexts of translational choices is a rare occurrence in non-academic publishing circles. The majority of literary translations aimed at a non-expert readership avoid such signposts of intervention. The all-important translator's invisibility (Venuti 1995), so influential in the majority of contemporary translation practice, does not allow the fluidity and readability of a text to be disturbed by the presence of footnotes, which highlight the translator's (creative and ideological) process.

Nonetheless, theatre offers an abundance of case studies that blur the distinction between adaptation and translation processes, as well as products. The dramaturgical processes necessary, the practices employed by directors, writers, and actors, and the nature of theatre that destabilizes notions of single authorship and 'originality' in the first place, disallows a distinction between adaptation and translation more decisively than other acts of writing. It is a Western theatre tradition rather than a universal law, that the source text, the 'original' play, is regarded as an authority that should be served by the performance. As Zarilli et al. point out: 'Aristotle had set the western pattern of privileging the text and the author in his *Poetics* [c. 330 BC]' while, for example, 'in indigenous theaters of India, Southeast Asia, and Japan, performances were never viewed as being as text-centered as they were in Western-influenced theaters' (Zarilli et al. 2006: 450). Similarly Pavis observes that: 'The fixing of texts and their infinite revivals [. . .] is a historical accident [. . .] according to which the text supposedly precedes the stage in both temporal and statutory terms' (Pavis 2003: 203).

Let us turn our attention for a moment to the very British contemporary practice of so-called 'literal' translation: it is common practice to commission this type of text from someone who is fluent in the languages concerned, and has a translation or at least a linguistic background. The source text is then transformed and reworked into a draft target text, which is subsequently reworked by a better-paid and better-known dramatist. Playwrights who undertake such a practice of rewriting are, for example, David Edgar, John Gielgud, and Frank McGuinness, who have been credited with rewriting Brecht's *Mother Courage,* Chekhov's *Cherry Orchard,* and Ibsen's *A Doll's House,* respectively. Leaving the important ethical dimension of better pay to one side (even though this is an important debate) this practice alone – a theatrical practice before we even enter the rehearsal room or the performance space – blurs the boundaries between adaptation and translation. Does this mean that the difference between the two is simply a question of nomenclature? Describing a piece of re-writing as either a 'translation' or 'adaptation' depends on the legal, ideological, and hierarchical status of the practitioners involved. As Christopher Hampton, a translator of Ibsen who does not have any knowledge of Norwegian, states: 'It's a terminology problem. *Hedda* was not translated by me because I don't speak Norwegian. But I don't much like (the term) 'new version', because that sounds like you've altered it. The problem is that there isn't a terminology which says I haven't done anything to this play except put it in English' (cited in Hale and Upton 2000: 10).

Probably less contentious examples can be found in any production of ancient Greek plays. Mike Pearson's production of *The Persians,* which formed part of the National Theatre of Wales' 2010 program, used a so-called version by Kaite O'Reilly of the classic play by Aeschylus, and it was performed on a military site in the Brecon Beacons. Not normally accessible to the public, the site includes a mock German village, constructed at the height of the Cold War, and is used as a place for testing battlefield scenarios. At no point is *The Persians* labelled an adaptation. Kaite O'Reilly attempts to establish trustworthiness by describing her re-writing process in the programme accompanying the performance:

> Although I'm not a linguist and therefore unable to read the text in Ancient Greek, through my close reading of 23 translations, made across three centuries, I like to think I caught a sense of the bass line. (O'Reilly 2010.)

Emphasizing the importance of the socio political contexts of those twenty-three translations, she describes the process of writing as one akin to translation in all but linguistic competence:

> I chose not to reinvent. I chose to be as faithful as far as I could perceive it, to that 'initial' voice and to trust that the extraordinary location in which the performance takes place would create a context with more resonance than anything I could ever fabricate. (O'Reilly 2010)

By employing terminology such as 'reinvention' as a negative, and 'faithfulness' as a positive description of the translation process, O'Reilly operates within the popular Western discourse of translation. Her commentary mirrors, of course, a view of translation identified by Oittinen (2000) as problematic: translation is faithful while adaptation changes and alters and thus reinvents a text. This perspective on translation still prevails, even though Walter Benjamin challenges it in *The Task of the Translator* (1923 [1999]). Benjamin argues that: 'It is the task of the translator to release his [or her] own language' (1923 [1999]: 80), while transmission as a goal or aim of translation is a 'characteristic of inferior translation, which consequently we may define as the inaccurate transmission of an inessential content' (1923 [1999]: 70–1).

Despite O'Reilly's attempts to distance her work from notions of adaptation and instead align it with ideals of translation, both her process of re-writing and the product itself comply with Sanders' definition of adaptation. Performing *The Persians* in a contemporary military range (characterized by a cold-war shell of a German village) reinterprets as well as relocates the source text's cultural and temporal setting. O'Reilly's and Pearson's production of *The Persians* raises a number of intriguing questions when considering processes and products of rewriting and reinterpretation. Is this a performance of a 'translation', so long as the audience does not read O'Reilly's program-notes? Or is it an 'adaptation', even though it labels itself a 'version', which seems to be a term used by rewriters who have no access to the source text's language yet claim to have been 'faithful' to their source? How can distinctions be drawn and what would their consequences be? Does the experience of the performance change according to the nomenclature used by the rewriter? Or has *The Persians,* belonging to the canon of classic drama, surpassed such labelling? Has the text been authenticated by its title alone?

Of course, not all these questions can be answered within the confines of this chapter, yet the sheer proliferation of them reveals how symbiotic the relationship between adaptation studies and translation studies actually is. The pleasure of watching this particular production of *The Persians* was mainly related to the site of performance, rather than any memory of a source text and its textual reinvention. Yet, Sanders argues that it is 'the survival of the source text that enables the ongoing process of juxtaposed readings that are crucial to the [. . .] ongoing experience of pleasure for the [. . .] spectator' (Sanders 2006: 25). The fact that the production is not labelled an 'adaptation' creates a certain horizon of expectation in the audience: It may be a version (a rewriting which claims to be 'faithful') but it is not necessarily the rewriting the audience appreciates; the setting takes centre stage. In Sanders' formulation, O'Reilly's *The Persians* is not an 'adaptation', because the pleasure of watching comes from the performance's location rather than the 'juxtaposed readings' of source and target text. Furthermore, O'Reilly's text makes sure to describe and define itself as faithful to Aeschylus' play, a characteristic most often ascribed to translations. Kaite O'Reilly's text may be a translation without having 'translated' a word.

Another example in which 'authentication' (Hermans 2007) may have been bestowed on a translation is Rufus Norris's *Hergé's Adventures of Tintin*. Referencing the animated television series (1959–1963) by using the same title, director Norris and writer Greig created a stage version of *Tintin in Tibet*, which managed to combine critical acclaim with popular success. The translators of the comic strip are not mentioned in the programme-notes, any of the reviews, or advertising of the show. It is as if Leslie Lonsdale-Cooper and Michael Turner (credited as translators in the Methuen version of the comic) are indeed invisible. Yet, the text of the performance is based upon and references on numerous occasions Lonsdale-Cooper's and Turner's text. Whether including Captain Haddock's exclamation ('Blistering Barnacles!'), or retaining the name of Snowy the dog, the Methuen version is used as the 'authentic' Hergé in this production, and the success of the performance is credited solely to the generic shift from comic-book heroics to real life action on stage. Hergé's estate, the Hergé Foundation, was present throughout most of the rehearsals, ensuring that the 'original' translation was adhered to (Lawson 2005); and thus the sameness, or rather equivalence, to the French was not brought into question. Such authentication of course, allows any reading of the performance to disregard linguistic elements of reinterpretations and rewritings and the translational aspect is subsequently ignored by almost all paratexts, including programs, posters, and reviews. The audience shared a collective memory of the characters and possibly even the story; and it is the points of mediation (Tintin and Haddock *do* climb the Andes on stage!), and refraction – (Snowy is transformed in front of the audience's eyes from a dog into a human being) that account for the pleasure of watching the performance. According to Van Coillie and Verschueren: '[I]t may be argued that all translation [. . .] is an act simultaneously involving mediation and refraction' (Van Coillie and Verschueren 2006: v). Adaptation studies has much to offer to an analysis of mediation and refraction, with regards to both the process and the product of rewriting, as the majority of comparative case studies are built around the investigation of both. Furthermore, seminal studies such as Geraghty (2007), Hutcheon (2006), and Sanders (2006) all investigate mediation and refraction, without necessarily offering a comparative approach that pays (excessive) attention to source texts.

These examples have been taken from contemporary theatrical practices and performances, where labelling of a text and/or performance as an adaptation or translation has legal implications. The translational and adaptational waters get even murkier when examining European practices prior to the Berne Convention for the Protection of Literary and Artistic Works (1886).[3] In 1819, John Pollidori published a short story entitled *The Vampyr* that told the story of Aubrey, a young English gentleman, who befriends Lord Ruthven on his travels to Rome. Once returned to London, Aubrey has become very much aware of Lord Ruthven's (un)deadly character yet cannot save his own sister from becoming one of the vampire's many victims. The story enjoyed instant success and was subsequently rewritten throughout Europe. For example, 1820 saw the performance of Planche's melodrama *The Vampire or the Bride of the Isle;* a year later a vaudeville piece by French dramatist Eugene Scribe appeared, with Ruthven as a main character; in 1829 a German opera was performed under the same title, yet the librettist Wohlbrueck Germanicized the spelling of Ruthwen. The list goes on and on, and includes important theatrical figures such as Dion Boucicault (*The Vampire: A Phantasm*, 1852), until we get to Bram Stoker's *Dracula* (1897), inspired by Lord Ruthven. It would be entirely impossible to distinguish clearly between adaptation and translation in any of these examples. Few if any of these pieces credit Polidori's or any other versions: generic shifts are part of Ruthven's history, from short story to melodrama to opera to vaudeville, while the settings move from London to Scotland to France to Wales. The provisions made by the copyright law of that time were not able to acknowledge such sophisticated forms of textual transformation. It was not until 1838 that Queen Victoria introduced the first copyright act, by which time a good many Ruthvens had populated Europe already.[4] Any attempt to distinguish between translation and adaptation at that time would have been futile.

None of these examples, either from past or present, prevents the academy, or the wider public for that matter, from trying to preserve the distinction between adaptation and translation, as if it were some sort of discursive safety blanket. In his introduction to 'Cracks in the Jug: Recent Translations/ Adaptations of Continental Plays by Irish Dramatists' (2004), Heinz Kosok cites Ewald Mengel, who declares that: 'Every translation is *per definitionem* an adaptation which changes the source text with regards to the needs of the target audience. The adjustment comprises not only the linguistic but also cultural and functional transformations' (Mengel 1994: 3, qtd. in Kosok 2004: 99). Yet, just like Mengel, Kosok concludes: 'It will have become apparent that, although from a strict theoretical position every translation must be considered an adaptation, on a more practical level it is possible and even necessary to distinguish between 'translations' and 'adaptations' (Kosok 2004: 115). Similarly, Perteghella's article 'Adaptation: 'Bastard Child' or Critique? Putting Terminology Centre Stage', (a significant contribution to the theoretical debate concerning adaptation and translation within a theatrical context), ends by admitting that: 'While we can agree then that it might be an impossibility to define adaptation comprehensively, and its relation to translation, I shall nonetheless attempt such a definition' (Perteghella 2008: 63). Perteghella continues: '[A]daptation, both as process and as product, critically supplements the source with subjective and cultural interpretations' (Ibid.: 63). This, of course, seems remarkably similar to a current definition of translation in which 'both the source text and the translation [are] products of historically specific moments, determined as well as nourished by many linguistic and extra-linguistic factors of a political [and] or cultural kind' (Hoenslaars 2006: 50).

The attempt to preserve differences, rather than embrace the convergence of adaptation and translation processes and products ignores the 'sobering thought that most, if not all people who participate in a given culture will never in their life be exposed to all the 'originals' on which culture claims to be based' (Bassnett and Lefevere 1998: 9). All rewritings 'effectively [. . .] function as the original' (10), for the majority of readers/viewers/spectators. A far more constructive and productive way forward would be to focus on similarities between both translational and adaptational processes and products, to investigate each other's methodologies and assumptions, and examine the culturally and historically determined differences in the reception of such rewritings. This is not so much a plea for adaptation studies to become part of translation studies or vice versa, but rather for both of these fields of enquiry to engage in an equal and mutually beneficial exchange of ideas, which will, no doubt, strengthen our understanding of contemporary as well as historic constructions of culture through the rewriting of source texts. As Jenny Spencer suggests: 'The Jacques Derrida of *Monolingualism of the Other* would contend that this summoning of a memory of an original that does not exist, or that exists only retrospectively alongside our complete lack of access to it, is the condition of all speech on which our identity is founded' (Spencer 2007: 408). This could be the 'tails' of this double-headed coin of translation and adaptation.

Notes

[1] Recent pivotal works which turn their back on the so-called fidelity debate include Hutcheon (2006), Sanders (2006), Smith (2009), etc.

[2] The notion of domestication has been given prominence in translation studies by Lawrence Venuti's work, especially his *The Translator's Invisibility* (1995). Tracing the rise of domestication, a technique which allows a translation to appear embedded in the domestic literary landscape rather than a foreign one, as dominant strategy in Western translation theories and practices, Venuti calls for 'readers to reflect on [such] ethnocentric violence of translation' (1995: 41). Since *The Translator's Invisibility,* and especially in work dealing with theatre translation, domestication has been conceptualized in a less ideologically charged context.

[3] America continued to treat non-resident authors as unprotected common property until 1891.

[4] For more detail on nineteenth-century British and American copyright law see: http://www.victorianweb.org/authors/dickens/pva/pva74.html (accessed June 7, 2011).

Bibliography

Aaltonen, Sirkku (2000). *Time-Sharing on Stage: Drama Translation in Theater and Society*. Clevedon: Multilingual Matters.

Allingham, Philip (2001). 'Nineteenth Century British and American Copyright Law'. http://www.victorianweb.org/authors/dickens/pva/pva74.html (accessed June 28, 2011).

Anderman, Gunilla (2005). *Europe on Stage: Translation and Theater.* London: Oberon Books.

Bassnett, Susan and Lefevere, André (1998). *Constructing Cultures: Essays on Literary Translation.* Clevedon: Multilingual Matters.

Benjamin, Walter (1923 [1999]). 'The Task of the Translator'. In *Illuminations,* trans. Harry Zorn, 70–82. London: Pimlico.

Frank, Armin Paul (1998). 'Schattenkultur and Other Well-Kept Secrets: From Historical Translation Studies to Literary Historiograph'. In *Translating Literatures – Translating Cultures: New Vistas and Approaches in Literary Studies.* Kurt Mueller-Vollmer and Michael Irmscher (eds), 15–30. Stanford: Stanford University Press.

Geraghty, Christine (2007). *Now a Major Motion Picture: Film Adaptations of Literature and Drama*. Lanham, MD: Rowman & Littlefield.

Hand, Richard and Krebs, Katja (2007). 'Editorial'. *Journal of Adaptation in Film and Performance* 1(1): 3–4.

— (2009). 'Editorial'. *Journal of Adaptation in Film and Performance* 2(1): 3–4.

— (2011). 'Editorial'. *Journal of Adaptation in Film and Performance* 4(1): 3–4.

Hermans, Theo (1999). *Translation in Systems: Descriptive and System-Oriented Approaches Explained*. Manchester and Kinderhook, NY: St. Jerome Publishing.

— (2007). *The Conference of the Tongues*. Manchester and Kinderhook, NY: St. Jerome Publishing.

Hoenslaar, Ton (2006). 'Between Heaven and Hell: Shakespearian Translation, Adaptation, and Criticism from a Historical Perspective'. *Yearbook of English Studies* 36(1): 50–64.

Hutcheon, Linda (2006). *A Theory of Adaptation*. London and New York: Routledge.

Kosok, Heinz (2004). 'Cracks in the Jug: Recent Translations/Adaptations of Continental Plays by Irish Dramatists'. In *Drama Translation and Theater Practice*. Sabine Coelsch-Foisner and Holger Klein (eds), 99–120. Frankfurt-am -Main: Peter Lang.

Krebs, Katja (2007). *Cultural Dissemination and Translational Communities: German Drama in English Translation, 1900–1914*. Manchester and Kinderhook. NY: St. Jerome Publishing.

Lawson, Mark (2005). 'Boy Wonder'. *The Guardian*, September 7, 2005. http://www.guardian.co.uk/stage/2005/dec/07/theater4 (accessed May 22, 2011).

Lefevere, André (1985). 'Why Waste Our Time On Rewrites?: The Trouble with Interpretation and the Role of Rewriting in an Alternative Paradigm'. In *The Manipulation of Literature: Studies in Literary Translation*. Theo Hermans (ed.), 215–43. London: Croom Helm Ltd.

Leitch, Thomas (2011). 'Vampire Adaptations'. *Journal of Adaptation in Film and Performance* 4(1): 5–16.

Milton, John (2009). 'Between the Cat and the Devil: Adaptation Studies and Translation Studies'. *Journal of Adaptation in Film and Performance* 2(1): 47–64.

Oittinen, Ritta (2000). *Translating for Children*. New York and London: Routledge.

O'Reilly, Kaite (2010). *Program-Notes: The Persians*. Cardiff: National Theater of Wales.

Pavis, Patrice (2003). *Analyzing Performance: Theater, Dance, and Film*, trans. David Williams, Ann Arbor: University of Michigan Press.

Perteghella, Manuela (2008). 'Adaptation: 'Bastard Child' or Critique? Putting Terminology Centre Stage'. *Journal of Romance Studies* 8(3): 51–65.

Sanders, Julie (2006), *Adaptation and Appropriation*. New York and London: Routledge.

Smith, Iain Robert (ed.) (2009). *Cultural Borrowings: Appropriation, Reworking, Transformation*. Nottingham: Scope.

Spencer, Jenny (2007). 'Performing Translation in Contemporary Anglo-American Drama'. *Theater Journal* 59(3): 389–410.

Stam, Robert (2005). 'Introduction: The Theory and Practice of Adaptation'. In Stam and Alessandra Raengo (eds), *Literature and Film: A Guide to the Theory and Practice of Film Adaptation*. 1–52. Oxford and Malden, MA: Blackwell.

Van Coillie, Jan and Verschueren, Walter P. (2006). *Children's Literature in Translation*. Manchester and Kinderhook, NY: St. Jerome Publishing.

Venuti, Lawrence (1995). *The Translator's Invisibility: A History of Translation*, London and New York: Routledge.

— (2007). 'Adaptation, Translation, Technique'. *Journal of Visual Culture* 6(1): 25–43.

Zarilli, Phillip B., McConachie, Bruce, Williams, Gary Jay, Sorgenfrei, Carol Fisher (eds), (2006). *Theater Histories: An Introduction*. New York and London: Routledge.

Chapter 3

The Authenticity in 'Adaptation': A Theoretical Perspective from Translation Studies

Cynthia S. K. Tsui

This chapter aims to explore the conceptualizing issue of adaptation from the perspective of translation studies. My position is as a scholar of translation studies who examines adaptation studies. This implies that I will treat adaptation studies as the subject matter, using translation studies as one of the possible ways to contribute new thoughts to adaptation studies. In this essay, instead of bridging the two disciplines through theoretical debates, I will try to elucidate the common ground found in the problems and challenges that face the two disciplines, while maintaining my translation studies perspective. I will utilize the concept of translation to reflect on the future of adaptation.

The wealth of research on adaptation, initially and chiefly built on 'literature on screen', has tended to regard literature as a primary text, and film as a secondary product. However, as the scope and quantity of case studies has expanded, the theoretical potential of adaptation studies has emerged. As Robert Stam observes, much of the past thinking in adaptation studies 'has focused on the rather subjective question of the quality of adaptation, rather than on the more interesting issues of (1) the theoretical status of adaptation, and (2) the analytical interest of adaptations' (Stam 2005: 4). With this in mind, Stam's article 'The Theory and Practice of Adaptation' provides a detailed analytical account of the fundamental characteristics of adaptation by associating the subject with various intellectual concepts. These include the long-standing debate over fidelity, postmodernism, narratology, difference, formalism, intertextuality, and transtextuality. While his analyses aptly address the theoretical status and analytical interest of adaptation, they are concerned primarily with deconstructing 'the unstated doxa which subtly construct the subaltern status of adaptation'

(Stam 2005: 4). Stam's concept of adaptation can be described as a kind of 'adversarial' stance, designed to eliminate misunderstanding of the process of adaptation. However, if we aim at conceptualizing adaptation in a 'positive' and 'authentic' manner, it seems that we need to look for definitions or theories that entirely break free from Stam's negative preconceptions. Julie Sanders (2006) calls for viewing adaptation as 'appropriation', while Linda Hutcheon (2006) suggests adaptation is a 'creative' and 'receptive' process. These two critics move away from the idea of adaptation as an inferior intellectual activity, and try and express an idea about what adaptation precisely is. These new theories provide a suitable framework for considering adaptation studies in relation to contemporary translation studies.

A major problem faced by adaptation studies is the notion that adaptation is somehow derivative or inauthentic, implying the presence of an 'original' text. The concept of translation parallels adaptation in this respect. Adaptation and translation, in fact, share a similar set of debates: these include fidelity vs. creativity; author vs. adapter/translator; and adaptation or translation practices as the interpretation, contextualization, and transformation of meaning. However, translation studies as an academic discipline has undergone transformative changes in the past three decades (Snell-Hornby 1994; Bassnett 2003; Duarte 2006; Riccardi 2008). Whereas once it was viewed as a linguistic activity, it is now treated as a conceptual tool and theoretical resource to explain cross-cultural transfers, the re-creation of meaning, issues in representation, and cultural dynamics in globalization. Perhaps adaptation studies could benefit from current debates in theorizing translation, as a way of establishing itself (and hence negotiating that negative perception outlined by Stam). Conceptualization inevitably involves the question of definition. What is the rationale behind the concept of adaptation? This is, of course, not an easy question to answer. The word 'adapt' is generally accepted to mean 'to fit' or 'to modify' for new uses, forms, or conditions. The very idea of 'adaptation' presumes an 'original/source text' that the 'adaptation' serves – a belief that lies at the heart of 'adaptation studies' subaltern status. Critics in adaptation studies have made attempts to liberate the notion from those negative connotations, and to open up new research areas on the centrality and contribution of adaptive practices. Sanders creates the five categories of 'intertextuality', 'hybridity', 'transposition', 'transgenre', and 'pleasure' in characterizing adaptation (2006: 17–25). Hutcheon (2006) proposes viewing adaptation as an 'intertextual' and 'palimpsestuous' product (Hutcheon 2006: 6), a process of 'creation' and 'reception'(8), and highlights the three modes of engagement in adaptation (i.e. 'telling', 'showing' and 'interacting') (22–32). Despite these notions, it may still be hard, however, to identify just what renders the concept of adaptation unique. If intertextuality is identified as the core value of all adaptive practices (Hutcheon 2006: xii; Sanders 2006: 1–3), it undermines the claim that adaptations need to be considered as novel, independent entities in forms and meanings (Hutcheon 2006: xiv; Sanders 2006: 41). Such a paradox is understandable in trying to arrive at a constructive theory of adaptation. On the one hand, it is mandatory to have an 'original/source text' as a means for understanding adaptations. On the other hand, adaptation is obviously in need of the kind of theories that break free of the confines of the 'original' text, and thereby legitimize artistic innovation and ideological sovereignty. Another crucial aspect in theorizing adaptation is the ways that the notion of '(re-)creativity' has been theorized. When Hutcheon describes adaptation as a 'creative process', she claims to adopt a theoretical approach that is both 'formal' and 'experiential', and refers to the 'various ways of engaging the audiences [for adaptations]' across different media and genres (Hutcheon 2006: xii). Practically, she identifies three models of adaptation ('telling', 'showing' and 'interacting') in the process of communicating a story to an audience. Sanders identifies the creative aspect of adaptation as 'appropriation', a kind of 're-imagination' of intergeneric transformation and expansion (Sanders 2006: 12). This elicits a range of progressive values such as variation, revision, echo, creativity, pluralism, and interrelationships.

These insights are all valid and valuable. However, for the concept of adaptation to be appreciated as a conceptual tool, we must formulate a more logical, comprehensive framework that describes the objective and detailed workings of the adaptive process. Put another way: what precisely is the unique aspect of adaptation that distinguishes it from other concepts of textual transformation? This problem has already been encountered in translation studies: is it an activity, a product, a process, a cultural metaphor? However, cutting-edge translation theories have been able to formulate an autonomous concept of translation, using a new set of critical tools. Lawrence Venuti's criticism of the 'translator's invisibility' (1995) disputes the secondary status of translation. His theory of 'violence' in translation (1995) further suggests the power of translation to reconstitute meanings in a cross-cultural context. André Lefevere's proposal of translation as 'rewriting' (1992) sees translations contributing to the afterlife of the source text, as well as regenerating the texts' meaning across different cultures, space, and time. Maria Tymoczko's analysis of the political element of translation (2000) shows it to be a powerful agent in cultural politics.

All these contemporary, cultural-oriented translation theories focus on the process of translation that is both complex and contradictory. The source text is rather treated as a textual-cultural resource offering ideas and contents for future meaning regeneration. This approach puts an end to the fidelity debates in translation. Moreover, translation as a target text is considered as a product created according to readers' needs in the target cultural context.

Translation and adaptation are very similar to each other – both involve an end product, an audience, and a re-creative process in which the interference of the translator/adapter is decisive. Nevertheless, there is a major difference between the two conceptualizations. Despite the diverse ways that translation theories hypothesize translation, the translation concept is always accommodated into the tripartite model of 'Source Text→ Translating Process→ Target Text', from which trans-lingual, cross-cultural, and metaphorical theories evolve. The duality of translation bridging two languages and two cultures constitutes the unique framework for applying translation theories for social, cultural, political, and other purposes. More significantly, translation is a site of operation between the art of literature and the science of linguistics, and hence rendering the discipline open to both aesthetic and logical concerns. It possesses a structural framework as well as hypothetical flexibility. By contrast, adaptation, with its origins in literary and film studies and its basis in semiotics, psychology, as well as literary studies, can be more abstract and complex to conceptualize.

Nonetheless the idea of adaptation requires a clear conceptual model to demonstrate its theoretical distinctiveness. Perhaps scholars of the discipline should bear in mind the comment of Doris Bachmann-Medick on the ways in which the practice of translation studies has acquired its theoretical foundation. She proposes three criteria that translation research should fulfil: first, the 'expansion of the object or thematic field'; second, 'metaphorization'; and third, 'methodological refinement, provoking a conceptual leap and transdisciplinary application' (2009: 4). Adaptation studies (that deal with the modes of representation and involve a wide range of artistic forms, socio-cultural discourses, and knowledge fields) has the potential to establish itself as a transdisciplinary conceptual tool. To achieve this, however, it needs to develop a systematic and refined methodology of its own.

Apart from the need for a conceptual model, there are some issues that need to be borne in mind when comparing current research in adaptation and translation. Although intertextuality is regarded as a core component of adaptation, it is doubtful whether an understanding of what constitutes an 'original' text is absolutely necessary. To an audience, the intertextual background of an adaptation may enrich their reading experience and affect their interpretation of meanings, but they might also approach the adaptation on its own terms. Hence, intertextual knowledge is not a prerequisite for the reception of an adaptation. Instead, it can be said that the real value of adaptation resides in disseminating a work to different audiences through different media. This idea derives from the fact that in translation, many readers of foreign literature treat the translated texts as 'originals' without thinking about the alterations made by translators. The idea of an 'original' becomes unimportant in the relationship between readers and translations. Translation recreates past texts and becomes an autonomous act creating solely sustainable texts for the present and the future. In the same vein, adaptation treats intertextuality as a kind of versatile creativity that generates multiple forms to meet the changing requirements of new readers and contexts.

More research needs to be done on the role of adapters as creators, and the adaptive process as a site of textual, semiotic, and trans-generic reproduction. If we are to understand what adaptation involves, we must be able to understand its contribution to the modes and processes of multicultural reproduction in the postmodern global age, in which imitations and variations of cultural flows are always a vibrant source of creativity. Finally, some aspects in adaptation theories need to be fine-tuned. For example, the 'pleasure' principle as the purpose of adaptation (Sanders 2006: 24) can be problematic since pleasure is an individual, subjective feeling that can be difficult to measure.

Such notions can be better understood by approaching adaptation studies through the experience of translation studies, a discipline that provides practical directions and theoretical inspirations that are highly relevant and useful in conceptualizing adaptation. As Hutcheon observes, adaptation can be put as 'translations in the form of intersemiotic transpositions from one sign system to another', in the specific sense as 'transmutation and transcoding' into 'a new set of conventions as well as signs' (Hutcheon 2006: 16). Her comment suggests while adaptation draws on the tripartite structure of translation, only adaptations work between sign systems. This is actually erroneous: adaptation, like translation, can involve the 'interlingual' aspect (what Hutcheon calls 'transcoding' between genres); and both disciplines involve the 'cross-cultural' aspect (i.e., in adaptation, 'transmutation' to fulfill new spatial-temporal requirements). To create an 'authentic' theory of adaptation, scholars need to analyse the adaptive practices in manipulating texts, themes, narratives, discourses, and other re-creative aspects by drawing on the tripartite 'translational' model. Perhaps we should bear Stam's comment in mind:

> [The] source-novel hypotexts are transformed by a complex series of operations: selection, amplification, concretization, actualization, critique, extrapolation, popularization, reaccentuation, transculturation. The source novel, in this sense, can be seen as a situated utterance, produced in one medium and in one historical and social context, and later transformed into another, equally situated utterance, produced in a different context and relayed through a different medium. The source text forms a dense informational network, a series of verbal cues which the adapting text can then selectively take up, amplify, ignore, subvert or transform. (2005: 46)

What Stam describes about the 'source novel' and 'a complex series of operations' parallels the elements of the source text and the translating process in the tripartite model of translation. His reference to adaptation as a 'situated utterance' represented by 'another medium' produced for a new socio-historical context meshes in with the theoretical status of the target text in translation as a reconstituted, functional product. The creative impulse of adaptation and translation as transcoding, transforming, and transmutative processes encourages more comparison, contrast, and analyses between the two disciplines. They are mutual inspirations, kith and kin in the network of interdisciplinarity; not only can they benefit from one another's insights, but their profound interrelationships are awaiting to be explored.

Bibliography

Bachmann-Medick, Doris (2009). 'Introduction: The Translational Turn'. *Translation Studies* 2(1): 2–16.

Bassnett, Susan (2003). *Translation Studies: An Introduction* (3rd edn). London and New York: Routledge.

Duarte, João Ferreira et al. (eds) (2006). *Translation Studies at the Interface of Disciplines*. Amsterdam and Philadelphia: John Benjamins.

Hutcheon, Linda (2006). *A Theory of Adaptation*. London and New York: Routledge.

Lefevere, André (1992). *Translation, Rewriting and the Manipulation of Literary Fame*. London and New York: Routledge.

Leitch, Thomas (2008). 'Adaptation Studies at a Crossroads'. *Adaptation* 1(1): 63–77.

Riccardi, Alessandra (ed.) (2008). *Translation Studies: Perspectives on an Emerging Discipline*. Cambridge: Cambridge University Press.

Sanders, Julie (2006). *Adaptation and Appropriation*. London and New York: Routledge.

Snell-Hornby, Mary et al. (1994). *Translation Studies – An Interdiscipline*. Amsterdam and Philadelphia: John Benjamins.

Stam, Robert (2005). 'Introduction: The Theory and Practice of Adaptation'. In Stam and Alessandra Raengo (eds), *Literature and Film – A Guide to the Theory and Practice of Adaptation*, 1–52. Oxford and Malden, MA: Blackwell.

Tymoczko, Maria (2000). 'Translation and Political Engagement – Activism, Social Change and the Role of Translation in Geopolitical Shifts'. *The Translator* 6(1): 23–47.

Venuti, Lawrence (1995). *The Translator's Invisibility*. London and New York: Routledge.

Chapter 4

Translation and Rewriting: Don't Translators 'Adapt' When They 'Translate'?

João Azenha and Marcelo Moreira

The present study deals with the notion of adaptation in translation. By means of a case study, a number of features of a 'retold story' – the book *A Saga de Siegfried* [Siegfried's saga], by Tatiana Belinky (1993) – will be compared with a translation into Brazilian Portuguese of the same excerpt, taken from the book *Deutsche Heldensagen* [German Heroes' Sagas] (1951). In translating from the German version, the concept of 'documentary translation' (Nord 1989) will be specially considered, the main objective of this methodological procedure being to discover whether the final translation from the German original and the published retold story differ a lot. However, this chapter will show that there exist certain significant discrepancies between the two texts, indicating that procedures like modernization, universalization, and simplification have been adopted by the retold story's author. The retold story retains features from the *saga* genre (defined as the history of a people condensed in the narration of a family's or a national hero's history), in which fantasy and reality are combined. More significantly, a considerable number of rewritings have been introduced into the documentary translation from the German, so as to render the text comprehensible to Brazilian readers. Such processes demonstrate that translation and adaptation, far from being mutually exclusive concepts, complement each other at different levels and cannot therefore be rigidly separated.

4.1 Theoretical Dilemmas

The distinction between the concepts of translation and adaptation has been discussed in translation studies for some five decades.[1] In spite of systematic treatment, a sizeable proportion of it carried out in other areas,[2] a review of the bibliography reveals a difficulty in establishing a clear-cut theoretical distinction between the two concepts. When one discusses translating a work, this seems to entail an assumption that requires no qualification. On the other hand, if one discusses adapting a work, other questions will invariably arise: What will be adapted? For whom? On whose initiative? Such assumptions are based on so-called commonsense conceptions: translating is to approximate oneself, to remain 'faithful' to a source text in a twofold sense, not only with regard to content and ideas (i.e., at the level of semantics or coherence), but also on the textual surface (at the cohesive and stylistic level). Adapting, on the other hand, is to distance oneself from one of these dimensions or both: the semantics of content and ideas (for instance, when the story is transferred to another setting, when names and other topical elements are modified), and the textual surface (as when additions, suppressions, and reformulations are made). Each of these moves is subsequently given a direction: toward a source text, in the case of translation, or, in the case of adaptation, away from the source text so as to suit other purposes: to serve the target text, the conditions for its reception, the projected audience, or the medium into which the story will be transferred (in intersemiotic translation, for example).

Be that as it may, the conceptions supporting a would-be dichotomy between translation and adaptation are not always applicable, precisely because they try to dissociate subjects and objects involved in the translation process: the attempts at differentiation are either centred on products (the source text on the one hand and translated text on the other); subjects (the author on the one hand and the translator on the other); the media conveying the products (the written or electronic media); or on the agents involved (the writer and the publisher). Any attempt at dissociating what cannot be dissociated has been challenged by three matrices that have appeared in translation studies over the past three decades: functional and cultural translation studies, descriptive translation studies, and the deconstructionist perspective. From the first of these matrices comes the primacy given to the *function* of the translated text, which directs attention away from the surface level of the source text: instances of distancing and dissimilarity on the cohesive level are justified, so long as the translated text retains the function of the source text and as long as this is the *skopos* of the work. In a pioneering article, Reiss (1982) – with Hans Vermeer, a leading figure in translational functionalism in Germany – tries to devise, on the basis of Klingberg's works (1974), a typology of procedures differentiating, in a case study, the boundaries that separate the concepts of translation and adaptation. However, in spite of her attempts toward a systematization of procedures that are observable in practice, there still lingers a view of difference centred on approximation to and distancing from a source text:

> Adaptations, as *departures from a text in the source language*, manifest themselves in translation either as reductions or expansions, or inaccurate translations, or, still, as substitutions. In this study, we are concerned only with adaptation in the sense of adjustment to a different social and cultural context within the target language community (*for all other adaptations [Adaptationen] basically lead to a rewriting [Bearbeitung] of the source language text, which – it is true – carries an underlying translating process, but can no longer be said to be the translation of a text from a source language*). (Reiss 1982: 10–11, our italics)

In her own proposal for a translation typology, Nord (1989) cites the example of children's literature as an *instrumental translation*, which often departs significantly from the conventions of the source text. This is clearly the case of the great works of literature such as *Gulliver's Travels*, by Jonathan Swift, or *Robinson Crusoe*, by Daniel Defoe. Nord states that these translations may help these texts to survive, given the fact that they have now lost their original function of social satire (Nord 1989: 103–104). On the other hand, the concept of *documentary translation*, as defined by Nord (ibid) and applied in our study, suggests a greater degree of correlation between source and target texts. Whereas Reiss still insists on the translation versus adaptation dichotomy, the same cannot be said for Nord. Although she insists on the importance of loyalty for all those involved in the translation process, including the source text author, she categorizes all textual transformations under the umbrella-term 'translation'.

Parallel to the studies of Reiss, Vermeer, and Nord in Germany, whose work was mainly based on texts of a pragmatic nature, scholars following the work of Itamar Even-Zohar and Gideon Toury in Tel Aviv, whose work dealt with literary translation, introduced, almost at the same time, a related change in the centre of interest. Snell-Hornby (2006) comments:

> The breakthrough came in 1985 with the publication of that volume of essays edited by Theo Hermans, with the now famous title *The*

> *Manipulation of Literature* [Hermans 1985]. The aim, as the editor stated in his introduction was 'quite simply, to establish a new paradigm for the study of literary translation, on the basis of a comprehensive theory and ongoing practical research'. (Snell-Hornby 2006: 10)

The new paradigm, to which Hermans (1985) refers, is centred on:

> A view of literature as a complex and dynamic system; a conviction that there should be a continual interplay between theoretical models and practical case studies; an approach to literary translation which is descriptive, target-oriented, functional and systemic; and an interest in the norms and constraints that govern the production and reception of translations, in the relation between translation and other types of text processing, and in the place and role of translations both within a given literature and in the interaction between literatures. (Hermans 1985: 10–11)

This approach opposes to a great extent the widespread idea of the source (literary) text as a (prescriptive) model for the production and evaluation of translations, and states instead that the dominant criterion is the *function* of the translated literary text in the target culture (cf. Snell-Hornby 2006: 49). However, in contrast to the perspective of functional and cultural translation studies, as developed in Germany, the function in this case is fundamentally the position that the translated work will occupy in the receiving literary system. Toury (1985) explains:

> Semiotically speaking, it will be clear that it is the target or recipient culture, or a certain section of it, which serves as the initiator of the decision to translate and of the translating process. Translating as a teleological activity *par excellence* is to a large extent conditioned by the goals it is designed to serve, and these goals are set in, and by, the prospective receptor system(s). Consequently, translators operate first and foremost in the interest of the culture into which they are translating, and not in the interest of the source text, let alone the source culture. (1985: 18–19)

The concept of 'norms' is of utmost importance to Toury (1995): translation, like other human activities, is influenced by socio cultural factors, which take on importance through norms, understood as:

> the key concept and focal point in any attempt to account for the social relevance of activities, because their existence, and the wide range of

> situations they apply to (with the conformity this implies), are the main factors insuring the establishment and retention of social order. (Toury 1995: 55)

From this point of view, the translation of literary texts is thus subject to

> norms [that] can be expected to operate not only in translation of all kinds, but also at every stage in the translating event, and hence to be reflected in every level of its product. (58)

A detailed examination of Toury's (1995) analysis of the norms to which a literary text is subject to is beyond the scope of this Chapter, but we can say that the change in focus, as proposed by Even-Zohar and Toury, brings with it important consequences. First, there is a change in the role of translators: instead of acting alone, what is now required from them is a view from 'outside the box' – that is, the translator is now one of the links in the extensive chain of agents and acquires the role of an administrator, a manager of variables; moreover, the notion of authorship is diluted as there will now be various agents taking part in the process. Secondly, the agenda of the subject-translator shifts away from the source text (retrospective view), to the conditions of reception (prospective view). Therefore, the various procedures used in accommodating the (new) text into the projected reception conditions result in the boundaries between translating and adapting being diluted. Besides, the translated text is included in a dynamic and complex system of relationships, and the description of the process gains primacy at the expense of the notion of normativeness.

Finally, there is the idea of non-dissociation of subject and object, from the deconstructionist perspective: all the material to be processed in translation is meaningful and gains meaning and sense only through the action of a historically rooted subject. Therefore, a 'text' only constitutes itself as such by being read by a subject, who is conditioned by the speech community to which he/she belongs. This is to say that a source text, from this perspective, is nothing else other than one particular reading:

> What the translator *recreates* is not the mark of 'authentic expressiveness' of the Other, but rather a view or reading committed to stereotypes of the Other crystallized in his/her culture. (Amorim 2003: 28; our italics)

So, if seen as rewriting,[3] translation necessarily *trans*forms and checkmates the concept of fidelity, usually associated with the notion of neutrality.

By extending these considerations to the discussion on the boundaries between translation and adaptation, Amorim (2003: 31–2) remarks:

> For instance, a translation of a novel which presents considerable alterations such as suppression of characters, abridgment of chapters, and omission of poems or songs, might be described in certain speeches and interpretive communities as a transgression or domestication. Such a rewriting is often considered an 'adaptation'. This classification may be explained in part by the fact that adaptation is usually considered a minor practice, on the allegation that it springs from readings that violate the 'integrity' of original texts, and therefore should be distinguished from translation. However, the boundaries separating adaptation and translation are neither 'natural' nor as sharp as assumed, and there is no theoretical unanimity as to the possibility of an objective delimitation.

He concludes: 'The difference between translating and adapting would not be found in ahistorical or 'intrinsic' features of translation or adaptation' (37). The contributions of these three matrices are forcefully synthesized in the process of translating for young adults and children. In this setting, the features of this literary genre, conditioned by the target audience and the activity of agents,[4] rather than by distinctive features intrinsic to the realm of text and speech, define procedures that decree the failure of all attempts at establishing a distinction between translation and adaptation, at least in theoretical terms.

An example of this may be found in the limitations imposed on translators who wish to remain 'faithful' to a source text and preserve, as much as possible, some degree of foreignness in the translated text: their efforts must take into account not only the development of the receptors' linguistic skills, still being formed, but also their discernment and understanding. Thus, the yearning for a 'faithful' translation may pose a serious threat to the playful aspect of the work that is responsible for stirring and retaining the reader's interest.[5] In this sense, readability affects the decision as to whether to translate or adapt: a text full of strange and foreign elements, not only with regard to content, but language as well, impairs the reader's understanding and so the acceptance and endurance of the work over time.

The influence of these theoretical matrices in conjunction with the very features of translation for children and young adults determine another sort of move and stance: a prospective move toward the receptor and the conditions of reception, on the one hand, and a stance that recognizes creativity as an integral part of the translating process, on the other.

Thus, from the perspective of an *integrated* consideration of agents and objects of study and work, all of them historically grounded, there cannot be a boundary defining translation and adaptation as two mutually exclusive categories, with separate identities, closed and impervious to conflict or contamination. Translating and adapting, from a theoretical point of view, are complementary moments, inherent to the practice of producing sense in language through translation.

In an effort to test these assumptions, we conducted a case study in which some features of a story told anew – a 'retold story' – were set against a translation of the same story into Brazilian Portuguese. The main objective in this methodological procedure was to confirm (or not) the hypothesis that a translation from the German 'original' would be highly different from a retelling of the same story.

4.1.1 The dilemmas of practice

Among publications directed to children and young adults, one often finds world literature classics in abridged form, bearing the description 'a retelling of' or 'a retold' story. These indications elicit from the reader specific ideas about a certain kind of text, marked, for instance, by a freer narrative style and written in a language considered more appropriate to an audience of children and young adults. If these works were originally published in a foreign language, there is the further assumption that cultural differences will not be a hindrance to the understanding of young readers, whatever the devices used to deal with them in the retold story.

In spite of these assumptions, there remains the question of determining whether in practice, differences between receptors and, specially, the functions of these texts, may justify procedures differing from those employed in works labelled as 'translations' and whether these differences in processes are really meaningful.

In order to examine the features of these two processes – translating and retelling – we selected a discrete case: a comparison of *The Siegfried Saga: The Hoard of the Nibelungs*, as retold by the well-known Brazilian author and translator of children's literature, Tatiana Belinky (Belinky 1993), and a version of the same saga we translated into Brazilian Portuguese (Heberle 1951) originally intended for older readers. The works chosen for our study share the fact that both stress in their titles the relationship of the story to the *saga* tradition, in which the history of a family or worthy hero condenses the history of a people, while presenting historical facts interspersed with fantastic events.

As part of our study, the translation of the first part of *Die Nibelungensage* was guided by a specific theoretical notion – *documentary translation*, as formulated by Nord (1989). We chose documentary translation, because, on the one hand, it would allow us to identify more clearly the different levels of textual transformation, and, on the other, to establish a counterpoint to the adaptation, or, more specifically, to the retold story. Although this translation was made for strictly academic purposes, it did not allow for a purely retrospective move directed to the source text, but rather permitted a 'coming and going' in both directions. The principle guiding this move was readability: the transformative procedures went beyond sheer syntactical and lexical adjustment, and included phraseology and wordplay, as shown in the excerpt below:

> *Ach, Mutter, ich weiß auch noch einen anderen Spruch, 'daß Wehe nahe bei Wonne wohne und Liebe zuletzt mit Leiden lohne!' Davor nehme ich mich in acht und will mich vor der Liebe hütten!* (Heberle 1951: 53)
>
> *Ah, mãe, conheço ainda outro provérbio: 'junto com o amor mora também a dor' ou 'o amor com a dor se paga!' Quanto a isso sou cuidadosa e estou precavida contra o amor!* (Unless otherwise specified, all translations from the German into Spanish and English are by the authors.)
>
> [Ah, mother, I know still another proverb: 'together they come, love and pain; try to part them, work in vain' or 'fall in love and you fall forever!' I am careful about it and am forewarned against love!]

The excerpt presents proverbs used by Kriemhilde to counter her mother's efforts, as her mother tries to coax her into accepting love and marriage. Since they are no longer idiomatic, these proverbs had to be reconstructed in Brazilian Portuguese on the basis of proverbial formulations in a Portuguese-speaking culture. This strategy based on the functionalist approach imparted fluency, readability, and an idiomatic quality to the translated text, based on the importance of rendering it suitable to prospective readers' expectations. These expectations, on their turn, are largely determined by the publishing traditions favoured by the target culture at the time of publication.

So, when considering a retold story, one has to take into account the Brazilian publishing tradition in children's literature, which is specially shaped by a limited popular appeal and an emphasis on the fantastic element, the prime example of which is the fairy tale. The use of the term 'fairy tale' to classify this retold story confirms this tradition of fantastic fiction in the Brazilian market.

In descriptive translational terms, the publishing tradition establishes its own norms, and these are maintained largely through the action of consumers. In our study, the outstanding example is how violence is treated: descriptions of death and its repercussions are reshaped and mitigated in retold stories. Representations of violence in children's literature are very different from those found in other media, especially cartoons and video games, where the violent content is kept largely intact. By contrast book publishers in Brazil adopt a stricter attitude toward violence, based on the belief that violence is a part of people's daily lives.

In spite of interference by the agents involved in the translating process, translators who wish to bring to their cultures a work deeply rooted in another culture have to reflect on several important issues. Paloposki (2009) observes that whereas it is up to publishers to decide what and how to translate, translators may influence publishers' decisions (or even decide for them) as specialists when they have a credible or reliable reputation. This seems to be the case for Tatiana Belinky, who has an excellent reputation in the area of children's literature. Notwithstanding the freedom the 'retold story' label seems to imply, she chooses to maintain foreignness rather than change the setting; to sustain this 'foreign' element, she relies on an afterword that outlines the historical and cultural setting for her translation. This text acquires a didactic function and provides details on the origin of the myths and the outlook of medieval nobility for an audience whose 'official history' begins with the twentieth century. The afterword offers a rereading of the source text in which the cliché of the virtuous hero is questioned according to the ideas of our own time; an instance is the discussion on women's status in society:

> *É curioso notar, no entanto, que em momento algum da narrativa da saga de Nibelung aparece uma só palavra de crítica ou reprovação do narrador à ação do puro Siegfried, quando, para ajudar seu amigo, o rei Gunther, ele derrota, invisível, a invencível e orgulhosa Brunhilde, ludibriando-a de maneira nada menos que desleal, para, mais tarde, não só desmentir e desautorizar a palavra de sua esposa amada Kriemhilde, como mentir, negando o fato, até sob juramento falso – coisa inconcebível para um homem de honra, um guerreiro de sangue real.*
>
> *Não há dúvida de que, se o estratagema tivesse sido usado para enganar e derrotar um adversário masculino, esse fato teria manchado a notável reputação do herói.*

> *De onde se conclui que, naqueles tempos de tanta ética, enganar uma mulher, mesmo sendo uma rainha guerreira, não constituía falta grave, capaz de empanar o brilho da honra de um homem. E Siegfried passou para a história como um herói perfeito, 'sans peur et sans reproche', paradigma do Held exemplar, digno de ser admirado e amado sem restrições. O que não deixa de ser um tema para um momento de reflexão.* (Belinky 1993: 31)
>
> [It is curious, however, that not for a single moment in the Nibelung Saga is a word said to criticize or disapprove the actions of pure Siegfried, as when, in order to help his friend, King Gunther, he becomes invisible to defeat the invincible and proud Brunhilde, deceiving her in a most treacherous way, or later, when he not only refutes and discredits his beloved wife Kriemhilde, but also lies and denies the fact, resorting even to a false oath – an inconceivable act for a honourable man and warrior of royal blood.
>
> There is no doubt that if the ruse had been resorted to in order to deceive and defeat a male opponent, the fact would be a blemish on the hero's notable reputation. Therefore, one may conclude that in those times, so concerned with ethics, deceiving a woman, even a warrior queen, was not a serious fault, of the sort that might diminish the honour of a man. And Siegfried entered History as a perfect hero, 'sans peur et sans reproche', an exemplary Held paradigm, worthy of admiration and unconditionally loved. This can provide some food for thought.]

It is interesting that she refers to the narrator as a third person, as if she, who is retelling the story, had no power to relativize the hero's character in the translation itself. Her stance emphasizes her decision to keep the archaic and foreign element, rather than to interfere in the character's depiction, although an interpretive line on the basis of contemporary values is later suggested. However, the illustrations are the most important element supporting the foreignizing technique. According to Oittinen (1998), illustrations establish a dialogue both with the written text and the reader's emotions. They portray the characters and their world and may lead to a deeper reading, stir the reader's interest, and anticipate events. They are found throughout the book—on the sleeve, occupying the whole page surface at every four pages, and opening every chapter – and serve a variety of purposes in the work. Their functions are as follows:

- *Illustrative/informational* – illustrations bring the archaic, foreign element closer to young readers (still in the process of building their own cultural background), provide visual information on the customs and traditions of the time that are essential to the work (contributing to textual cohesion), and give form to magical elements (the dragon, the mountain people, etc.);

- *Auxiliary* in describing the setting – the images clearly show that the events are not taking place in the contemporary Brazilian cultural context;
- *Interpretive* – illustrations provide a very clear depiction of some scenes, which are almost always portrayed from alternative points of view – from above, below, or laterally, rarely from the front. Readers thus see events from a unique perspective, as if they were witnessing them;[6]
- *Introductory* – inside chapters, accompanying subtitles, there are images drawn in Indian ink. Besides their ornamental effect, they synthesize the contents of each chapter.
- *Aesthetic* – the use of illustrations is also justified by marketing considerations – in this case, producing a book that is appealing to consumers.

Since Belinky decided to preserve the foreign element, it is no wonder that, while comparing the retold text with the translated text, only a few differences in plot were found. These differences especially refer to elements that might appear confusing to a young Brazilian reader, or perhaps contradict the publisher's norms for children's literature. However, even though such differences are minimal – permitting a degree of coherence between source and target texts, the same cannot be said about plot-construction. Belinky's narrative style in the retold story is more concise, and focuses on events rather than details. The excerpt below comes from the passage in which the charcoal seller warns Siegfried about the dangers in the path to the cave of Fafnir, the dragon watching over the hoard of the Nibelungs:

> *'Dorthin geht der Weg zur Heide und über sie ins Land der Nibelungen. Doch noch einmal warne ich dich, hüte dich, diesen Weg zu ziehen. Fafnir ist schrecklich, kein Schwert kann ihn bezwingen, selbst des Donnerers Hammer schlägt ihn nicht!' So warnte die Köhler. Aber Siegfried lachte hell, und kampfeslustig schwang er sein Schwert, daß es durch die Luft pfiff und der Köhler ängstlich zur Seite wich.*
>
> *So eilte Siegfried, den das Abenteuer lockte, weiter. Er kam in ein wildes Gebirge, finsterer wurde der Wald, die Berghänge waren zerklüftet, Felsen sperrten oft den Weg, und Schluchten gähnten vor ihm. Dazu heulten die Wölfe, schrien die Eulen, tauchten Zwerggesichter auf und verschwanden wieder in Erdspalten. Ist*

hier der Weg zu Hel, zur 'Unterwelt?' So fragte sich Siegfried. Aber je schauerlicher der Wald wurde, desto höher schlug des Helden He

Da, nach einer Wegbiegung, stand er unversehens vor einer Höhle. (Heberle 1951: 45)

'É por ali o caminho que leva à charneca e, depois dela, à terra dos nibelungos. Mas devo alertar-te mais uma vez: pensa bem antes de trilhar por esse caminho. Fafnir é terrível! Nenhuma espada pode derrotá-lo, e até mesmo o Martelo de Thor não o abate!' Assim advertiu o carvoeiro. Siegfried, porém, deu uma gargalhada, e, com sede de luta, balançou sua espada, de modo que ela sibilou no ar e fez o carvoeiro se afastar de medo.

Então Siegfried, atraído pela aventura, retomou seu caminho a passos apressados. Ele chegou a uma região montanhosa e intocada: a floresta foi ficando cada vez mais sombria, as encostas das montanhas eram íngremes, rochedos bloqueavam com freqüência o caminho, e gargantas abriam-se diante dele. Então os lobos uivaram, as corujas piavam, rostos de anões emergiam e desapareciam novamente nas fendas da terra. Será este o caminho para Hel, para o 'Reino dos Mortos'? Assim perguntava Siegfried a si mesmo. Mas quanto mais amedrontadora ficava a floresta, mais forte batia o coração do herói.

Então, após uma curva no caminho, ele se deparou com uma caverna. (. . .)

['That's the way to the heath and the land of the Nibelungs lies beyond. But I must warn thee once again: think ere thou takest this path. Fafnir is terrible! No sword can defeat him, and even Thor's Hammer cannot slay him!' Thus the charcoal seller warned him. Siegfried laughed, however, and thirsting for war, swung his sword in such a way that it hissed in the air and the charcoal seller shrunk way in fear.

So Siegfried, drawn by adventure, went quickly along his way. He reached a mountainous, untouched region: the forest was increasingly dark, the mountain slopes were steeper, boulders often blocked his way and gorges opened before him. Then wolves howled, owls hooted, and the faces of dwarfs appeared and disappeared through cracks in the earth. Can this be the path to Hell, to the 'Realm of the Dead?' Thus Siegfried asked himself. But as the forest grew spookier, the stronger beat the hero's heart.

Then, after a bend in the path, he found himself before a cave.]

Muito contente com esse resultado, Siegfried continuou seu caminho até a casa do carvoeiro, a quem contou a aventura. Este então lhe falou de um tesouro inestimável, acumulado pelo rei dos anões, Nibelung, e escondido nas entranhas de uma montanha próxima. Após a morte do rei dos anões, seus filhos, Schilbung e Nibelung, brigavam constantemente por causa da divisão do tesouro do pai. Mas eles nem sequer podiam pôr as mãos em todas aquelas riquezas, porque a entrada da caverna era guardada pelo dragão enfeitiçado Fafner, o mais terrível de todos os dragões.

Ao ouvir isso, Siegfried imediatamente desistiu de voltar para a forja de Mime, pensando consigo: 'Quem matou um dragão, mata dois – ainda mais agora, que nada me atinge!' E lá se foi o herói Siegfried – porque agora ele já era um herói – ao encontro de seu dragão, maior e mais medonho que o primeiro.

Pouco depois, Siegfried chegou até a cavern. (Belinky 1993: 4–6)

[Very glad with this outcome, Siegfried followed his path to the charcoal seller's house and told him his adventure. The charcoal seller then told him about a priceless hoard amassed by Nibelung, the king of the dwarfs, and hidden in the entrails of a nearby mountain. After the death of the king of the dwarfs, his sons, Schilbung and Nibelung, were in constant strife over the division of their father's hoard. However, they could not even put their hands on the hoard, for the entrance to the cave was protected by a bewitched dragon, Fafner, the most dreadful of dragons.

On hearing this, Siegfried immediately decided not to go back to Mime's forge, and thought to himself: 'One who has slain a dragon, can slay two – now even more so, since no harm can reach me!' And there went Siegfried, the hero – for now he was a hero – to meet his dragon, even bigger and more dreadful than the first.

Before long, Siegfried reached the cave.]

These excerpts reveal dominance of narration over description in the retold story: the charcoal seller anticipates and summarises events that are told by the dwarfs in the German text. On the other hand, Siegfried's temerity in accepting the challenge (expressed by the gloominess surrounding the path to the cave and its inhabitant) is hardly stressed. His response differs considerably in the two texts: in the German saga, his brandishing the sword and his laughter suggest that the charcoal seller's frightening description, instead of dissuading him from the adventure, urges him on; in Belinky's retold story, the same response is conveyed by outlining his thoughts.

The excerpt we have used here reveals two recurring procedures in the retold story: an emphasis on the narration of events and a clear establishment of interpretive lines through the adoption of an explanatory stance toward the plot. Hence, Brazilian readers have only to follow the lines laid down by the narrator. The source text's plot loses its local specificity and is hence universalized in the retold story – for example, through the omission of elements of daily life:

> *Da gab es der König auf, den Sohn umzustimmen, aber fürsorglich wollte er Siegfried eine Heerschaft mitbringen, da das Recht nur bei der Macht sicher sei. Doch Siegfried lehnte auch das ab, nur zwölf auserlesene Recken wollte er bei sich haben. Wichtiger dünkte ihm ein feines Gewand aus Seide, bestes Linnen aus der Truhe und Pelzwerk als Überwurf.* (Heberle 1951: 52)
>
> *Então o rei desistiu de dissuadir o filho, mas, por precaução, quis que Siegfried fosse acompanhado por uma tropa, uma vez que, para eles, a justiça só seria assegurada pela força. Siegfried também a recusou; apenas doze guerreiros da melhor qualidade ele quis ao seu lado. A ele lhe pareceu mais importante vestir de fina seda, do melhor linho da arca e de pele de animal como capa.*
>
> [The king then gave up the intent of dissuading his son, but, out of caution, he wanted Siegfried to be accompanied by a posse, since, for them, justice would only be secured by force. Siegfried refused that too; only twelve of the best warriors he wanted by his side. To him it seemed the best thing was to put on the finest silk, the best linen from the trunk, and an animal hide as a cloak.]
>
> *Porém, como de costume, o obstinado Siegfried não quis ouvir os conselhos paternos, e partiu para Worms, com uma companhia de vassalos e cavaleiros, dispostos a conquistar e a trazer de volta consigo a difícil princesa Kriemhilde, fosse por bem ou por mal.* (Belinky 1993: 10)
>
> [As usual, however, the obstinate Siegfried did not take heed of fatherly advice, and departed to Worms with a company of vassals and knights willing to bring the reluctant princess Kriemhilde with them, whether she liked it or not.]

According to Köhler (1993), the basic garments for German men during the eleventh to the thirteenth centuries were broad silken or woollen tunics worn over a linen shirt and covered by a cloak fastened over one of the elbows. Suppressing this piece of information might render the story more acceptable to those reading the retold story; on the other hand, however, an opportunity is lost to inform readers about habits in the source culture in an attempt to modernize the story.

Modernizing procedures also manifest themselves when the main character's heroic deeds are made to conform to Western Christian values.

An example may be found in the episode where Siegfried, after beating Fafnir, helps the dwarf kings to share the hoard of the Nibelung kingdom. Instead of his fierce and fearless self, Siegfried exhibits pity and temperance:

> *Die Zwerge aber waren nicht zufrieden, sie geiferten, Siegfried habe unrecht geteilt. Jeder glaubte, er sei zu kurz gekommen, und sie riefen das Gewimmel des großen Zwergenvolkes auf, gegen Siegfried zu kämpfen. Siegfried durchzuckte der Zorn. Mit Balmung erschlug er Schilbung und Niblung und noch siebenhundert Zwergenrecken.* (Heberle 1951: 47)
>
> *Os anões, porém, não estavam satisfeitos. Eles diziam vitupérios, afirmando que Siegfried não havia dividido de forma justa. Cada um acreditava ter recebido a menos. Eles, então, convocaram a massa do grande povo dos anões para lutar contra Siegfried. A fúria tomou conta de Siegfried. Com [a espada] Balmung ele matou Schilbung e Niblung e ainda setecentos outros anões-guerreiros.*
>
> [The dwarfs, however, were not contented. They got angry and said Siegfried had not made a fair division. Each one thought they had received less than his fair share. They summoned a mass of the great dwarf people to fight against Siegfried. Siegfried was enraged. He took Balmung [his sword] and slew Schilbung and Niblung and seven hundred dwarf warriors.]
>
> *[Siegfried] fez o possível para repartir tudo eqüitativamente, mas os anões nunca ficavam satisfeitos, fazendo-o recontar e repartir as riquezas de novo e de novo. Por fim, cada vez mais irritados, os dois ficaram tão furiosos que, junto com seus súditos, atacaram Siegfried de todos os lados.*
>
> *Rebatendo seus golpes com a espada, Siegfried, esquecido de que Balmung era sempre mortal, tocou os anões de leve – e eles caíram mortos. Então todos os outros desistiram de atacar o herói.* (Belinky 1993: 7)
>
> [Siegfried did his best to divide everything fairly, but the dwarfs were never happy, and made him count and divide the wealth again and again. Increasingly annoyed, they were finally so enraged that they and their subjects attacked Siegfried from all sides.
>
> Fending off the strokes with his sword, Siegfried forgot that Balmung was always deadly and lightly touched the dwarfs – and they fell dead. Then, all the others ceased to attack the hero.]

Siegfried, as an epic hero, embodies the values of Germany in the Middle Ages. In our society, however, his behaviour might affect his virtuous image.

Hence his deeds are altered according to current moral and educational norms, while at the same time stressing the playful side of the text. The same thing happens to his opponents:

> *'Siegfried muß sterben', grollte auch Hagen, wenn er den Helden sah. Er ließ nicht ab, dem König zuzureden und ihm zu sagen, wie Brunhilde langsam sterben müsse, weil der Gram ihr den Lebensodem abschnüre. Er ließ nicht ab, ihm vorzustellen, welchen Vorteil Siegfrieds Tod Burgund einbrächte. Er sprach vom Nibelungenhort und von der Krone, die am Niederrhein winke. So lockte Hagen seinem König endlich doch die Zustimmung zu diesem Plane ab.*
>
> *[. . .] Der König schauderte, doch stimmte er dem Höllenplane zu.* (Heberle 1951: 68–9)
>
> *'Siegfried terá que morrer', resmungava também Hagen, sempre que via o herói. Ele não desistiu de tentar persuadir o rei, dizendo-lhe como Brunhilde acabaria morrendo, pois o desgosto roubava-lhe o sopro de vida. Ele não desistiu de mostrar a Gunther as vantagens que a morte de Siegfried traria à Burgúndia. Ele falou da fortuna dos nibelungos e da coroa que o esperava como recompensa no Baixo Reno. Assim Hagen conseguiu conquistar a aprovação de seu rei para esse plano [. . .] O rei estremeceu, mas consentiu com o plano diabólico.*
>
> ['Siegfried must die', grumbled Hagen whenever he saw the hero. He did not stop trying to persuade the king, and said Brunhilde would eventually die, for sadness was extinguishing the breath of life in her. He did not stop telling Gunther the advantages Siegfried's death would bring to Burgundy. He talked about the wealth of the Nibelungs and the crown waiting for him on the Lower Rhine. Thus Hagen conquered the approval of his king to this plan [. . .] The king shuddered, but gave his assent to the devilish plan.]
>
> *O rei Gunther, por sua vez, começou a se tomar de raiva contra Siegfried, pois este cometera leviandade de confiar o segredo à esposa, sua irmã, que num momento de ira o revelara a Brunhilde. Além disso, Gunther pensava cada vez mais no famoso tesouro de Nibelung, que pertencia a Siegfried, cuja riqueza ele no fundo invejava. E foi assim que, ao fim de algum tempo, Gunther e Hagen conspiraram para matar Siegfried.* (Belinky 1993: 17–18)
>
> [King Gunther, in turn, started to hate Siegfried, for he had jokingly told the secret to his wife, his very sister, and she, in a moment of anger, had revealed it to Brunhilde. Besides, Gunther now thought more often about the famous Nibelung hoard that belonged to Siegfried, whose wealth he envied deep down. And so it happened, that after a while, Gunther and Hagen conspired to kill Siegfried.]

The alterations to the target text create an unequivocal interpretive line, allowing little room for interpretation. The different approaches revealed by translating on the one hand and adaptation/retelling on the other, pose different requirements and challenges to readers. This has been shown, albeit partially, through this exercise of translating under controlled conditions and contrasting the results with the retold story. On the other hand, this exercise has also shown that other factors, outside the text, affect the results, the most significant of which are the receptors, the communicative situation, and purpose of the two versions. These factors notwithstanding, we have seen that different processes result in functionally similar texts, guided by a shared notion of readability and adequacy to a target audience.

As to the literary classification of the retold story, we have seen that, for cataloguing purposes, it is no longer recognized as a saga, but rather as a 'fairy tale'. This classification, however, is based not so much on theoretical criteria as on a tradition governing publications for children, which has established a close association of folk children's literature and fairy tales. In this way, even though we stated clear-cut objectives for our use of theory, in the association of theory and practice we could not define actual criteria for translation and adaptation, expressed here in the relationship between an academic translation and a retold story.

4.1.2 A solution from outside

As we have seen in this study, from a theoretical point of view, there is no way of solving the dilemma of establishing boundaries separating translation and adaptation. The issue seems to rest on the old dichotomy, 'fidelity versus translating freedom' and seems to be closely related to specific conceptions of translation: for some theoreticians procedures toward adaptation are part and parcel of translation; for others such procedures fall outside the purview of translation and are classified as adaptation. Perhaps the translating process should be approached through an integrated perspective, where subjects and objects in translation are inseparable. Translating and adapting are not such mutually exclusive categories, but complementary moments, inherent to the rewriting process, the process of producing sense in language through translation This study has shown that, for the sake of readability, 'adaptive' procedures have to be incorporated in a framework that is avowedly 'translational'. On the other hand, in the retold story, the decision to maintain a degree of 'foreignness' is guided by a wider conception of text that includes the illustrations and afterword. Besides showing the interpenetration of these two processes, this chapter has also outlined certain distinctive features of the 'retold story' genre. The decision as to whether to translate or to adapt is frequently the sole province of the publisher, who takes into account not only the potential requirements of the readership but acknowledges the fact that the source text was in the public domain. The decision as to whether to label the target text a 'translation' or an 'adaptation' is invariably motivated by marketing concerns – a notion that bypasses ideas described in the theoretical section of this chapter, which refer to such dichotomies as 'word-for-word translation' versus 'translation for meaning', or 'literal translation' versus 'free translation'. Sometimes publishers don't even bear such considerations in mind, as they label a published work an 'adaptation' (or 'retold story'), and thereby sever the connection between the retold text and the 'original'. This approach regards the target text as a 'new' text, whose visibility – in this specific retold story – is expressed in the afterword, in the interaction of text and illustrations, and in the articulation of the new work with the publishing proposition.

Notes

[1] Cf., Störig 1969, Reiss 1971, 1982, Nord 1989, Johnson 1984, Gambier 1992, and Stolze 2003. In Brazil: Zavaglia & Cintrão 2007, Bertin 2008, Amorim 2003.

[2] Amorim (2003), for example, remarks that it has been given more attention in intersemiotic studies.

[3] We mean here the concept of translation as rewriting, as described in Lefevere (1992).

[4] In this sense, cf. Dias (2001) and Azenha Jr. (2008)

[5] Lajolo and Zilberman (1984) stress the playful aspect in children's and young adult literature as the element responsible for the 'text's permeability to the reader's interest'. For this, cf. also Azenha Jr. (2005).

[6] As in the text, the selection of images and perspectives also expresses the action of other agents. An example is the way war and death are suppressed or reduced to a minimum in the illustrations, even though they refer to essential passages in the story.

Bibliography

Amorim, Lauro Maia (2003). '*Tradução e Adaptação*: Entre a Identidade e a Diferença, os Limites da Transgressão'. Unpubl. MA Thesis. Instituto de Biociências, Letras e Ciências Exatas, UNESP.

— (2005). Tradução e adaptação: Encruzilhadas da Textualidade em Alice no País das Maravilhas de Lewis Carroll e Kim de Rudyard Kipling. São Paulo: UNESP.

Azenha Jnr., João (2005). 'A Tradução Para a Criança e Para o Jovem: a Prática Como Base da Reflexão e da Relação Profissional'. *Pandaemonium Germanicum*, Sept: 367–92.

— (2008). 'Dependências, Assimetrias e Desafios na Tradução Para a Criança e o Jovem no Brasil,. In *Vozes, Olhares, Silêncios: Diálogos Transdisciplinares Entre a Lingüística Aplicada e a Tradução*. Elizabeth Ramos and Denis Scheyerl (eds), 97–114. Salvador: EDUFBA.

Belinky, Tatiana (1993). *A Saga de Siegfried: O Tesouro dos Nibelungos*. São Paulo: Companhia das Letrinhas.

Bertin, Marilise Rezende (2008). "'Traduções', Adaptações, Apropriações: Reescrituras das Peças *Hamlet, Romeu e Julieta* e *Otelo* de William Shakespeare'. Unpubl. MA thesis. Faculdade de Filosofia, Letras e Ciências Humanas, USP.

Cintrão, H. P. and Zavaglia, A. (2007). 'Domínios Culturais e Função Poética Como Condicionantes da Adaptação Dentro da Tradução: Sobre o Conceito de Adaptação'. In *XI Encontro Regional da ABRALIC – Associação Brasileira de Literatura Comparada, 2007, São Paulo. Anais do XI Encontro Regional da Associação Brasileira de Literatura Comparada 2007*. 45–78. São Paulo: ABRALIC.

Dias, Renata de Sousa (2001). 'Traduzir Para a Criança: uma Brincadeira Muito Séria, Vol. I e II'. Unpubl. MA thesis. Faculdade de Filosofia, Letras e Ciências Humanas, USP.

Gambier, Yves (1992). 'Adaptation: une Ambiguïté à Interroger'. *Meta: Journal des Traducteurs/Meta: Translators' Journal* 37(3): 421–5.

Heberle, Eugen (1951). *Deutsche Heldendsagen*. Heidelberg: Keysersche Verlagsbuchhandlung.

Hermans, Theo (ed.) (1985). *The Manipulation of Literature: Studies in Literary Translation*. London: Croom Helm.

Johnson, M. A. (1984). 'Translation and Adaptation'. *Meta: Journal des Traducteurs/ Meta: Translators' Journal* 29(4): 421–5.

Köhler, Carl (1993). *História do Vestuário*, trans. Jefferson Luís Camargo, rev. Silvana Vieira. São Paulo: Martins Fontes.

Lajolo, Marisa and Zilberman, Regina (1984). *Literatura Infantil Brasileira: História e histórias*. São Paulo: Ática.

Lefevere, André (1992). *Translation, Rewriting, and the Manipulation of Literary Fame*. London and New York: Routledge.

Moreira, Marcelo Victor de Souza (2009). 'O Reconto Como Categoria de Tradução: Projeto de Iniciação Científica'. Unpubl. Paper. Faculdade de Filosofia, Letras e Ciências Humanas, USP.

Nord, Christiane (1989). 'Loyalität statt Treue: Vorschläge zu einer Funktionalen Übersetzungstypologie'. *Lebende Sprachen* 3: 100–5.

Oittinen, Riitta (1998). 'Kinderliteratur'. In *Handbuch Translation*. Mary Snell-Hornby et al (eds), 250–3. Tübingen: Stauffenburg-Verlag.

Paloposki, Outi (2009). 'Limits of Freedom: Agency, Choice and Constraints in the Work of the Translator'. In *Agents of Translation*. John Milton and Paul Bandia (eds), 189–208. Amsterdam and Philadelphia: John Benjamins.

Reiss, Katharina (1971). *Möglichkeiten und Grenzen der Übersetzungskritik: Kategorien und Kriterien für eine Sachgerechte Beurteilung von Übersetzungen*. München, Max Hueber Verlag.

— (1982). 'Zur Übersetzung Von Kinder- und Jugendbüchern: Theorie und Praxis'. *Lebende Sprachen* I: 7–13.

Snell-Hornby, Mary (2006). *The Turns of Translation Studies: New Paradigms or Shifting Viewpoints?* Amsterdam and Philadelphia: John Benjamins.

Stolze, Radegundis (2003). 'Translating for Children – World View or Pedagogics?' *Meta: journal des traducteurs/Meta: Translators' Journal* 48(1–2): 208–21.

Störig, Hans Joachin (ed.) (1969). *Das Problem des Übersetzens*. Wege der Forschung; Band VIII. Darmstadt: Wissenschaftliche Buchgesellschaft.

Toury, Gideon (1995). *Descriptive Translation Studies and Beyond*. Amsterdam and Philadelphia: John Benjamins.

Chapter 5

Adapting, Translating and Transforming: Cultural Mediation in Ping Chong's *Deshima* and *Pojagi*

Tanfer Emin Tunç

Born in 1946 in Toronto, Canada, and raised in New York's Chinatown, postmodern playwright, avant-garde performance artist, and world-traveller Ping Chong is the ultimate Chinese/American cultural mediator. As an individual who has, in numerous interviews, positioned himself as personally, politically, and artistically 'in-between' cultures, Chong lives and works in the interstices of Chinese American culture, privileging hybridity, as well as the liminal, marginalized Other in almost all of his professional endeavours. His background as a filmmaker and visual artist has not only allowed him to transform images into written text and stage performance, but has also provided him with the tools to function as an intersemiotic translator of the Chinese American experience. In his capacity as a cultural interpreter, Chong has successfully woven a dense pastiche of words and symbols into the fabric of his mixed media theatrical works, which, collectively, have come to embody the nature of cross-cultural intertextuality.[1]

The fact that Chong has and continues to struggle with his cultural identity perhaps renders him the most suitable type of spokesperson for the Chinese American experience since he can look at both societies from a more objective perspective. He actively resists assimilation because it involves the 'self becoming the Other, giving up your cultural identity, [and] that schizophrenia of being and not being' (Steinman 1995: 54). Chong's self-admitted 'in-between' identity and his use of such a diversity of eclectic materials and innovative theatrical techniques has led his work to be classified as 'fragmented', a label that Chong rejects, arguing that it only seems fragmented when considered from a Western linear perspective: 'It isn't really fragmentary [. . .] I think that it's not understood [. . . .] while it looks fragmented, it's really three dimensional chess. It's all interrelated, but not in a linear manner. They are connected, but they're not connected A-B-A-B, that's all' (qtd. Kaye 1996: 150). Chong's unconventional and experimental theatrical approach thus functions as an intercultural – and intertextual – *transformative process of adaptation, translation, and interpretation* with 'each element . . . expressing its own discrete point or view, rather than . . . merging in a conventionally unified artwork' (Wilmeth and Bigsby 2000: 43).[2] Consequently, 'thematically as well as aesthetically, Chong evokes the sense that beneath the simple order of the surface there are layers of [knowledge] and identity constantly moving over other layers [. . .] [His works] establish a dichotomous relationship between surface and depth, forcing us to question our sense of surface simplicity' (Frieze 2002: 157). More significantly, Chong's work resists easy classification: we cannot identify whether he is 'adapting', 'transforming', or 'translating' material. Perhaps the distinctions are not really important: Chong functions simultaneously as an intercultural interpreter, translator, and adapter of different artistic and creative media. This process is evident in his *East/West Quartet* – four dramas (*Deshima*, 1990; *Chinoiserie*, 1995; *After Sorrow*, 1997; and *Pojagi*, 1999) that deal with the inter- and intra-cultural clashes (e.g., racism and prejudice) arising between East (Japan, China, Vietnam, and Korea, respectively), and West (e.g., the Netherlands, the British Empire, and the United States), as well as between Asians themselves (Chong 2004). More significantly, the quartet also serves as a space for the examination of the processes involved in adapting, translating, rewriting, and staging texts (or in this case historical and cultural narratives) from the margins. It is in this space that we discover that for Chong, adapting, translating, and interpreting are parallel – and often (de)constructive – ventures, which intersect to produce powerful cross-cultural critiques of both Eastern *and* Western societies.

This chapter will examine the ways in which Ping Chong has used adaptation and translation as both a means to reconcile his own struggle with identity (i.e., negotiating a place for himself – both physically and psychologically – in-between cultures, ultimately deciding to adopt the 'whole world' as his culture) and as methods to transfer/transform the building blocks of culture (e.g., visual images, music, material objects, and historical texts) into staged works (a process which Chong, alluding to French anthropologist Claude Lévi-Strauss, calls 'bricolage'). By taking the first and last works of *The East/West Quartet* – *Deshima,* which focuses on Japan, and *Pojagi,* which takes Korea as its central focus, this chapter will also illustrate how both translation and adaptation have the potential to revolutionize theatrical performance, especially through works which, like those produced by Ping Chong, incorporate and interpret a mélange of media and nuanced cultural references.[3] It will pay particular attention to Chong's techniques as a writer, director, and producer of avant-garde theatre (e.g., his use of foreign languages and American sign language to marginalize the white observer and render uncomfortable monolingual individuals; his incorporation of Chinese, Japanese, and Korean theatrical aesthetics; and his integration of Eastern and Western dance techniques, still photos, music, and historical dialogues/texts), with the intention of exposing the rich fusion that can result when adaptation and translation are used simultaneously.

5.1 Adapting and Translating Ping Chong's World

Although Ping Chong was raised in the shadow of Broadway, and as a child participated in family excursions to Radio City Music Hall and Times Square, unlike several of his theatrical contemporaries, he did not draw inspiration from the mainstream resources that existed in New York City in the 1960s and 1970s. Chong lived in the ethnic neighbourhood of Chinatown; however, he rarely ventured beyond its borders into Manhattan. Consequently, his position as a liminal figure – living within, yet between, two cultures – was formed during childhood. As Chong admits, 'I am always this person who is a part of yet not a part of. That's my metaphysical condition' (Kaye 1996: 150). It is not surprising, then, that Chong's works deal abstractly and metaphorically 'with the broader issues of culture: the Other, displacement, and alienation' (Lee 2006: 112). As he delineates: 'this sense of 'otherness' can prove useful to a writer. It can result in a kind of double vision that allows one to work at the intersection of forms, at the crux of cultures, at the critical junctures where ethnic, aesthetic and social identities blur and blend' (Berson 1990: xii).

While in the New York of the 1960s 'anything seemed possible', Chong gravitated toward stage performance, and saw 'art as a way of surviving' (Lee 2006: 113). He studied filmmaking and graphic design at the Pratt Institute's School of Visual Arts, and began his theatrical career in the mid 1960s with Meredith Monk's *House Company*. In 1975 he went solo, establishing *Ping Chong and Company* (formerly known as the *Fiji Theater Company*) in order to explore performances and multimedia installations that combine contemporary theatre aesthetics, multicultural issues, movement (dance), and art. Over the years, his dramatic work has become increasingly difficult to categorize and describe because it adapts all of these elements, and many more.

'His influences, hence, are many and his works are filled with allusions to history, philosophy, science, religion, literature and popular culture' (Sugano 2002: 34). However, according to Douglas Sugano, 'what is most impressive about Ping Chong's works is the ingenuity and variety of media that he uses to convey complex, engaging and enduring ideas' (34, 36–7).

Because Chong maintains that '*whole* cultures are unable to interact harmoniously' (Berson 1990: 3, my emphasis), he developed a unique 'talk, reveal, and seek to understand' approach to theatre that simultaneously involves adaptation, translation, and interpretation in order to move audiences 'towards unification, diminishing the barriers between peoples, and [. . .] embracing all that is good in civilization' (Masters 2004: 10). Like French Surrealists such as Magritte, to whom he admittedly owes a debt of gratitude, Chong 'comprehends the ordinary by making it strange' (Banes 1998: 234), specifically through the technique of *bricolage* – a concept Chong adopted from anthropologist Claude Lévi-Strauss. *Bricolage* involves creating a 'new world [. . .] out of any and all available materials [drawn] from an old world' (Mehta 1984: 169). According to Chong, it is the most effective technique to translate his experiences as a Chinese American into art: 'I use old materials [such as film and video clips, paintings, sculptures, quoted material, recorded sound, historical documents, still images, slides, choreography, and elements from Chinese operatic theatre] to give [my world] a new resonance. That's what I was thinking with *bricolage*, recombining old materials that were not in those combinations before . . . to create a kind of luminosity' (Kaye 1996: 148).

Chong's use of *bricolage* helps him to create dense plays with hybridized allusions to numerous disciplines, and remarkably, accomplishes this with very little dialogue. He, instead, uses multivalent symbolism, semiotics, sign language, images, Eastern and Western choreography, music, exaggerated robotic gestures and stylized body language, bold facial expressions, and artistic makeup found in traditional Chinese theatre, thereby illustrating the needlessness of words, especially in postmodern 'post-verbal' societies, where computer communication is permanently replacing the spoken and the handwritten word (Steinman 1995: 62). Stylistically, as we observe, 'there is [. . .] no fourth wall here, a convention that is reinforced when the . . . performers speak presentationally [. . .] [or when] Chong translates text spoken in [Japanese, Dutch, Javanese, or Korean], thus literally becoming the artist as translator, to say nothing of the artist as lecturer, raconteur and master of [sacred] ceremonies' (Dillon 1996: 20–1).

Chong's narrative interpretations rely on his unique heteroglossia, which includes elements adapted from the Asian aesthetics of his parents and grandparents (who were Chinese opera performers), nonlinear/achronological structure, and surrealism as opposed to realism (Westfall 1992: 360). As Kent Neely observes: 'it is the combination of a plastic space of representation and the network of symbols and events that creates this sensation of liminality that continues throughout [his] performances' (Neely 1992: 130–1). Moreover, Chong often adapts and fuses different media simultaneously, which translates into a multi-referential, imagistic spectacle that establishes a mood or 'aura' of alienation. Music, in particular, is a 'crucial element in Chong's work. It never settles mildly into the background but often commands more attention than the actors onstage. Sometimes wordless singing seems to imitate human speech; sometimes the music is in a well-known religious or popular genre. Frequently it has a haunting quality. The music feels like a meaningful sign; it takes the form of significance, but signifies nothing in particular. It is the music's presence rather than its message which preoccupies spectators', and impacts their own personal translation and interpretation of Chong's message (Carroll 1983: 73).

Through his works, Chong is able to render white, Anglo-Saxon, Protestant, American culture, and its predominantly white, male, univocal, linear, hegemonic historical narrative, irrelevant by deconstructing, translating, and interpreting it from the margins. His polyvocal (or polyphonic) 'voicing back' successfully 're-embodies [history through multiple perspectives] in order to embody it differently' (Shimakawa 2002: 22). However, Chong's process of historical deconstruction, which also involves adaptation and transformation, does not attempt to reflect specific events, but, more importantly, 'fundamental human behaviors [and emotions], which transcend individuality and temporal or spatial specificity' (Neely 1992: 126). While, initially, 'works appear confusing, audiences must trust that Chong will fill in the blanks that will allow then to construct [or intuit] meaningful responses. Until the audience becomes familiar with Chong's method of signification, however, the kernel [. . .] remains elusive and allusive, and must often be reconstructed in retrospect, after the theatrical experience has ended' (Westfall 1992: 360). Thus 'in attempting to absorb Chong's theater performance, we must construct stories; we must mythologize', and create our own translation/interpretation, or (counter) narrative to history (Frieze 2006: 98).

Chong inevitably lies outside the societies he describes, and is a perennial Outsider – not 'Chinese' and not 'American' (Kaye 1996: 147). As the only Chinese student in his high school, Chong explains: 'I felt like I was sitting on a fence staring at two cultures. You go out into the bigger world, and start looking at it with the kind of objectivity an anthropologist has'.

However, rather than dwelling on this difference, Chong has transferred this feeling of estrangement into his work: 'characters often seem to be strangers in their environment, and the images he creates are made strange by seeming out of context. The audience is distanced from them in such a way that they experience the strangeness'. He underscores this alienation by incorporating languages other than English, which, as he has conveyed, reconfigures the 'exclusive English speaker [. . .] [as] the outsider: 'I want the audience to understand the other side of the fence, what it feels like not to comprehend' (qtd. Shank 2002: 253–4). In his 'multicultural, multilingual, and multi-media', it is the 'average American theater patron [who is ultimately cast] as the outsider' (Westfall 1992: 362).

5.1.1 *Deshima* (1990)

Ping Chong's *East/West Quartet* was born out of a desire to adapt, translate, and locate a '2000 year old culture' (Chinese) within 'a 200 year old one' (American). This involved the personal 'need to synthesize the antagonistic traditions which he found in himself, what Chong describes as 'creating the world out of necessity'. *The East/West Quartet* thus functions as a 'meditation on East–West relations, historiography, and the concept of Otherness woven through a stylized, often episodic, portrayal of historical encounters, 'real' and imaged, significant and incidental. Taken as a whole, the *Quartet* presents a history of the United States' and Europe's . . . military, colonial, economic and diplomatic encounters with Asia (or parts of it) and how that history . . . constructs contemporary relations within and between those sites' (Frieze 2002: 172). Chong's formal work on what was to become *The East/West Quartet* began in 1988, when he was commissioned by the famous Dutch Mickery Theatre (located in Amsterdam, the Netherlands) to create a piece in commemoration of the centennial (1990) of Vincent van Gogh's death (1890). While conducting his research, Chong realized that Van Gogh was born in 1853, 'the year that Commodore Admiral Perry of the United States Navy went to Japan to open its door to trade, after Japan had been closed for two hundred years' (Frieze 2002: 172). Chong became increasingly curious about what happened between Japan and European colonial powers in the mid-seventeenth century that had necessitated a closing of trade routes with the West. Consequently, he shifted his central focus away from Van Gogh and chose to focus on Dutch relations with the East, specifically its contact, colonial exploits, and competition with Japan. His critique of European economic and cultural imperialism eventually translated into *Deshima*, which was named after the artificial quarantine island that the Daimyo (or powerful territorial lord who was lieutenant to the Japanese Shogun) established off the coast of Nagasaki after commencing trade with the Dutch in the late sixteenth century (Westfall 1993: 10).

Deshima is structured around a series of *intersections*: 'cultures collide, histories and eras are juxtaposed, and aesthetics clash to create a prismatic sense of history, time and implication' (Chong 2004: 5). Relaying back and forth in chronology, the play spans four centuries of Japanese–Western contact, including Dutch trade negotiations with the Daimyo, the Japanese domination of Indonesia, World War II, the internment of Japanese Americans, and the trade wars of the 1980s. The purchase of Van Gogh's *Vase with Fifteen Sunflowers* for a record $39.9 million by Japanese investor Yasuo Goto in 1987 serves as a framework for the play's critique of the bi-directional East/West colonization, imperialism, and cultural commodification that has spanned the past four centuries.[4] According to Suzanne Westfall, the purchase of *Vase with Fifteen Sunflowers* 'stirred widespread speculation about the problematic relationship between Japan and the West, between art as aesthetic object and art as commodity – and propelled Chong on his leap to *Deshima*. Fascinated by the Japanese economic colonization of the West, Chong began to see Van Gogh as the inheritor of the exile at *Deshima*' (Westfall 1993: 10). In other words, an 'outcast controlled by foreign economic forces' (Shank 2002: 256).

As a fluid exploration of history through sensory association that focuses on the universal themes of 'xenophobia, racism, commercialism, and amnesia', *Deshima* adapts layers of contradictory themes and aesthetics – Eastern and Western choreography (Indonesian and Japanese court dances, as well as the Swing, Waltz, and Jitterbug), images, semiotics, text, props (Japanese shoji screens juxtaposed on black walls and flooring), music, languages (English, Japanese, Dutch, French, and Javanese), first-person accounts, archival photos, sound recordings, and 'the most discursive of performance modes, the lecture' – 'to blur the audience's sense of time, space, dimension', fact and fiction (Lee 2006: 116, Chong 2004: 5). With the exception of the Narrator (played in the original production by African American actor Michael Matthews), all the performers in *Deshima* are of Asian descent. Interestingly, 'the Narrator assumes many roles throughout the piece – servant, metaphysical commentator, Japanese businessman, American businessman, and Van Gogh' (Chong 2004: 7). Asians 'play Anglo roles such as the Dutch Ambassador, missionary Jesuits, and colonial governors; Van Gogh himself is played by a woman, a child, and a black man [Matthews] simultaneously' (Westfall 1993:10). Chong's cross-cultural casting highlights the irony and insidiousness of the racism inherent in East–West interactions: 'I decided to do *Deshima* with all Asians, so that the Asians play both the oppressor and the oppressed' (Chong 1989–90: 65–6). According to Chong, this form of interracial historical adaptation allows the audience to transcend 'people and their associated skin colours' and interpret the nature of racism itself. The casting of the play also reinforces 'the fluidity of identity and the impact of history on identity', as well as the common experience of racism that links Asian and African Americans. As we are reminded in *Deshima*, during World War II 'black men [were] killed fighting yellow men for the protection of white men' (Chong 2004: xxi, 40).

As Chong has repeatedly stated, 'I think every society should have a mirror held to it by an outsider'. *Deshima*, as well as the other works in *The East/West Quartet*, function as these transnational mirrors, adapting, translating, interpreting, and reflecting the prejudices of generations past, present, and future. Throughout *Deshima*, the audience is presented with the manifestations and ramifications of bi-directional racism: in Scene 1, for example, the Dutch trader and Daimyo refer to each other as 'cannibalistic monsters' and 'man-eating beasts', and consistently dehumanize one another rather than attempting to bridge the physical (e.g., 'red hair/black greasy hair', 'eyes like a fish/slanted eyes', and 'huge nose/no nose'), cultural (e.g., beer vs. sake), and religious elements that divide them (Chong 2004: back cover, 16). Despite their differences (especially in interpreting and translating each other's cultures), East and West are united in their desire for wealth, and come to a mutually beneficial plan to exploit one another. This, as foreshadowed by the Latin hymn *Dies Irae* in Scene 2, will result in a 'Day of Wrath' for the Japanese at the hands of Dutch traders and Portuguese missionaries, who not only converted them but also destroyed their Shinto and Buddhist temples and sold them into slavery.

Scene 3 brings the bigotry and hypocrisy that characterized the colonial era into the contemporary period by satirizing an American World War II fundraising radio programme as a hotbed of racism. As the disc jockey, who works for 'WKKK' (an allusion to the Ku Klux Klan) informs us, the 'Top Ten' songs of the year are all anti-Japanese propaganda tunes – such as 'I'm Going to Find a Fellow Who's Yellow and Beat Him Red, White and Blue' and 'To Be Specific, It's Our Pacific' (Chong 2004: 23–4). These songs not only illustrate the intolerance and violence suffered by Japanese Americans, but also serve as good examples of the way in which Chong routinely adapts elements of popular culture in his works in order to satirize them and suggest ulterior meanings. In this case, these songs translate the notion that Americans are just as guilty of prejudice, jingoism, and imperialism as Europeans. Moreover, the fact that unsuspecting 'wholesome' teenagers are happily dancing the Jitterbug to these tunes during a fundraiser also conveys the idea that racism has insidiously been normalized as part of popular culture.

Scene 4, which consists of an adaptation of David Frost's interview with Akio Morita, President of the Sony Corporation, signals the entry of the Japanese into the world economic market after World War II. Morita's description of the 'sunny boys of Sony' as the brains behind the technological revolution is juxtaposed with a map of Indonesia, divided in two by the Japanese characters for 'East' and 'West' (Chong 2004: 26). The court dancing in this vignette serves as a prelude for Scene 5, which depicts the Dutch enslavement and exploitation of another group of colonized peoples – the Indonesians. This scene, subtitled *Nuit Blanche* or 'a white night in the heart of history', begins with a conversation between the Javanese Regent and a Dutchman about civilization and barbarity. By Scene 6, the audience realizes who the true barbarians are (the Dutch) when they casually decide how to divide Africa at a ball. The incivility of this behaviour is accentuated in the next scene when a 'European' woman's elaborate bodice and white colonial wig are forcefully removed to reveal a Javanese dance costume and black hair. Not only does this metaphorically suggest the Dutch rape of Indonesia, but it also implies that civilization is merely a façade and that the Other is located in each of us.

Scene 7, which deals with the 'liberation' of the Indonesians from European influence by the Japanese during World War II, simultaneously exhibits the damage that Asians have inflicted on one another. Although they were welcomed with cheering crowds, the Japanese soon deployed soldiers in the region, transforming it from a landscape of Dutch-controlled cultural and economic imperialism to one of Japanese military and social domination. As the Indonesians are informed, they have become a part of the 'Empire of the Rising Sun': 'From now on, you will perform [. . .] a ritual bow toward the emperor in Tokyo at public assemblies. The local calendar will be changed to the Japanese. 1941 will become 2601. Japanese holidays will become your holidays. The Japanese language will be promoted as the *lingua franca* of the new Imperium. Are there any questions?' (Chong 2004: 39). By the end of the scene, it is clear that both Manifest Destiny and racism connect Japan and the United States, the latter of which reciprocated with its own brand of colonization through the forced internment of Japanese Americans during World War II (Scene 8).

At 'Internment Camp, USA' we meet a series of six Japanese Americans who inform us about their 'all-American' jobs (e.g., teaching, dentistry, and farming), while a list of ten 'relocation centres', with their locations and populations, is projected behind them. As the Narrator reads an absurd adaptation of Franklin Delano Roosevelt's Executive Order 9066, which ordered all 'alien and non-alien' Americans of Japanese descent to internment camps, the music shifts from the Christian spiritual song 'Go Tell it on the Mountain', to 'Dardanella', a rumba-like tune with a warbling Japanese female voice and lots of static. One by one, we see families evacuated, selling their possessions to 'white vultures' below market value, set against a backdrop of authentic black and white period photographs of the relocation of first, second, and third generation Japanese Americans. Although, as we are told, no evidence of sabotage was ever found concerning Japanese Americans, they are punished once again with the bombing of Hiroshima and Nagasaki in Scene 9. As the interned engage in a joyous dance of 'displacement' after V-J (Victory in Japan) Day, in the background we hear President Harry Truman and General Douglas MacArthur discuss their reasons for dropping the atomic bombs and their plans for a post-war Japan.

Between Scene 9 and the last scene of the play, Scene 10, is a historical timeline juxtaposing both significant and trivial events in history and popular culture (such as '1960: John F. Kennedy is elected President of the United States'. Song of the Year: 'Itsy Bitsy Teeny Weeny Yellow Polka Dot Bikini') (Chong 2004: 50). The timeline begins with the surrender of the Japanese in 1945, and ends with the selling of Van Gogh's *Vase with Fifteen Sunflowers* to a Japanese investor and the collapse of the Berlin Wall in the late 1980s. The Narrator, now dressed in an expensive business suit, represents the new face of capitalism in the late twentieth century and a player in 'East Meets West 2', the subtitle of Scene 10. Once again, we hear the Frost and Morita interview, but this time set against a portrait of a Japanese schoolgirl and the running projection 'In the Name of Profit', which thematizes the final scene as well as the entire work. As we hear the details of Sony's marketing strategy, the Narrator conveys the notion that in the United States, Morita's financial status protects him from being treated like a second-class citizen (i.e., like an African American). However, ultimately, both Morita and the Narrator are connected by the fact that they are not white. The Narrator disapproves of Morita's patronizing tone and criticism of American workers as lazy: what connects the two cultures is money (which is an allusion to the East/West negotiations between the Japanese and Dutch in Scene 1).

In the final moments of *Deshima*, the Narrator removes his jacket to reveal Vincent Van Gogh's peasant costume underneath, suggesting that all of us, despite our designer exteriors, are bound together by the same cycle of globalization, capitalism, and commodification that is exemplified in the play (Lee 2006: 116, Westfall 1993: 112). Resembling a subject from one of Van Gogh's pastoral scenes (e.g., *The Sower (after Millet)* or *Crows in the Cornfield*), the Narrator begins to sell postcards of Van Gogh's works to the audience, reinforcing the exploitation of the painter by both the Dutch and the global art market 'in the name of profit'. The scene, which is crosscut by two Japanese farmers returning home with firewood strapped to their backs (an adaptation of Van Gogh's *Japonaiserie: The Bridge in the Rain, After Hiroshige,* 1887, which was his imitation of a Japanese painting) (Shimakawa 2002: 139), ends with Van Gogh's prediction that Arles, a small 'backwater' city in southern France, 'will be the Japan of the future' (Chong 2004: 56). Today, Arles, which served as the inspiration for some of Van Gogh's most famous works including *Yellow Room, Starry Night Over the Rhone, The Night Café,* and *L'Arlésienne,* and was the setting of the infamous ear-severing incident, has become a tourist trap – part of the growing global network that commodifies humans and the art they produce.

As Chong conveys throughout *Deshima*: 'nations don't own up to past historical wrongs'. While the age of colonization is over, globalization, and the trade wars that support cultural imperialism, have clearly just begun. By staging a theatrical adaptation of history written from the margins, Chong compels his audience – which was originally the Dutch themselves – to translate imperialistic and racist events that occurred centuries ago (e.g., nation-building in someone else's nation) in order to find their relevance in today's world. Moreover, he also encourages critical self-interpretation, and an 'owning up' to forgotten or erased aspects of history: 'an audience, confronted in the theatre by acts of casual or intentionally vicious racism, can congratulate themselves for 'not being like that' – or can they? (Dillon 1996: 20–1, Chong 2004: xix). However, what makes *Deshima* truly transformative is that it underscores the oppression of Asians by each other (specifically, the power struggle between Japan and its weaker neighbours in the 1930s and 1940s), as well as the Eastern objectification of other peoples of colour. By doing so, Chong 'calls attention to the ways that Asians and Asian Americans have at times colluded with white racism and at other times suffered similar abjection by white culture' (Shimakawa 2002: 157). In Scene 1, the Narrator lists the tributes offered by the Dutch to the Japanese during their first encounter: 'Among the most cherished gifts were black people, whom the Japanese were particularly fond of' (Chong 2004: 15). As Karen Shimakawa conveys, 'spoken by a black man directly addressing the audience, this statement [accentuates the fact that] both the Dutch and the

Japanese were guilty of the racist exploitation of [Africans]' (Shimakawa 2002: 157).

5.1.2 *Pojagi* (1999)

As the fourth and final work in *The East/West Quartet*, *Pojagi* (1999) 'is a poetic exploration of Korea's culture and history in the turmoil of global power dynamics'. As Gang-Im Lee conveys: 'it is a historical *bricolage* collaged from the detritus of Korean history from sixteenth-century encounters of Koreans and Europeans to the present socio-political conundrum of the unification' of North and South Korea (Gang-Im Lee 2006: 181). By adapting, translating, and interpreting the complex relations between the 'privileged' and the 'marginalized' throughout Korean history, Chong is able to transcend binaries that posit the East as 'victim' and the West as 'victimizer'. Consequently, *Pojagi*, like *Deshima*, conveys the reality that the East can be the source of both 'oppressors' and the 'oppressed'. When Japan began its colonization of Korea in the sixteenth century, Korean rulers almost immediately aligned with Japanese imperialists, thus functioning as the source of their own oppression by creating a circular power struggle within the nation. *Pojagi* seeks to heal these divisions by serving as a 'neutral ground . . . a ceremony of recognition and reunification for the divided Korean soul' (Chong 2004: 168).

Pojagi adapts ethnography, historiography, 'found text, traditional Korean and minimalist choreography, and a thrilling wraparound sound score', all of which he uses to interpret and construct his own 'impressionistic journey through Korean history' (Solomon 2000). By relying on a 'poetics of detachment and fragmentation' that 'blurs distinctions between museum exhibition, illustrated lecture, and theatre', Chong uses his skills as a cultural interloper and intermediary to recuperate, and translate, historical vignettes, artefacts, eyewitness accounts, and long-forgotten events into a comprehensible narrative. The detachment and isolation in *Pojagi* is heightened by its stark production style, which includes the adaptation of Brechtian alienation techniques (such as direct audience-address, pantomime, and sound effects as opposed to music); the use of masks, symbols, and cultural semiotics (e.g., Chong evokes the bear and tiger from 'Dan-Gun', the Korean creation myth that explains the origin of their nation); minimal physicality (Chong incorporates simple Korean folk dance poses and Chinese opera gestures); an absence of colour (the stage is dark, and all the cast members are clad in white, the traditional colour of Korean shamans); sparse narration; and few visual projections (only key words are illuminated by the light box located in centre of the 'no-man's land' of the vast empty stage) (Chong 2004: 167–8). The result is a destabilization of the 'national and international conditions which perpetuate hierarchies among people and nations', as well as the startling realization that Korea's history is circular: it does not 'progress . . . it has pitfalls, contradictions and ironies' (Gang-Im Lee 2006: 181, Chong 2004: xxxiii).

Covering a broad sweep of time, from opening scenes depicting 'sea-tossed Europeans landing on the 'deserted island', encountering men 'clad after the Chinese fashion', to recent recollections of elderly South Koreans reuniting with relatives from the North', *Pojagi* attempts to present a neutral landscape for the peninsula's troubled history and shifting values (Solomon 2000, Chong 2004: xxxii–xxxiii). Moreover, it functions as a metaphoric attempt to summon Korea's dead ghosts back to life. Unlike *Deshima, Pojagi* focuses on the Asian (i.e., Korean) experience in Asia (Korea) and does not examine the diaspora. It weaves European/U.S. involvement in Asia into its plot; however, not to the same extent found in *Deshima. Pojagi* does refer to the Pacific as the 'ocean bride of America' where 'East meets West', and China, Japan, and Korea, 'with their innumerable islands, hanging like necklaces about them . . . [as] the bridesmaids'. Chong extends this metaphor by portraying the U.S. as the 'bridegroom', and California as the 'bridal chamber, where all the wealth of the Orient [was] brought to celebrate the wedding', but does little else to critique American involvement in the region until the end of the play when he examines the post-World War II era. Moreover, *Pojagi* is, for the most part, chronologically ordered, which contrasts greatly with Chong's other works. Nevertheless, it uses the same adaptive and translational elements, exploring the concept of 'moving vocabulary' through American sign language, which Chong uses as the 'silent language' of the Koreans. Here, however, sign language does not serve as a substitute for the Korean language itself, which is also used at critical junctures throughout the play. Rather, it is Chong's way of translating the fact that 'Korea is a country whose voice is not really heard, because Korea's fate was in the hands of larger nations and their political machinations' (Chong 2004: xxxii, 184). In this context, sign language is used to visually represent the lost or erased voices of the Korean people, which have fallen upon 'deaf' ears for centuries.

Chong's translation of the Korean experience is also embodied in the *pojagi* itself, traditional square or rectangular 'Korean cloths which were used for centuries [. . .] to wrap, carry and store things [. . .] In the twentieth century, *pojagi* were replaced [. . .] by ready-made carriers, such as bags and suitcases. [However, metaphorically], *pojagi* represent containers, or vessels, for the [historical baggage] of [Korea], and also the traditions that have vanished in the modern world'. *Pojagi* thus serves as 'a theatrical rite of discovery and longing, a summoning of the dead to give witness to the present' (Chong 2004: 167). Our introduction to these metaphorical vessels of burden comes at the beginning of the work when, after enacting a stylized version of a Korean folk-dance, the male and female leads of the play toss *pojagi* (represented by pom poms) into the sea (symbolized by the sound of crashing waves). After this 'unburdening', Chong adapts the Korean 'Dan-Gun' myth in order to explain the origins of the Korean people and their interactions with the Mongolian, Chinese, and Japanese Empires. European missionaries then 'testify' to their 'mental adroitness and quickness of perception, and their talent for the rapid acquisition of languages'. This Western racism is underscored by the 'observation' that Koreans 'have the vices of suspicion, cunning and untruthfulness that all Orientals have'. Even though we are told that 'women are secluded, and occupy a very inferior position' in Korean society (Chong 2004: 177), we soon learn that they actively challenged the Japanese invasion of Korea in 1592 through a symbol of their domesticity – the *pojagi* – which they filled with rocks and threw off cliffs at the enemy. This exertion of power clearly disrupts the Western tendency of viewing Asian women as 'sentimental icons of peasant simplicity . . . Orientalist emblems of feminine passivity', for in this case her *pojagi*, her 'bulging bundle . . . [is her] weapon of resistance' (Solomon 2000).

Inter/intra-Asian struggle is also expressed through Chong's depiction of Korea's Yangban, the wealthy, pipe-smoking aristocratic ruling class of the Joseon Dynasty (1392–1910), who enslaved other Koreans 'with the terrible misfortune of being born into the wrong class' (i.e., the peasantry). Not only did the Yangban maintain social order, they ensured Chinese domination in Korea by importing and adapting Chinese culture, and characterizing Korea as 'the little brother of China' (Chong 2004: 180–1). They not only betrayed their own heritage through their explicit sinophilia, but they also compromised the integrity of their nation by exploiting their fellow countrymen through indentured servitude. As Chong illustrates, however, the Yangban paid the price for their appeasement of other Asian powers. They were eventually overthrown by the Japanese, who ruled Korea in all but name only during the reign of Queen Min 1851–95 – empress between 1873 and 1895. Since Great Britain and the United States were content with their trade agreements and did not want to interfere in Korean politics, Min had no choice but to side with Russia against the Japanese. On October 8, 1895, Japanese soldiers dressed as Korean civilians invaded the palace, and stabbed Min and her ladies-in-waiting to death, doused them with kerosene, and set them on fire (Chong 2004: 185).

After Min's assassination, members of the Korean family fled abroad, and in 1910 Japan annexed Korea. Like in *Deshima* when the Indonesians were forced to adopt Japanese customs during World War II, Koreans were also forced to engage in ritual bowing to the emperor in Tokyo, abandon their calendar, celebrate Japanese holidays, speak Japanese, and change their names to those approved by the colonial administrative government. Koreans were transported to Japan to serve as menial labourers, and as conveyed by a vignette in *Pojagi*, were also killed/wounded when the United States dropped atomic bombs on Hiroshima and Nagasaki. The aftermath of World War II was just as painful for the Koreans as it was for the Japanese: Korea was arbitrarily divided along the 38th Parallel into Russian (North) and American (South) spheres of influence, and separated by the Demilitarized Zone (DMZ). As Chong conveys, 'around midnight on August 11, 1945, two young [American] colonels, Charles Bonesteel and Dean Rusk [. . .] who had no knowledge about Korea [. . .] without consulting Korean leaders [. . .] [and] with only a map borrowed from a *National Geographic* magazine' divided the nation in half along a straight imaginary line of latitude (Chong 2004: 188). Min's dream of uniting Koreans against foreign influence thus never came to fruition – a legacy against which a divided Korea still struggles today.

Despite its name, the DMZ is surrounded by military forces and is 'home to the densest minefield in the world'. Yet, as Chong elucidates in the eloquent closing lines of *Pojagi*, there is hope – the ban on civilian habitation in the area has transformed it into a wildlife sanctuary: 'two of the world's most endangered birds, the white-capped crane and the red-crowned crane winter there [. . .] it is now home to [. . .] nine mammals and numerous plants which were thought to be rare or extinct'. As Chong conveys through this thoughtful theatrical adaptation of Korean history, humans are the cause of destruction, and nature flourishes where they do not exist. The DMZ, which is '4.8 miles wide, stretching one hundred and forty-eight miles long across the Korean peninsula, separating ten million families for more than [sixty] years' is simultaneously Korea's metaphoric burden or *pojagi* as well as its 'Garden of Eden, confounded by sorrow and pain' (Chong 2004: 193).

As critics have noted, Chong's works raise important questions but do not answer them. Instead, his dramas are open-ended, yet so full of rich historical and social fragments that audiences cannot help but draw their own conclusions with respect to the complex nature of East–West relations. In a 1987 interview, Chong himself confessed 'I'm not a mapper, I'm a blind man [. . .] one idea feeds off another [. . .] I'm not so much a creator as an editor' (Gussow 1988: I, 17); thus admitting that the task of deconstructing and reinterpreting history is always a work-in-progress, especially for cultural mediators narrating from the margins. Nevertheless, Chong has learned to embrace his liminality, and has used his hybridity to reconfigure the Asian American experience as a polyvocal one, filled with intertextual resources waiting to be rediscovered, reassessed, and, of course, simultaneously adapted and translated as part of the broader East–West narrative. As Chong elucidates, this process (of adapting, translating, rewriting, and staging East–West cultural elements) is always political, and for those of Asian descent, always personal: not only does it deal with coming to terms with multiple, and often contradictory, aspects of their identity, but it also involves transcending the stereotype of the 'monster [. . .] the outsider, the scapegoat, or any symbol onto which you can throw all your negatives' (Westfall 1992: 360).

As this chapter has illustrated, Chong has used adaptation and translation as both a means to reconcile his own identity struggle, and as a technique to transfer/transform the building blocks of culture into staged works through *bricolage.* As conveyed by *Deshima* and *Pojagi,* translation and adaptation have the potential to revolutionize theatrical performance, because as conceptual tools,they facilitate a rich fusion of experiences through the simultaneous interpretation of multiple resources (e.g., Eastern and Western dance techniques, still photos, music, multilingual dialogue, and historical texts). Clearly, this contributes to the deconstruction of social tropes and binaries that continue to compartmentalize individuals and their complex cultural heritages. Furthermore, as parallel ventures, translation and adaptation also possess the ability to render the personal political. This, for Chong, a self-proclaimed realist, is perhaps the ultimate objective of his works: 'If you can change [the minds of] one or two people, that's something' (Masters 2004: 10).

Notes

1 For more information on intertextuality, see Wong 1993. Intertextuality is analogous to Mikhail Bakhtin's concept of dialogism, as developed in his seminal work *The Dialogic Imagination.* According to Bakhtin, dialogic literature engages in a continuous dialogue with other works and authors. It does not simply augment, revise, or respond to previous work, but rather communicates with, and is continuously informed by, other works. Moreover, the meaning of dialogic literature, and the works with which it communes, can change over time, as new interpretations surface and fresh layers of significance are added by cultural, social and historical events. Both intertextuality and dialogism are intimately linked to another Bakhtinian concept – polyphony – or the existence

of simultaneous multiple voices (akin to polyvocality) in a work of literature, each of which echo a diversity of interpretations, and culminate in a crescendo of voices.

[2] In this chapter, adaptation, translation, and interpretation are defined as transformative processess which serve as cultural and epistemologic bridges, especially between East and West. These processes can be both constructive (creative) and destructive, and involve adjusting, modifying or reworking (and not simply 'rewriting') to accommodate different conditions and environments (adaptation); changing, rendering, or converting from one form (e.g., verbal, visual, or theatrical language) into another (translation); and explaining or elucidating behaviours and expressions to convey a stylistic individuality (interpretation). In Chong's case, these processes involve personal experience (as a Chinese American) and history (of the East and West), both of which are unifed through his theatrical techniques.

[3] For an in-depth analysis of *Chinoiserie* and *After Sorrow*, see Tunç 2010. Parts of this article 'Razing/Raising the Literary Canon' – in particular the biographical material on Chong – appear in this chapter.

[4] In the 1980s and 1990s, foreign investors, especially those from the Middle and Far East, began purchasing major symbols of the West, both for investment purposes and self-aggrandizement. This became a Western concern, especially after Harrods in London and Rockefeller Center in New York were bought by the Al Fayed Brothers and Mitsubishi Group, respectively.

Bibliography

Banes, Sally (1998). *Subversive Expectations: Performance Art and Paratheater in New York*. Ann Arbor, MI: University of Michigan Press.

Berson, Misha (1990). *Between Worlds: Contemporary Asian American Plays*. New York: Theater Communications Group.

Carroll, Noel (1983). 'A Select View of Earthlings: Ping Chong'. *The Drama Review* 27(1): 72–81.

Chong, Ping (2004). *The East/West Quartet*. New York: Theater Communications Group.

— (1989/90). 'Mumblings and Digressions: Some Thoughts on Being an Artist, Being an American, Being a Witness. . . '. *MELUS* 16(3): 62–7.

Dillon, John (1996). 'Three Places in Asia: Ping Chong Delves into the East–West Collisions of History'. *American Theater* 13(3): 18–22.

Frieze, James (2002). 'The Interpretation of Difference: Staging Identity in the United States, 1986–1992'. Unpubl. Ph.D thesis, University of Wisconsin–Madison.

— (2006). 'The Mess Behind the Veil: Assimilating Ping Chong'. *Theater Research International* 31(1): 84–100.

Gussow, Mel (1988). 'Ping Chong's View of History in *Maraya*'. *The New York Times*, January 16: Section I, 17.

Kaye, Nick (1996). *Art into Theater: Performance Interviews and Documents*. London and New York: Routledge.

Lee, Esther Kim (2006). *A History of Asian American Theater.* Cambridge: Cambridge University Press.

Lee, Gang- Im (2006). 'Poetic Exploration of the East and the West in Ping Chong's *Pojagi'. East–West Comparative Literature Journal* 15: 181–206..

Masters, A. (2004). *Window on the Work.* New York: Lincoln Center Institute.

Neely, Kent (1992). 'Ping Chong's Theater of Simultaneous Consciousness'. *Journal of Dramatic Theory and Criticism* 6(2): 121–35.

Shank, Theodore (2002). *Beyond the Boundaries: American Alternative Theater.* Ann Arbor: University of Michigan Press.

Shimakawa, Karen (2002). *National Abjection: The Asian American Body Onstage.* Durham, NC: Duke University Press.

Solomon, Alisa (2000). 'The Poetry of the DMZ'. *Village Voice,* February 29. http://www.villagevoice.com/2000-02-29/theater/the-poetry-of-the-dmz/ (accessed May 11, 2011).

Steinman, Louise (1995). *The Knowing Body: The Artist as Storyteller in Contemporary Performance.* Berkeley, CA: North Atlantic Books.

Sugano, Douglas I. (2002). 'Ping Chong'. In *Asian American Playwrights: A Bio-Bibliographical Critical Sourcebook.* Miles Xian Liu (ed.), 32–7. Santa Barbara, CA: Greenwood Press.

Tunç, Tanfer Emin (2010). 'Razing/Raising the Literary Canon: Ping Chong's *Chinoiserie, After Sorrow,* and Chinese American Postmodern Theater'. In *Positioning the New: Chinese American Literature and the Changing Image of the American Literary 'Canon',.* Tanfer Emin Tunç and Elisabetta Marino (eds), 84–113. Newcastle-upon-Tyne, UK: Cambridge Scholars Publishing.

Westfall, Suzanne R. (1993). 'Invasion of a Cornfield'. *American Theater* 999): 10–11.

— (1992). 'Ping Chong's Terra In/Cognita: Monsters on Stage'. In *Reading the Literatures of Asian America.* Shirley Geok-Lin Lim and Amy Ling (eds), 359–73. Philadelphia, PA: Temple University Press.

Wilmeth, Don B. and Bigsby, Christopher (2000). *The Cambridge History of American Theater.* Cambridge: Cambridge University Press.

Wong, Sau-ling (1993). *Reading Asian American Literature: From Necessity to Extravagance.* Princeton, NJ: Princeton University Press.

Xerxes, Mehta (1984). 'Some Versions of Performance Art'. *Theater Journal* 36(2): 165–98.

Chapter 6

The Transadaptation of Shakespeare's Christian Dimension in China's Theatre – To Translate, or Not to Translate?

Jenny Wong

In this chapter, I will use the causal model for translation studies proposed by Andrew Chesterman (2000) to analyse the adaptation of religious material in the Chinese version of *The Merchant of Venice. The Merchant* (1980) is the most popular Shakespearean adaptation in China to date, with over 500 performances recorded between 1980 and 1986. It is an adaptation in Julie Sanders' terms (2006: 26), as it contains omissions, rewritings, additions, but acknowledges the contribution of the source text's author. It is widely different from its 'prior materials', and is subject to differing degrees of manipulation and revision (Venuti 2007: 29). Additionally, *The Merchant* is an interlingual, intersemiotic translation, involving transfer between languages and from text to sounds, movements, and lighting, among others. But the distinction between theatre translation and adaptation is often blurred. Unlike other forms of translation, where translators are expected to make only minor deletions or additions, where the source text is granted the ultimate authority over the translation, every theatre translation is in fact a different interpretation and adaptation of the text (Zatlin 2005). Actors, directors, and translators are adapters in the play. These agents of translation are engaged in an act of adaptation, or what Linda Hutcheon called (2006: 20) 'a double process of interpreting and then creating something new'.

Traditionally, studies in adaptation draw on intralingual, intersemiotic versions but not interlingual issues. Translation models were only occasionally touched upon until the groundbreaking work of Lawrence Venuti (2007), who criticized the lack of theoretical basis in adaptation studies, and John Milton (2011), who drew attention to the lack of attention to linguistic aspects in adaptation studies. This chapter aims to fill the gap by approaching adaptation using well-developed models from translation studies.

The causal model is the most suggestive model in this context, together with the comparative model and the process model. The comparative model deals with charting equivalences and relations between source and target texts, while the process model sees translation as a dynamic process, representing a change of state over time, which is useful in analysing sequential relationships between different phases of the translation process. Chesterman's causal model does not see translation explicitly as an effect, nor does it explain why translations look the way they do (Chesterman 2000). Rather the comparative model deals with what might be described as the 'what' question, the process model deals with the 'how' question, while the causal model deals with the 'why' question.

The causal model is particularly relevant in analysing Shakespearean translations and adaptations in China, because these plays span different time periods. However, I propose that the causal model should be modified to take into account the socio-cultural conditions that affect the religious content of Shakespeare's plays in translation, as well as issues of identity, homosexuality, and gender. Such conditions determine the ideologies of adapters, individual translators, and directors. The socio cultural conditions influence the operations of theatre companies, the choice of play and adapters, and the dynamics among various adapters.

This chapter will conduct a linguistic analysis of the 1980 revival of *The Merchant of Venice* in Beijing, to show how and why religious material has either been adapted or translated. I will draw on two linguistic concepts: thematic structure and discourse analysis. The thematic structure is a structure that runs through a text, the function of which is to provide a sense of organization, hierarchy, and relations between different aspects or properties of the text, and between different units of the text,that is, sentences and paragraphs (Deacon 1999: 169). Using a thematic approach is important because different productions of the same play highlight different themes.

Discourse analysis is characterized by its attention to language as social interaction. The analysis of discourse, the use of language in social life, is an important concept in the field of critical linguistics (Deacon 1999: 146). Behind the concept of discourse analysis is the importance it attaches to ideology. So far there are very few critical discourse analysis oriented studies on translation, much less on adaptation (that deals more with intralingual issues).[1] The textual analysis in this chapter employs critical discourse analysis in order to uncover the ideological force at work in shaping the theatre text.

Shakespearean productions in China had a tradition of mirroring the socio-political background of Chinese society. In 1942, *Hamlet* was staged by the National Drama School in Sichuan, whose purpose was reportedly to prompt a spirit of resistance to the Japanese invasion (Huang 2004). The pragmatic function of foreign literature translation has long been advocated in its history. For example, during the Anti-Japanese war, 1937–45, foreign literary works that promoted patriotism were translated. Mao Zedong reinforced this didactic function further in his 'Talks at the Yan'an Forum on Literature and Art' in 1942, which has impacted the history of Chinese drama to this day. Mao believed that literature and art should serve the political agenda, while political interests should be the first priority in creative arts.

6.1 Socio-Cultural Conditions

The Merchant became the first Shakespearean play brought on to the Chinese stage in the post-revolution era. The early 1980s saw a revival of interest in Shakespeare's plays – they were the first examples of Western literature that were reincorporated into the post-secondary educational curriculum. This period also witnessed the formation of the first Chinese Shakespeare Centre in 1984, and the Shakespeare Society of China in 1995 by renowned playwright Cao u. There are three reasons behind the rise of Shakespeare in the early 1980s: first, China had just emerged from a feudal system and political turmoil; hence the people could strongly identify with the 'radical [i.e., non-feudal] consciousness' underlying Shakespeare's works. It was a time of transition that recalled Elizabethan England; according to one Chinese commentator this was a period characterized by a 'youthful, glorious and radical cultural temperament' (Shih 2000: 200). Second, in the post-revolution era, the Chinese people were drawn to Shakespeare's humanistic optimism; they could walk out of the shadow of distorted ideological value and appreciate the individuality and humanity in his works. Third, they hoped to reconnect to non-Chinese, Western arts in the hope of discovering new techniques and insights. The 1980s witnessed the importation of feminist ideas from the West to China, leading to the publication of writings by women such as *On the Same Horizon* by Zhang Xin Xin (1981), which showed the difficulties and challenges of women in a patriarchal society.

However, there were certain constraints prevailing at that time. While there was no explicit state censorship of theatre productions, there were still sensitive areas subject to censorship – for example, explicit references to sex, or sensitive political issues (Chang 2008). In the revival of *Measure for Measure* in 1981, over five hundred lines on sex, religion, and politics were deleted.

6.1.1 Situational and cognitive conditions

When Zhang Qi Hong decided to stage *The Merchant*, she consulted experts and did extensive research, but was preoccupied with a number of questions, including whether the play should be staged as a comedy or tragedy, what to cut, and how to approach its religious and racial issues. After discussions with theatre practitioners, she enlisted Cao Yu, a renowned playwright, the 'Shakespeare of the Orient' as the artistic director (Zhang 1983: 280–7), who decided that *The Merchant* should be interpreted as a comedy (Wu 1981: 55).

Zhang Qi Hong chose the published translation of playwright Fang Ping (1954): there were two main reasons for this decision. First, Zhang did not read English, so Fang's translation was crucial to the director's interpretation. At that time Fang was a prolific theatre critic who had published articles on Shylock (1979) before the production was staged. Second, Fang's translation seemed particularly suitable for the Chinese context, particularly in its rendering of the play's religious material. In Portia's mercy speech at the trial scene (IV, i), Fang adopts a domestication strategy: the line 'him that gives and him that takes' in Portia's 'quality of mercy is not strained' speech (IV, i, 194) becomes '施主 shi zhu' and '受施的人 shou shi de ren', undergoing a semantic modulation shift. '施主 shi zhu' is a Sanskrit translation that means those who share clothes and food with the monks (according to the Buddhist dictionary). The term 'mercy' (in Portia's line 'the quality of mercy is not strained' (191)) is translated into a Buddhist term '慈悲 ci bei' – a polysyllabic word where '慈ci' means the provision of happiness out of the Buddha's love of all living things, and '悲 bei' can be translated as the rescue of human beings from disaster. The Buddhist gods who advocate non-violence are known to show these qualities to all living beings. 'Earthly power' (203) – in the same speech – is translated as '替天行道 ti tian xing dao' or '天道 tian dao' (the way of heaven). This term has a Confucian connotation, in which heaven prepares the way for human beings. But it is the cosmos not the deity that possesses such power. The mercy that is 'enthroned in the hearts of kings' (201) is translated into 'gong feng' (worshipped), an act of Daoist worship of God involving the offer of incense and cooked meat as sacrifices.

Despite Fang's adaptation of the religious material into locally understood terms, the text proved problematic for Zhang, who favoured a humanistic reading of the play. She set forth her views in her article 'Some Points in the Process of Implementation and Exploration – Discussions on the Directorship of *The Merchant of Venice*' (1983), which I translate as follows:

> In assessing the meticulousness of a production, we should not focus on whether directors can 'reproduce' the play, but on whether they can do full justice to the writer's [or the adapter's] intention, to the substance of the script, and whether the play's main themes are explored in-depth. Based on these criteria, we inevitably deleted conflicts that are not essential to the main theme. For instance, scenes of religious conflict (between Jews and Christian), racial conflicts were deleted or downplayed, and we retained only three soliloquies of Shylock. We retained all the speeches that praised the Jews, and kept the Jewish costumes on stage to give a real sense of the play's socio-historical background. In the source text, the author objectively describes religious conflicts and racial conflicts. But we believe that such conflicts are not the essential conflicts in this play. They do not constitute the main theme according to Shakespeare [. . .] Owing to the differences across time periods, countries and races, another reason we adapted the storyline is that we wanted to give general audiences a sense of what *The Merchant of Venice* was about. The conflicts between Christianity and Judaism that took place hundreds of years ago, as well as the racial conflicts, are relatively obscure for the Chinese audience. In order to let the Chinese audience have a clear understanding of Shakespeare, I omitted these non-essential conflicts while at the same time not jeopardizing the spirit of the play. (1983: 285–6)

With this in mind, she tried her best to omit much of the play's religious content, in the belief that this might detract from its basic humanism. More significantly, she made such changes in the belief that her audiences might misinterpret her production as an allegory of the Israeli–Palestinian conflicts prevailing at the time of staging (1983: 286). Zhang's approach was criticized by the theatre critic and scholar Zhang Long Xi on the grounds that '[the deletion of lines on the religious conflicts between Shylock and Antonio] fundamentally alters Shakespeare's intention which is unacceptable' (Sun 2009: 65). Other performers of the Chinese National Youth Art

Theatre nonetheless agreed with her interpretation, as the interaction between a Jew and a Christian was not meaningful to Chinese audiences. They upheld the prevailing ideology, which focused attention on individual rights and creative potentialities in the post-Cultural Revolution era (Zhang 1996: 241–2). The Chinese audience was not widely exposed to Western cultures and beliefs, and hence indifferent to religious conflicts between Christians and Jews – to the Chinese, Christians and Jews were simply outsiders (Sun 2009: 65).

Additionally, she significantly adapted Portia's speech in Act IV. In Fang Ping's 1954 translation, the allegory of mercy and justice was removed. The king's rule became a close equivalent of justice. In Zhang's 1981 text, the Christian concepts underwent further adaptation: the Lord's Prayer that teaches people the deeds of mercy (IV, i, 209), was altered into '心地的善良显示出灵魂的美好' (A kind heart shows a good soul)'; no prayer was mentioned, and gentleness of spirit was foregrounded instead. The Chinese translation of 'mercy' is '仁慈 (ren ci)', rather than '慈悲 (ci bei)'. '仁Ren' is a key Confucian term in Book IV of *The Analects*, where 'ren' can mean humanity, benevolence, true virtue, etc. It is too diverse a term to be pinned down by Confucius' disciples. Sayings on *Ren* abound in *The Analects*, 'If one sets one's heart on *ren*, there will be none he hates' (4. 4), 'The Master said, Those who are not *ren* cannot long dwell in straitened circumstances, and cannot long dwell in joy. The *ren* person is at peace with *ren*. The wise person makes use of *ren*' (4. 3). The mercy speech was only one of the seven instances where Christian mercy was domesticated into Confucian term 'ren' in Zhang's play text. Using a cultural equivalent term in the adaptation permitted a Confucian interpretation of Shakespeare's play, as later scholarly critiques of *The Merchant* show (Luo 1997: 27).

The decision to delete lines on religious grounds was not an individual one, but emerged out of Zhang's collaboration with the actor Wang Jing Yu, who was cast as Shylock (Wang 1981: 61). In rehearsals he explained that while the biblical allusions could enrich the character of Shylock as a Jewish money-lender, the audience might not understand them. After the deletion, the conflict between Antonio and Shylock would be even more prominent. Apart from removing the Christian identity of Antonio, the biblical allusions disappeared altogether. Daniel, an Old Testament prophet whose name is used to describe Portia's clever judgment in the court scene (IV, i, 230), was rendered instead as 'a clever judge'. The story of Jacob and Laban in the Old Testament, cited by Shylock (I, iii, 70) as a way to indicate how he could match Jacob's cunning, is deleted to avoid confusion (Wang 1981: 61). The only translated reference to Christianity that remains in the Chinese text is the following reference by Antonio in Act 1, scene iii: 'The devil can cite Scripture for his purpose/ An evil soul producing holy witness' (98–9). However, the retention of this line does not make much sense, because in the source text these lines follow Shylock's citation of the biblical story of Jacob and Laban.

Zhang and Wang made further adaptations to the Shakespearean text. The reason for Shylock's hatred toward Antonio ('I hate him for he is a Christian' (I, iii, 37)), while the famous line 'Hath/ Not a Jew eyes?' (I, iii, 53–4) became 'just because I am a money-lender'. Although Jessica's and Lorenzo's elopement was retained, the storyline was altered on account of the deletion of Lorenzo's Christian identity. Now Shylock was infuriated because Lorenzo had no money to support his daughter, not because he was a Christian, as implied in Shakespeare's play text. The adaptation of Shylock's Jewish identity was necessary, according to actor Wang Jing Yu: Jews have suffered enormously in history, and were persecuted in the Second World War. Hence it would not be fair to show them in an adverse light: 'We assume, if Shakespeare is still alive, he with his humanistic spirit, probably will not highlight Jewish identity of Shylock and subsequently humiliate him' (Wang 1981: 62). More importantly, this adaptation did not influence Shylock's characterization; he was still the money-lender who grinned at the signing of the bond, suffered for the loss of daughter and his money, and expressed his anger against Antonio in his celebrated speech.

6.2 Translation Profile

At the trial scene, Shylock's conversion to Christianity (IV, i, 401) as a condition for his release was omitted from Zhang's script, even though it had been retained in the three main literary translations in circulation in the early 1980s, including Fang Ping's. Zhang believed that the audience might find the forced conversion irrelevant to the Chinese context. This view can be traced back to China's history where religious conflicts were rarely in evidence. People were generally tolerant toward religious differences in a culture rooted in harmony.[2] To date there has never been a forced religious conversion in Chinese public culture. This is due to the strong influence of Buddhism and Taoism that persists in the country. Hence the omission: to show a change of religion might cause discontent among the audience, as suggested by Hui (1983). Another possible source of discontent relates to the anti-Christian tradition in China since the nineteenth century, during which the unequal treaty system in the aftermath of the First Opium War between China and Britain, including the Treaties of Tianjin and the Sino-French Convention of Beijing, permitted foreign missionaries to live, own property, and preach in China (Cohen 1963: 44). The treaties that remained in effect until 1943 inspired a phenomenal growth of missionary enterprise, which only served to increase the people's hostility toward Christianity (as witnessed in the growth of anti-Christian pamphlets and tracts) (Cohen 1963: 45). Missionaries were often associated with colonial invasion and cultural imperialism.[3] Hence Zhang adapted Fang's translation in an attempt to placate her audiences.[4]

Just as interesting as what was deleted is what was added or modified. In this two-hour adaptation, one-third of the scenes were dedicated to Portia's selection of her future husband. In the casket-scene, each casket was personified: a glamorous lady brought in the gold casket, a well-dressed lady in silver brought in the silver casket, while a humbly dressed lady held the lead casket, positioned toward the back of stage. Her modesty highlighted Bassanio's nobility. The large portrait of Portia's late father hanging on the wall of Portia's room suggested the bondage of patriarchal society – something that Portia obviously hoped to escape through marriage. Zhang's adaptation aptly illustrated the truth of the phrase: 'All that glitters is not gold' (Lin 1981: 22). Another addition to the play is that this lady with the lead casket was later married to Lancelot Gobbo; three pairs of lovers tied the knot on the same day, enhancing the liveliness of this romantic comedy.

Zhang admitted in an interview that she liked Portia, who was clever and unconventional in her efforts to liberate herself from her family:

> I like Portia, the new female, very much. As a director, I like freedom, I like her courageous, clever scheming which frees her from the bondage. She dresses as a male to be a female lawyer and strikes hard at the greedy and selfish Shylock. He is only interested in his pound of flesh, no more no less. I think this shows Shakespeare's passion for women in the Renaissance period and his respect for female dignity. He commends women's liberation as reflected in Portia's wisdom, which finds its expression in a bright sunny space. (Zhang 1983: 280)

6.3 Cognitive and Behavioural Effects

Zhang's adaptation attracted mixed reviews. At the post-performance symposium held on October 23, 1981, attended by Zhang, theatre critics, and drama scholars, the majority agreed that the simplification of Shylock's complex character was attributable to the deletion of religious and racial conflicts. Director Sun Jia Sou did not agree with her decision: if the German poet Heinrich Heine, (who showed sympathy toward Shylock and saw the humiliations suffered by Jews) was still alive, Sun asked, would one see sympathy in him? The scholar Zhang Long Xi believed that the Judeo-Christian conflict was less apparent in performances of *The Merchant* staged in Great Britain and America, as there is a large Jewish population in these countries, but in China this is not the case. So Shylock should not be given a black-or-white portrayal, but the complexity of his character should have been retained. Zhang's adaptation over-simplified his character (Wu 1981: 56, Zhang Long Xi 1981: 60).

The personification of the three caskets was highly commended by critics (Lin 1981: 24), in an alteration that livened up what is customarily a most static, boring sequence. However, Zhang's emphasis on Portia weakened the source plot of the pound of flesh (Wu 1981: 56). Moreover, the omission of the play's religious and racial conflicts, plus the emphasis on liberation, produced an over-romanticized adaptation.

At the same time Zhang's adaptation was considered bold in traditional Maoist terms, as audience went away recalling that: 'there [was] kissing on the stage' (Li 2003: 2). The *Beijing Evening Post* published a letter from an official on September 7, 1980, who was disturbed for weeks after watching the production (Li 2003: 2) on account of its being 'harmful to public morals', as the performers 'embraced and kissed each other in front of such a big audience' (Li 2003: 2). His letter created a storm of protest – the majority of respondents disagreed with him, but still there were dozens of letters expressing concern that certain sex jokes in Act V of Zhang's adaptation were 'vulgar and dreadful' (2).

6.4 Socio Cultural Effects

The performance of this highly acclaimed adaptation had a significant socio-cultural impact:

1. It was conducive to restoring and establishing an ethos where friendship and love involve self-sacrifice. The notions of pure love and friendship championed by Shakespeare four hundred years ago could cultivate noble thoughts, especially in a corrupt society;

2. Zhang's adaptation increased the audience's knowledge of Western humanist writers and their works during the Renaissance era, helping them to understand early capitalist societies and their historical conditions, people, and ethos;
3. Zhang's adaptation was conducive to the development of theatre in China. As Shakespearean plays have structures similar to Chinese traditional drama (*xiqu*), the quick pace and the detailed portrayal of character could inspire the development of new Chinese drama. (Wu 1981: 57)

Prof. Zhu Guang Qian, professor at Peking University, in a letter to the post-performance symposium, wrote: '*The Merchant of Venice* opened a new Chapter for Shakespearean plays in our country's theatre'. Attendees at the symposium agreed that more 'elaborate, foreign and ancient' plays should be staged.

As the adage goes, every translation is an interpretation. The same is true for Zhang's adaptation. Drawing on Andrew Chesterman's causal model, we have seen how ideological forces led to the displacement and domestication of religious references in *The Merchant.* The model, initially used in translation studies, is applicable in adaptation studies, as both acknowledge the function of ideology in the shaping of translated or adapted literature. Robert Stam (2005) argued that: 'many of the changes between novelistic source and film adaptation have to do with ideology and social discourses'. Similarly, Lawrence Venuti (2007) proposes the concept of thematic interpretants, which are essentially codes, values, and ideologies, as an essential category for studying translations and adaptations. Thematic interpretants can be interpretation, taste, or morality used to appeal to a particular audience, or a political position that reflects the interests of a social group (Venuti 2007: 33). The question of what to cut should be situated in the larger context of the socio-political ideology, which differs across time and cultures. In *The Merchant,* the director and performers participated in the collaborative process of transadaptation to come up with a version embodying their political viewpoints. The resulting product is a version where religious material was filtered out layer after layer to suit the taste of local audiences and the ideology of adapters. This reminds one of the famous teaching of the linguist Wilhelm von Humboldt,[5] who proposed that every language should be seen as a particular view of the world. In short, language-views are world-views. To translate from one language to another inevitably means to exchange one worldview for another. When Shakespeare's text written some four hundred years ago was translated into contemporary Chinese, translation was not purely a linguistic process, but an adaptation or an appropriation that reflected a hybrid of two cultures, a Jewish moneylender with a Chinese shadow, a Venetian merchant showing Confucian and Buddhist mercy. Is this adaptation still Shakespeare? What's in a name – by any other name would smell as sweet.

Notes

[1] John Milton attributes the lack of attention to interlingual issues to that fact that most contemporary studies in adaptation originate from the monolingual departments of Theatre Studies, Film and Media Studies, Dance Studies, Music Studies, Cultural Studies, and English Literature (Milton 2009).

[2] Harmony is a core Confucian value, where harmony in the midst of differences is a quality of gentlemen.

[3] An Anti-Christian Student Federation, founded in 1922, issued a manifesto denouncing an imperial alliance of Christianity and capitalism under American leadership. For more details, please refer to Hunter 1984.

[4] The conflicts that theatre translators face are discussed in Zatlin 2005.

[5] Quoted in Gadamer 2004: 439.

Bibliography

Bassnett, Susan (1985). 'Ways Through the Labyrinth: Strategies and Methods for Translating Theatre Texts'. In *The Manipulation of Literature: Studies in Literary Translation.* Theo Hermans (ed.), 87–102. London: Croom Helm.

Chang, Nam Fung (2008). 'Censorship in Translation and Translation Studies in Present-Day China'. In *Translation and Censorship in Different Times and Landscapes.* Teresa Seruya and Maria Lin Moniz (eds), 229–40. Newcastle-upon-Tyne, UK: Cambridge Scholars Publishing.

Chesterman, Andrew (2000). 'A Causal Model for Translation Studies,'. In Maeve Olohan (ed.), *Intercultural Faultlines.* Maeve Olohan (ed.), 15–28. Manchester and Kinderhook, NY: St. Jerome Publishing.

—. (2002). 'Semiotic Modalities in Translation Causality'. *Across Languages and Cultures* 3(2): 145–58.

Cohen, Paul (1963). *China and Christianity.* Cambridge, MA: Harvard University Press.

Deacon, David, Pickering, Michael, Golding, Peter and Murdock, Graham (1999). *Researching Communications: A Practical Guide to Methods in Media and Cultural Analysis.* London: Bloomsbury Academic.

Fairclough, Norman (1995). *Critical Discourse Analysis: The Critical Study of Language.* London: Longman.

— (1989). Language and Power. London: Longman.

Fang, Ping (1954). *The Merchant of Venice*, Shanghai: Ping Ming Chu Ban She.

— (1979). 'On Shylock [Lun Xia Luoke]'. *Foreign Literature Studies Collections [Waiguo Wenxue Yanjiu Jikan]*: 213–33.

— (1981). 'Return to Basics – The Presumptions in Performing *The Merchant of Venice* [Fanpu Guizhen Weinisi Shangren de Yanchu Shexiang]'. *Foreign Literature Studies [Waiguo Wenxue Yanjiu]*, (4): 8–19.

— (2000). *New Shakespeare Translations [Xin Shashibiya Quanji]*. Shijiazhuang: Hebei Education [Hebei Jiaoyu].

Gadamer, Hans-Georg (2004). *Truth and Method*. London and New York: Continuum International Publishing Group.

Hawthorn, Jeremy (1992). *A Glossary of Contemporary Literary Theory*. London: Edward Arnold.

Hermans, Theo (1999). *Translation in Systems*. Manchester and Kinderhook, NY: St. Jerome Publishing.

Huang, Alexander Cheng-Yuan (2004). 'Shakespeare on the Chinese Stage, 1839–2004: A History of Transcultural Performance'. Unpubl. Ph.D. thesis, Stanford University.

Hui, Ji (1983). 'Discussions on the directorship of *The Merchant of Venice*'. *Shakespeare Research*, 302–6. Hangzhou: Zhejiang People's Press.

Hunter, Jane (1984). *The Gospel of Gentility: American Women Missionaries in Turn-of-the-Century China*. New Haven: Yale University Press, 1984.

Hutcheon, Linda (2006). *A Theory of Adaptation*. London and New York: Routledge.

Lee, Elaine Tzu-yi (2010). 'Translators as Gatekeepers: Gender/Race Issues in Three Taiwan Translations of *The Color Purple*'. Unpubl. Ph.D. thesis, University of Newcastle-upon-Tyne.

Lefevere, Andre (1992). *Translation, Rewriting and the Manipulation of Literary Fame*. London and New York: Routledge.

— (1985). 'Why Waste Our Time on Rewrites? The Trouble with Interpretation and the Role of Rewriting in an Alternative Paradigm'. In *The Manipulation of Literature: Studies in Literary Translation*. Theo Hermans (ed.), 215–43. London: Croom Helm.

Li, Ruru (2003). *Shashibiya: Staging Shakespeare in China*. Hong Kong: Hong Kong University Press.

Lin, Ke Huan (1981). 'The Light of the Ideal Dimension: Post-Performance Reflections on *The Merchant of Venice* [Lixiang Guodu de Guangmang: Weinisi Shangren Guanhou]'. *Peking Arts [Beijing Yishu]* 1: 22–4.

Luo, Wen Jin (1997) 'Viewing the Differences and Similarities between Christian Doctrine and Confucian Thinking from Shakespeare's *The Merchant of Venice* [Cong Shaju Weinisi Shangren Kan Jidu jiaoyi Yu Yujia Sixiang Zhi Yitong]'. *Zigong College Journal* [Zigong Shizhuan Xuebao] 3(41): 27–9.

Milton, John (2009). 'Translation Studies and Adaptation Studies'. In *Translation Research Projects 2*, Anthony Pym and Alexander Perekrestenko (eds), Tarragona: Intercultural Studies Group: 51–8.

Shakespeare, William (1961). *The Merchant of Venice*. John Russell Brown (ed.), The Arden Shakespeare, 2nd series. London and New York: Routledge.

Shih, Wen-Shan (2000). 'Intercultural Theatre: Two Beijing Opera Adaptations of Shakespeare'. Unpubl. Ph.D. thesis, University of Toronto.

Simpson, Paul (1993). *Language, Ideology and Point of View*. London and New York: Routledge.

Stam, Robert (2005). 'Introduction: The Theory and Practice of Adaptation'. In *A Companion to Literature and Film*. Robert Stam and Alessandra Raengo (eds),1–52. Oxford and Malden, MA: Blackwell Publishing.

Sun, Hui Zhu (2009). *Who's Butterfly?* Beijing: The Commercial Press: 65.

Venuti, Lawrence (2007). 'Adaptation, Translation, Critique'. *Journal of Visual Culture* 6(1): 25–43.

Wang, Jing Yu (1981). 'Debates on the Characterization of Shylock [Guanyu Xia Luoke Renwu Xingxiang de Zhengming]'. *Foreign Theatre* [Waiguo Xiju], (1): 61–2.

Woods Wilkins, Leah (1947). 'Shylock's Pound of Flesh and Laban's Sheep'. *Modern Language Notes* 62(1): 28–30.

Wu, Fu Rong (1981). 'Post-Symposium Afterthoughts of *The Merchant of Venice* [Weinisi Shangren Zuo Tan Hui San Ji]'. *Foreign Theatre* [Waiguo Xiju] (1): 54–7.

Xi, Hui Ling (2001). 'Review of the Characteristics of Feminist Writings in the 1980s and 90s [Ba Jiushi Nian Dai Zhongguo Nuxing Xiezuo Tezheng Huimou]'. *Commentaries on Literature and Arts* [wenyi pinglun] (5): 47–50.

Zatlin, Phyllis (2005). *Theatrical Translation and Film Adaptation*. Clevedon: Multilingual Matters.

Zhang, Long Xi (1981). 'On Shylock [Lun Xia Luoke]'. *Foreign Theatre* [Waiguo Xiju] 1: 57–60

Zhang, Qi Hong (1983). 'Some Points in the Process of Implementation and Exploration – Discussions on the directorship of *The Merchant of Venice* [Zai Shijian He Tansuo Zhong De Jidian Tihui: Shitan Weinisi Shangren De Daoayan Chuli]'. *Shakespeare Research [Shashibiya Yanjiu]*, Hangzhou: Zhejiang People's Press: 280–287.

Zhang, Xiao Yang (1996). *Shakespeare in China*. Newark, NJ: University of Delaware Press.

Chapter 7

'Tradaptation' *Dans le Sens Québécois*: A Word for the Future

Susan Knutson

In the terminological chaos making its way through translation and adaptation studies, one neologism worth keeping is *tradaptation*, in the sense developed by theatre practitioners and scholars in Québec.[1] Michel Garneau, Québécois poet, playwright, and public intellectual, coined the term to describe his three Shakespeare translations, *The Tempest / La tempête* (1973/1982),[2] *Macbeth* (1978),[3] and *Coriolanus/Coriolan* (1989), which reached global audiences in 1993, when Robert Lepage 'created a *Cycle Shakespeare* for the National Arts Centre in Ottawa, for the *Festival de Théâtres des Amériques* in Montreal, and for a world tour: a production of all three Garneau translations' (Lieblein 2007: 104). Or, we might insist, his three Shakespeare tradaptations.

Composed of *translation* and *adaptation*, *tradaptation* in Québec and English Canada has been studied by scholars including Annie Brisset, Leanore Lieblein, Denis Salter, and Jennifer Drouin. Born in the white heat of Québec's national awakening, its emergence shaped by that epoch during which Québec declared its identity and its language to itself and to the world, the concept of tradaptation can help us to think clearly about theatrical translations/adaptations, particularly when they are created by and for small, threatened, and/or minority societies; and it can help to illuminate the relationship between *transculturation* and translation, as I will begin to suggest below, following Lucien Pelletier's thoughtful and lucid 'Postface' to *Canadian Cultural Exchange/Échanges culturels au Canada: Translation and Transculturation/Traduction et Transculturation*, the book he co-edited with Norman Cheadle (Pelletier 2007: 363–78). *Tradaptation* is also immediately useful insofar as it redefines aspects of that comprehensive field known or decried as 'creative translation', with its sometimes dubious intentions – censorship, ethnocentrism, or worse. As Albert Braz argues in 'The Creative Translator': 'if the translator becomes creative to the point of ignoring the original work, no cultural exchange – that is, no translation – can take place' (Braz 2007: 17). My argument here is that tradaptation, in the Québécois sense, *does* permit cultural exchange, but it shapes it, with intentionality and transparence, so that those elements entering into the exchange are visibly and audibly the ones that artists have wished to bring onto the 'stage'.[4] The others are left by for the occasion.

For tradaptation, there must always be an occasion: tradaptations have intentions with respect to the past and the future, but they intervene in the *here and now*, as Lepage indicates when he states that he chose to work with Garneau's scripts for their 'immediacy of effect' and 'local color' (Salter 1993: 71). Denis Salter sharpens the point, arguing that 'tradaptations should be exercises in radical contingency, responsible only for the particular historical moment in which they attempt to decolonize and reinterrogate the Shakespearean text. They should vanish once their particular historical moment has passed and new tradaptations should take their place' (Salter 1996: 126). Both Lepage and Salter are addressing the original occasions within which Garneau evolved his tradaptations: the here and now of (quietly) revolutionary Québec, as it received or appropriated 'William Shakespeare'. Other social and cultural constellations, however, have the potential to foster tradaptation in the Garneau-Lepage-Salter sense. One striking example features a beleaguered francophone minority culture in North America: the theatre of Normand Godin, who as Artistic Director of *Les Aragnées du Boui-Boui* from 1973 to 2004, created and performed tradaptations of French and English authors from Molière to Longfellow to Topor and Yourcenar, in varieties of Acadian French including French as it was spoken in rural Nova Scotian Acadian communities, two or three generations ago (Godin 1993: 12–18)

Joël Beddows, citing his own experience as a theatre practitioner in Québec, uses the concept of tradaptation to speak of his non-Shakespearean work, which was shaped by the Quiet Revolution in the early 1960s, when an intense and almost exclusive preoccupation with the local contributed, as Beddows argues, to a creative surge of adaptations in the subsequent two decades: 'The tendency to adapt source plays, often associated with ethnocentrism, exists elsewhere in the Western world. However, the legitimacy of this approach is often questioned by foreign theatrical institutions, free from the cultural insecurities that permeated French language practices in this country until recently' (Beddows 2000: 11). Beddows goes on to cite one of the arguments made in Annie Brisset's groundbreaking study *La Sociocritique de la Traduction* (1990), where she describes and underlines the temporal and affective synergies at work in Québec during the years of national awakening:

> Naturalization of foreign plays is a prerequisite for their acceptance into [Québec's] [. . .] literary institution, as well as their relevance in a *wider* field of the discourse permeated by the nationalist doxa. To give a text from outside Québec a profile that conforms to the symbolic representations of the Québécois collectivity in social discourse, the translator 'forgets' markers of alterity, obliterating them through transference of the context of the utterance. In other words, the translator reverses the normal communication in translation. The translator's task is no longer to introduce the receiver to that which is unusual or original in the foreign work, but rather to turn the foreign work into a vehicle for representing the 'Québécois fact'. (Brisset 1996, 196, qtd. Beddows 2000: 11)

That this may be true, or may have once been true, does not change the fact that Brisset's own work clearly demonstrates that tradaptation does not end here: there is more to it than the desire of a radicalized public to reaffirm its identity, to focus on the local and immediate, and to reject lending an ear to the same old chauvinistic thing. Particularly at this distance, in 2011, we miss the point if we fail to note that tradaptation is not only about audiences and historical contingency, but is also very much about a particular kind of translation. Tradaptation is not translation on one hand and adaptation on the other; rather it is a kind of translation/adaptation that exists at a particular conjuncture of memory and intentionality with respect to the language(s) of the past and of the future, and with respect to the collectivity brought into being and speech by the theatrical event.

The linguistic techniques that comprise tradaptation have been explored in detail by critics with specific reference to Garneau's work. Drouin, for instance, writes that 'the systematic and complete substitution of 'Scotland' with 'chez-nous' [home] or 'pays' [country] is Garneau's foremost means of appropriation in his tradaptation of *Macbeth*' (Drouin 2004). This metonymic technique draws on the constructive capacity of *deixis* – the linguistic register of the here and now – to activate affective rapport and to place the action of the play in Québec by implication. Other metonymic techniques reinforce the deictic evocation of the Québécois context: for example, the names of local animals are spoken, as Salter points out:

> In *Garneau's Macbeth* we can hear [. . .] the vivid names of North American animals species ('*un chat sovage*', '*un grand ours noér*', '*l'portépique*', '*L'orignal*

ac'son panache', and '*L'vieux loup*') for the wildlife with which Shakespeare heightens the supernatural in his original text. (Salter 2000: 195)

Another tradaptation technique identified by Brisset is the intertextual referencing of motifs and themes found in the work of Garneau's fellow patriots and contemporaries, including poets Paul Chamberland, Gérald Godin, and Gaston Miron (Drouin 2004). Garneau's overarching technique, however, and the one that Leanore Lieblein references when she writes of Lepage's *Shakespeare Cycle* as 'a journey into the evolution of a language' (Lieblein 2007: 104), was to write the three scripts in three varieties of Québec French, corresponding to the language as it has evolved across generations, culminating in *Coriolan*, written in a 'courageous', and 'mature' manner (Lepage, qtd. in Salter 1993: 72, 73). This linguistic history is explored most radically in *Macbeth*, which brings into the present tense of the theatre space an idealized version of French as it was spoken in Québec two or more generations ago. In itself, this was an old language, for Québec French preserved, over the years, many of the words, structures, and pronunciations of the French of Rabelais' day, as is also the case with respect to the French of *Acadie*, that part of the French colonial empire in North America that included parts of eastern Québec, the Maritime provinces, and modern-day Maine.[5]

Salter notes the use of 'anachronisms, archaisms and neologisms, all reworked from the type of Québec French we find in the pre-1950s period (Salter 2000. 195); in his interview with Robert Lepage and *Le Théâtre Repère*, he asks about it:

> SALTER: Why did you choose the Michel Garneau 'tradaptations', as he calls them?
>
> LEPAGE: They give us an interesting double perspective. We're working with different kinds of Québécois and – at the same time – we're preoccupied with Shakespeare's original texts [. . .]
>
> SALTER: The language of Garneau's *Macbeth* tradaptation is certainly powerful but, in comparison [with that of *The Tempest* and *Coriolanus* is] sometimes very difficult to understand.
>
> LEPAGE: Yes, the language is as different for contemporary francophone actors as Elizabethan English is for contemporary anglophone actors. We, of course, recognize the words from our Québécois grandparents so we can say them with the proper accent. But it isn't the way we speak now. It's a kind of poetic proposition of how rural Québécois used to speak. (Salter 1993: 72)

'A poetic proposition of how rural Québécois used to speak': the language of *Macbeth* constructs an identitary point of reference, a navigation marker; an intentional 'proposition', as Lepage says, in relation to the origins and the history of the Québécois.

The practice of tradaptation has contributed to the survival of Québec's language, and to the relative position of strength of French in Québec today. Garneau's tradaptations 'enthrone[d]' (Lieblein 2000: 182) the Québécois language, proving that it was rich and flexible enough to carry the literary weight of 'le grand Will' (Lieblein 2000: 174 ff.); and carry him it did, all the way from the centre of the anglophone cultural capital to Québec. Although the Garneau tradaptations correspond to what Braz calls 'creative translations', they enact the kind of cultural exchange which is not dependent on power, but represents a liberating combination of elements retained for the future: *la langue québécoise, les animaux, les ancêtres, la contemporanéité*, and *la fierté de la société québécoise*. Salter, in 'Between Wor(l)ds', outlines a vision of the future when he argues that

> The key word in negotiating borders, is 'survival'. Who is trying to survive, and why? What values are being preserved? How? And who is likely to win the struggle? Garneau's twofold project of translation *and* adaptation is a sustained exercise in linguistic preservation of a kind peculiar to minority cultures struggling for autonomy on many different front(ier)s at once. (Salter 2000: 193)

Pelletier also addresses the question of survival 'of a kind peculiar to minority cultures', working with Cheadle to bring forward *transculturaciòn* (transculturation): a term and a paradigm for cultural exchange that was developed by Cuban ethnologist Fernando Ortiz in order to provide a non-Eurocentric alternative term to *acculturation*, that would express the complex processes of intercultural contact, conflict, loss, and acquisition without privileging European culture as the paradigm for human evolution. Pelletier believes that transculturation establishes a dynamic synthesis that depends upon 'the discrete refusals of a minority culture to forget' ('*les mouvantes synthèses et tensions d'une culture, ses asymétries internes, en un refus de subsumer et occulter certains éléments*', Pelletier 2007: 363) The particular complexities of a 'small' or threatened society – in this case Québec – survive, in spite of the powerful Other's agenda. In his essay, which interrogates both Canadian multiculturalism and the fraught history of Canada and Québec, Pelletier traces the terms of a possible cultural exchange 'free of domination' ('*exempts de domination*') and the possibilities of 'truly reconciliatory transcultural synthesis' ('*des synthèses transculturelles véritablement réconciliatrices*'). A long and complex passage traces the path that leads from a society's attachment to elements of its past toward a modernity free of coercion and open to a creative and transcultural future:

> *Charles Taylor a monté de façon convaincante que la référence à une tradition [. . .] se maintient au cœur même de la modernité, sous les traits de l'[expressivisme]* (Taylor 1992: 153, fn. 6), *cette vaste posture culturelle éprise d'authenticité et disposée à encourir les risques d'une identité individuelle ou collective incertaine qui, pour se connaître et s'affirmer, doit d'abord être exprimée et reconnue comme significative et valide. Cette reconnaisance de la part des individus et des collectivités est cruciale: elle introduit, au cœur même de la culture, un moment théorique, en ensemble de valeurs susceptibles d'être jugées vraies ou valides par autrui et par ce même sujet qui d'abord les exprime. C'est à hauteur de ce jugement, de ce partage philosophique du vrai que des échanges exempts de domination peuvent s'instaurer entre les cultures et que des synthèses transculturelles véritablement réconciliatrices deviennent possibles.*
>
> *Ce jugement s'élabore dans un travail d'autoréflexion où les membres d'une société non seulement se reconnaissent une certaine identité commune, un imaginaire hérité, mais, par le biais de leurs lettrés et de la discussion publique, entreprennent la recherche d'une intentionnalité inhérente à leur parcours historique. Celle-ci n'a rien d'une essence ou d'un sens nécessaire à la marche de la civilisation: elle est le dessin qu'une culture qui se souvient cherche à deviner dans le sillage tracé par son propre parcours contingent, et dont les enseignements permettront peut-être un destin plus librement choisi.* (Pelletier 2007: 368)[6]

My belief is that when Pelletier, with the help of Charles Taylor, speaks of the search for intentionality in relation to the past and to the future (a search framed by the 'theoretical moment' of a society's awareness of itself), the historical and social processes he references share crucial elements with the moment(s) of tradaptation, as practised by Garneau, Lepage, and others. By such means Pelletier's ideas may be integrated into the dimensions of discourse, textuality, and performance, tracing and leaving traces of the *parcours* of a small society making its way. I would like to place the terms transculturation and tradaptation together, in the tool kit or on the message board, as our little networks and collectivities continue to find their way in a globalized and often threatening future.

Recent discussions of translation in Québec have not, however, referenced these terms. 'Tradaptation', in particular, fails to be showcased in either Sherry Simon's *Translating Montreal: Episodes in the Life of a Divided City* (2006) or *Québec Studies: The Politics and Poetics of Translation in Québec and Canada,* (Forsyth 2010–11). The term may have fallen out of use because of its intense association with Garneau's work, and the cultural/social matrix within which that work developed: a matrix and a time immediately preceding the radical interpenetration of 'linguistic, political, and socio-cultural identitary horizons' (Forsyth 2010–11: 3), which renders the articulation of discrete identities so problematic. Simon acknowledges Garneau's 'translations' and their importance in Québec dramaturgy, but does not express interest in the difference between translation and the practice, as he modelled it, of tradaptation:

> For Brisset, Garneau's translation represents everything a translation should not be. His language represents a 'linguistic myth of origin for Québec', says Brisset, a language reconstituted from a lost past. The translation is selective in its references to the historical specificity of the action, so that in *Macbeth,* for instance, Scotland becomes a stand-in for a miserable 'chez nous', a land in conflict with the British crown, reduced to poverty and bitter defeat. Brisset's study is brilliant and rigorous. She shows how the array of terms Garneau uses correspond to the terms current in the Québec of the seventies to express the myth of victimization of Québec. Instead of being a window onto Shakespeare, Brisset shows, the translation throws a screen over Otherness, using theatre to reproduce the discourses of home. (Simon 2006: 157)

Simon's comments are puzzling from several points of view. As experimental literary 'translations', Garneau's tradaptations provide a rich instance of what Simon calls creative or 'perverse translations' similar to Erin Mouré's 'explicitly irreverent' translations (Simon 2006: 151), Nicole Brossard's 'pseudotranslations' (144–51), and Agnes Whitfield's 'translation without the original' (141). Second, tradaptation, as a word and as a concept, clearly references adaptation, and it does so in a sense that acknowledges the origins of adaptation in classical rhetoric, which proposes that one must adapt one's discourse to the rhetorical situation,that is, to the audience of the moment. This insight has recently resurfaced in an important international context: the World Health Organization-sponsored discourse concerning the cultural determinants of health, which now recognizes the necessity for cultural fit in the design of public and individual health services interventions.[7] The old is new again; adaptation is an intrinsic element of communication, and cultural interventions must fit the specificities of their target destinations. Simon finds fault with Garneau's work as translation, but does not address the question of adaptation.

Finally, I return to the linguistic texture and function of tradaptation as it has been formulated by Garneau. All commentators agree that tradaptations recreate for performance a kind of ancestral speech, a 'poetic proposition of how rural Québécois used to speak', in Lepage's phrase. Such a strategy is not for everybody, nor for all times, but in certain minority situations, the technique has real pedagogic, artistic, and philological value. The Garneau (and the Godin) tradaptations provide, and in fact perform, a linguistic point of reference in the performance space that negotiates the opposition between a relatively colourless or wooden international French or *synchronien* (which nobody speaks), and the less prestigious Canadian varieties of French, which, to a greater or lesser degree, tend to be considered 'incorrect'. This opposition is referenced in several articles in the recent issue of *Québec Studies*, and receives rigorous scholarly treatment by Luise von Flotow, Louise Forsyth, and Patricia Godbout.[8] It is not only significant in Québec: recently, in the Nova Scotian Acadian milieu, the opposition provoked a heated debate at a public lecture given by Pierre Igot, a highly respected local translator (Igot 2011). The ancestral speech of tradaptation addresses this problematic opposition creatively, referencing French as it may have been spoken two or three generations ago, imagining the language as it might have been in a safer place; a kind of elsewhere, free of the pernicious effects wrought by the mass media, which have produced the kind of lexical and syntactical impoverishment that threatens everyday French in the minority francophone communities across contemporary Canada. The depth and colour and history of this re-imagined French can recuperate for performance a linguistic music that would otherwise be simply lost. It also seems particularly appropriate for certain kinds of theatre, including Shakespeare, whose English is richly archaic to our ears, and including the tragic story of the Acadian Deportation of 1755–61. These instances suggest that there are and will continue to be places and times where tradaptation as it developed in Québec in the 1970s and 1980s may be useful beyond the social and cultural matrix in which it first evolved.

This judgment evolves by means of a self-reflection process within which the members of a society not only recognize that they share a common identity, an inherited imagination, but also undertake, through their writers and public debate, a quest for an intentionality that would be inherent to their history. This intentionality is nothing like an essence or a purpose required to advance civilization; it is the design of a culture that remembers, a culture that seeks to divine within the trail of its own contingent path, and whose teachings might allow for a more freely chosen fate. . . (translation Pierre Igot).

Notes

1 In other places and times, 'tradaptation' has various meanings, and sometimes refers to over-dubbing, subtitling, and voice-over. Anthony Panetto speaks of it in relation to an ideal: Il convient avant tout de rappeler qu'en matière de culture et de biens culturels, la *tradaptation*, qu'elle soit littéraire, audiovisuelle ou autre, vise cet *idéal de compréhension globale* [emphasis in original] sans jamais l'atteindre totalement. 'La Passion du Langage' (Panetto 2011).

2 *La Tempête* was Garneau's first Shakespeare translation but was revised. See Salter 2000: 194.

3 For publication and performance history of Garneau's *Macbeth* see Drouin 2011.

4 In the internet era, it appears that, more than ever, 'All the world's a stage' (William Shakespeare, *As You Like It* [II, vii, 139]: Shakespeare 1975, 55).

5 See Maillet 1971.

6 Translation: Charles Taylor has shown convincingly that reference to tradition is maintained at the heart of modernity, in the guise of 'expressivism', that widespread cultural attitude that cherishes authenticity and which is ready to risk individual identities or uncertain collectivities, that, in order to recognize and affirm itself must have previously been expressed and recognized as valid and important. This recognition on the part of individuals and collectivities is crucial: it introduces, at the very heart of culture, a theoretical moment, a gathering of values that can be judged to be true or valid, both by others and by the subjects who express them. It is in relation to this judgment, to this philosophical sharing of the truth, that cultural exchange free of domination can be initiated between cultures, and that truly reconciliatory transcultural synthesis becomes possible.

7 For example, see Carillo et al. 2011: 562–75.

8 See Forsyth, 'Introduction'; von Flotow 2011, 27–45; and Godbout 2010–11, 19–26.

Bibliography

Beddows, Joël (2000). 'Translations and Adaptations in Francophone Canada'. *Canadian Theatre Review* 102 (Spring): 11–14.

Braz, Albert (2007). 'The Creative Translator: Textual Additions and Deletions in *A Martyr's Folly*. ' In *Canadian Cultural Exchange/Échanges culturels au Canada: Translation and Transculturation/Traduction et transculturation*, edited by Norman Cheadle and Lucien Pelletier, 15–28. Waterloo: Wilfred Laurier University Press..

Brisset, Annie (1988). *A Sociocritique of Translation: Theatre and Alterity in Québec, 1969–1988*, trans. Rosalind Gill and Roger Gannon. Toronto: University of Toronto Press.

Carillo, J. Emilio, Victor, A. Carillo, Hector, R. Perez, et al. (2011). 'Defining and Targeting Health Care Access Barriers'. *Journal of Health Care for the Poor and Underserved.* 22(2): 562–75.

Cheadle, Norman and Pelletier, Lucien (eds) (2007). *Canadian Cultural Exchange/ Échanges culturels au Canada: Translation and Transculturation/Traduction et transculturation.* Waterloo: Wilfred Laurier University Press.

Drouin, Jennifer (2004). '*Macbeth* (1978)': *Canadian Adaptations of Shakespeare.* Daniel Fischlin (ed.). http://www.canadianshakespeares.ca/a_garneau.cfm (accessed January 16, 2011).

Forsyth, Louise H. (2010–11). 'Introduction'. *Québec Studies: The Politics and Poetics of Translation in Québec and Canada.* Forsyth and Jane M. Koustas (eds), 50 (Fall/ Winter): 3–18.

Forsyth, Louise H. and Koustas, Jane M. (eds). *Québec Studies: The Politics and Poetics of Translation in Québec and Canada,* (2010–11),50 (Fall/Winter).

Godbout, Patricia (2010–11). 'Jean Simard, traducteur de Hugh MacLennon'. *Québec Studies: The Politics and Poetics of Translation in Québec and Canada.* Louise H. Forsyth and Jane M. Koustas (eds), 50 (Fall/Winter): 19–26.

Godin, Normand (1993). 'Acadian Parlance on Stage'. *Canadian Theatre Review* 75 (Summer): 12–18.

Igot, Pierre (2011). 'Les infiltrés : Les faux amis : voyage au pays de la méfiance'. April 7, 2011, Université Sainte-Anne. http://www.fauxamis.fr (accessed July 3, 2011)

Lieblein, Leanore (2007). 'Pourquoi Shakespeare?' in *Shakespeare – Made in Canada: Contemporary Canadian Adaptations in Theatre, Pop Media and Visual Arts*, Daniel Fischlin and Judith Nasby (eds), 97–109. Guelph: The Macdonald Stewart Arts Centre.

— (2002). "'The Re-making'" of le Grand Will: Shakespeare in Francophone Québec'. In *Shakespeare in Canada: 'A World Elsewhere'?* Diana Brydon and Irena R. Makaryk (eds), 174–91. Toronto: University of Toronto Press.

Maillet, Antonine (1971). *Rabelais et les traditions populaires en Acadie.* Québec: Presses de l'Université Laval.

Panetto, Anthony (2011). 'La Passion du Langage'. http://anthonypanetto.jimdo.com/tradaptation/définition/ (accessed January 16, 2011)

Pelletier, Lucien (2007). 'Postface: Transculturation et mémoire'. In *Canadian Cultural Exchange/Échanges culturels au Canada: Translation and Transculturation/ Traduction et transculturation*. Norman Cheadle and Lucien Pelletier (eds), 363–78. Waterloo: Wilfred Laurier University Press.

Salter, Denis (1996). 'Acting Shakespeare in Postcolonial Space'. In *Shakespeare, Theory, and Performance.* James C. Bulman (ed.), 113–32. London and New York: Routledge.

— (1993). 'Borderlines: An Interview with Robert Lepage and Le Théâtre Repère, *Theater* 24(3): 71–9..

— (2000). 'Between Wor(l)ds: Lepage's Shakespeare Cycle'. In *Theatre sans frontières: Essays on the Dramatic Universe of Robert Lepage,* Joseph L. Donohoe and Jane

Koustas (eds), 191–204. East Lansing: Michigan State University Press. This essay first appeared in *Theatre* 24(3) (1993): 61–70. It also appeared in Polish as 'Miedzy Slowami, Mienzy Swiatami', trans. Halina Thylwe, in *Dialog* (November 1994): [129]–136.

Shakespeare, William (1975). *As You Like It*, Agnes Latham (ed.). London: Thomson Learning.

Simon, Sherry (2006). *Translating Montreal: Episodes in the Life of a Divided City*. Montreal & Kingston: McGill-Queens University Press.

Taylor, Charles (1992). *Rapprocher les solitudes: écrits sur le fédéralisme et le nationalisme au Canada*. Saint-Foy: Presses de L'Université Laval.

Thériault, Joseph Yvon (2002). *Critique de l'américanité: mémoire et démocratie au Québec*. Montréal: Québec Amérique.

Von Flotow, Luise (2010–11). 'When Hollywood Speaks 'International French': The Sociopolitics of Dubbing for Francophone Québec'. *Québec Studies: The Politics and Poetics of Translation in Québec and Canada*. Louise H. Forsyth and Jane M. Koustas (eds), 50 (Fall/Winter): 27–45.

Chapter 8

Waltz with Bashir as a Case of Multidimensional Translation

Ayelet Kohn and Rachel Weissbrod

8.1 Introduction

The animated film *Waltz with Bashir* (2008) and the graphic novel based on it (Folman and Polonsky 2009) describe the search of the narrator (Folman) for a lost memory. As a young Israeli soldier, he was sent to Lebanon in 1982, at the time when the massacre in the refugee camps Sabra and Shatila took place. Now, in the first decade of the twenty-first century, he tries to find out how he relates to this event. Built like a psychological detective story,[1] *Waltz with Bashir* deals with guilt, trauma, repression, and the return of the repressed in dreams and hallucinations. Both the film and the novel end, like a documentary, with a succession of journalistic photos of the massacre.

The film enjoyed international success, which culminated in its receiving the Golden Globe Award and being nominated for the Academy Award in the Foreign Language Film category in 2009. This success, which led to the production of the graphic novel, can be explained by the decision to use animation, and thus promote a psychologically and politically charged film as a product of the entertainment industry.

The following discussion is based on the premise that the film and the novel (as separate entities and in relation to each other) can be addressed in terms of 'translation' in a broad sense of the word.[2] Conceiving of translation as more than interlingual transfer is well established in translation studies nowadays. This has led researchers to make comparisons between translation and adaptation and question the very distinction between them (Hutcheon 2006: 16). Acknowledging that such a distinction may be superfluous, we still use the term 'translation' in compliance with the main theories we have consulted. Our analysis is oriented toward Freud's view of translation as a process that takes place in the human psyche (Freud 2006). Freud's perspective is linked to Jakobson's notion of intersemiotic translation, or transmutation (Jakobson 1987), and with Mailloux's idea that when we interpret a work of art, we are also translating it (Mailloux 2001).

By applying these interrelated notions of translation to one case study, we hope to suggest a model that may be used in other types of texts and cultural transfer. In a more general vein, we hope to bring to the fore the complexity of the concept of 'translation' and the possibilities that open up when it is looked at not in terms of interlingual transfer, but rather as a transformative process involving cultural, psychological and other elements.

8.2 Processes of Translation in *Waltz with Bashir*

8.2.1 Psychological processes as translation

As mentioned, both the film and the novel deal with guilt, trauma, repression, and the return of the repressed in dreams and hallucinations. Such themes invite the application of Freudian ideas. When discussing these phenomena, Freud uses the term *Übersetzung*, translation,[3] which appears in his writing in various contexts and refers to a movement toward a higher level of consciousness.

According to Mahony, Freud was a theoretician of translation: 'Freud merits to be classed among the principal theorists and innovators of translation, for he gives it a scope and depth unprecedented in history' (Mahony 2001: 837). In his writings, Freud combined interlingual translation (which he engaged in himself) with translation within one and the same language (Jakobson's 'paraphrase') and translation that takes place in the human psyche. As a psychologist, he recognized translation processes in dreams, slips of the tongue, fetishes, hysterical symptoms, and more. In his letters to Fliess and in other writings (e.g., Freud 1964b, 1964c, 1964e, 1964f), he described the individual as an accumulation of translations, each entailing a move to a higher level of consciousness. He regarded repression – a defence mechanism that drives memories, emotions, impulses, and thoughts threatening the ego from the conscious to the unconscious – as a failure to translate (Mahony 2001).

Freud's *Interpretation of Dreams* (2006, published in German for the first time in 1900) is a good example of how translation functions in his theoretical framework. Freud distinguishes between the manifest content of dreams, partly retained in the dreamer's memory, and their latent content, or the 'dream-thoughts'. He focuses his attention on the relationship between the concealed thoughts and the manifest content, and traces the psychic processes by which the former are transformed into the latter (Freud 2006: 311). He refers to these processes as 'translation' (ibid. 312). Since they entail a transformation of abstract thoughts into sensory images, they can also be seen as a variation of Jakobson's transmutation – the re-creation of meaning by means of another sign system (Jakobson 1987). The uniqueness of Freud's version of transmutation lies in the idea that the 'original' consists of abstract thoughts, to be encoded in the 'target' (manifest dream content). The relevance of translation in general, and transmutation in particular, to Freud's theory is highlighted by the following statement:

> The dream-thoughts and the dream-content are presented to us like two versions of the same subject-matter in two different languages. Or, more properly, the dream-content seems like a transcript of the dream-thoughts *into another mode of expression*, whose characters and syntactic laws it is our business to discover by comparing the original and the *translation*. (Freud 2006: 311–12; our emphases)

Freud's theory of dreams is linked to translation in another way; when he points out the dependency of the dream, as a text, on the dreamer's language. This is also why he anticipated difficulties in the translation of his own book:

> Indeed, dreams are so closely related to linguistic expression that Ferenczi (1910) has truly remarked that every tongue has its own dream-language. It is impossible as a rule to translate a dream into a foreign language and this is equally true, I fancy, of a book such as the present one. (Freud 2006: 132, in a note added in 1911)

Freud's concept of translation encompasses not just the creation of dreams but also their interpretation. In this respect, too, there is a striking similarity to translation researchers (such as Steiner 1975), who have emphasized the interpretive aspect of translation, and to scholars who have equated interpretation with translation (Mailloux 2001). Nevertheless, the conception of the role of the analyst/interpreter/translator has changed considerably since the days of Freud. In the field of psychology, emphasis has shifted to the analyst/patient interaction itself as a source of insight. Consequently, it is believed that the meaning of the dream is created (rather than revealed) during their encounter (Lippmann 1996). In the field of literary/cultural theory, a similar change has taken place: the view of the text as a self-contained entity has been challenged by the premise that it has no 'objective' existence, since the meaning is created only when read/interpreted/translated (Mailloux 2001).

Even when seen in the light of the criticism it has triggered, Freud's approach enables us to understand the psychological processes presented in *Waltz with Bashir* as processes of translation. Moreover, the act of creating the film and the novel can be understood as part of Folman's attempt, as director and narrator, to return to memory what he has repressed. Following Mailloux (2001), who regards each act of interpretation as an act of translation, we propose to consider our own interpretation as an additional layer of translation.

8.2.2 Translation of the psyche into film and graphic novel

Folman's film takes advantage of the unique means developed in cinema for expressing psychological processes such as memory, trauma, and repression (Caruth 1995; 1996; Walker 2005; Gertz and Khleifi 2008). More specifically, his decision to translate his search for a lost memory into an animated film, and then to turn the film into a graphic novel, links him with other artists who have regarded animation as an appropriate medium for addressing weighty subject matter.[4] Similar to Folman in *Waltz with Bashir*, they deal with trauma related to war, violence, and bodily harm, thus expropriating animation from the realm of naive fantasy and children's entertainment, where it is generally encountered. By using animation to depict harsh reality, they are protesting against the naiveté of traditional comics and children's films. At the same time, they draw attention to the less naive aspects of those self-same comics and films. Disney's animated films such as *Snow White and the Seven Dwarfs* (1937), *Bambi* (1942), and *The Lion King* (1994) deal with the kind of traumatic situations that have inspired many of the fairy tales upon which such films are based. The life stories of some superheroes such as Spiderman and Batman also have traumatic aspects; however, in the works of Folman and others these aspects take centre stage.

The use of animation to depict trauma is more than accidental. According to Caruth (1995, 1996), trauma leaves a double wound. The first one is caused by the traumatic event itself, and the second by the person's inability to integrate it into their psyche. LaCapra (2001) describes two ways of dealing with trauma. One way is to treat it as being impossible to represent. According to LaCapra, when people are unable to give expression to their traumatic experience, the result is an uncontrolled repetition of post-traumatic symptoms (such a reaction in *Waltz with Bashir* will be discussed below). The other way of dealing with trauma is controlling it, albeit incompletely, by distinguishing between the remote traumatic event and the person's present life. This strategy of coping with trauma, referred to as 'working through', acknowledges the role of words, or writing, as a means to represent the trauma without getting too close to it, though it does not deny that some aspects of the trauma cannot be represented. Following this line of thought, we suggest that visual art is also a tool of representation, which supports verbal language while decreasing the reliance on words. The uniqueness of animation as a form of visual art is that it uses iconic symbols that represent reality without ever coming in touch with it, in contrast to photographs, which are created through contact with reality (before the digital era – the exposure of celluloid to sunlight); that is, their relationship with the real world is indexical (Yosef 2008: 2, based on Mulvey 2006: 65). The world created by animation is an alternative, autonomous world, a pure fiction. This makes animation a particularly fitting medium for dealing with trauma from a safe distance.

Viewed in this light, the making of the film and the novel *Waltz with Bashir* can be interpreted as a stage in a Freudian translation process leading to an increased consciousness and working through of a trauma. From another perspective, it involves intersemiotic translation, or transmutation, in the Jakobsonian sense, because the film and the novel transform psychological processes into verbal and visual modes of expression. Nevertheless, translations, including transmutations, are seldom if ever exact replicas of their originals (Toury 1995, Venuti 1998). Though the film and the novel reflect and take part in psychological processes, they are also – or primarily – artistic creations, made by a team of artists who do not necessarily share Folman's traumatic experience. As such, they manipulate the psychological processes so as to serve rhetorical goals (Kohen-Raz 2007), for example, to entertain, give the audience an artistic experience, and express political opinions.

Jakobson's concept of transmutation is also applicable to the transformation of the animated film into a graphic novel, which is also a visual medium, but has its own unique features. The graphic novel approximates comics in the way it arranges frames in strips, and is similar to cinema in the way it treats each distinct frame as a *mise-en-scène* and simulates camera movements. The visual images and written text function as co-narrators of equal status. However, the graphic novel does not use the characteristic symbols of comics such as speech and thought balloons (McCloud 2000);

the written text is presented as a succession of sentences, making it similar to both written stories and scripts.

In the graphic novel, breaking down the flow of action into single frames focuses the reader's attention on concise, frozen units embodying meaningful moments in the plot (Eisner 1996, Kan 1994). Returning to the origins of cinema – namely still photography – the graphic novel invites slow and gradual engagement, with the reader paying close attention to every visual image and its relationship with the written text. In *Waltz with Bashir*, this kind of reading allows us to trace, step by step, the arduous process of discovering and reconstructing lost memories. Another aspect of the graphic novel format is the association with comics and superheroes, in and of themselves, and also as objects of criticism (Weiner 2002). While translating the film (which is itself a translation of an inner world), the novel provides a different perspective on the same basic plot of searching for lost memories.

This broad framework of 'translation' serves as the background for taking a closer look at three sequences that reflect crucial psychological turning points, and play an important role in moving and organizing the plot. A further section will be devoted to the documentary photos shown at the end of the film and the novel. We shall discuss the significance of replacing the technique of animation (the principal means of representation in both the film and the novel) with the documentary format, and note the implications of this change for the process of translation that Folman implements.

8.3 Boaz's Dog Dream

Dreams are one of the links between cinema and Freudian psychology. Metz (1986) compared the condition of film spectators to that of people dreaming: they sit in the dark, disconnected from the world outside, and experience an alternative reality which is conceived as real due to the manipulative power of the cinematic means of expression – the moving picture and sound. The capacity of cinema to reconstruct the experience of dreaming explains the tendency of film, since its beginnings, to make use of dreams (Kohen-Raz 2007). This also applies to *Waltz with Bashir*, which opens with a dream – more specifically, a nightmare. The site of action in the dream is an urban landscape in Tel Aviv – apartment buildings, balconies, and garbage. However, as Freud (2003) has observed, strange and threatening occurrences in dreams are likely to take place in the midst of the most familiar and apparently safe surroundings. In Boaz's dream, one dog, and then another, and another – twenty-six in all – run in a frenzy toward an unknown destination, trampling and knocking down every human and non-human obstacle in their way. Finally they stop by a multistoried building. The face of the person they are looking for – Boaz, the narrator of the dream – appears in one of the upper floor windows. Only at this point, when Boaz's voice and the picture coalesce, does the dogs' intention become clear. They demand that Boaz's boss turn him over to them, otherwise they will devour anyone who tries to get into the building. Typical of nightmares, Boaz wakes up at this moment.

In Freudian terminology, Boaz has had an anxiety dream, 'in which that most dreadful of all unpleasant feelings holds us in its grasp till we awaken' (Freud 2006: 168). The origin of the 'unpleasurable feeling' becomes clear during the conversation between Folman and Boaz, following the narration of the dream. During the war, whenever Boaz's unit entered a Lebanese village to look for terrorists, his role was to shoot the stray dogs with a silencer, so that they could not draw attention to the soldiers' presence. The number of dogs in the dream is the exact number of dogs that Boaz shot. Ironically, he got this 'job' because he was too sensitive to shoot people. His dream implies that in his own eyes he is a criminal awaiting punishment. The fact that dogs are involved does not assuage his guilt, probably because they are innocent creatures, which have nothing to do with the war. At the same time, the dream humanizes them by making them talk and seek revenge, so that killing them is likened to homicide.

The spectator/reader watches the dream only once, but Boaz tells Folman that it has been coming back every night over the last two and a half years, simulating recurrent dreams in real life, which, according to Zadra (1996: 231), usually 'have negative content, arise during periods of stress, and dissipate once the stressor has been successfully dealt with'. Though it is related to Lebanon, the dream makes its first appearance twenty years after the war. This, too, is in line with real-life situations. Research in psychology has shown that people experience post-trauma dozens of years after the traumatic event took place (Hermann and Eryavec 1994, Dean 1998). The delay is due to the fact that people are haunted by something inaccessible and often unknown to them. As Caruth puts it: '[T]he event is not assimilated or experienced fully at the time, but only belatedly, in its repeated possession of the one who experiences it' (Caruth 1995: 4).

On the face of it, dreams that take place under post-traumatic conditions, with the dreamer experiencing guilt and anxiety, are not covered by Freud's theory, which assumes that every dream is the fulfillment of a wish (Freud 2006: 123, 168–9). Freud resolved the contradiction by claiming that such dreams, too, fulfil a wish – the wish to be punished (Freud 1964d: 218–19).[5] However, dreaming in itself does not solve the dreamer's problem. In the film Boaz turns to Folman for help, but Folman declines, using the excuse that he is a filmmaker not a psychologist. Boaz suggests that filmmaking is a kind of psychotherapy, and when one looks at the film as a whole, he seems to be right. Yet, as far as Boaz is concerned, Folman does not meet the challenge. After their meeting, Boaz stands by the stormy sea and for a moment he seems to be in such despair that he considers committing suicide.

On a personal level, Boaz's problem remains unresolved. However, cinematic dreams are rhetorical and not just mimetic devices. From the filmmakers' point of view Boaz's dream illuminates what he is going through, allowing the audience to share his experiences, while at the same time appreciating the film's ideological and political message. To make the spectators feel that they are sharing these experiences with Boaz, Folman does not at this point inform them that the wild dogs' sequence is a dream. They 'wake up' with Boaz, after sharing their horror with the characters in the dream (the mother who hugs her child tightly, e.g.). According to Bluestone (1968), cinema knows only one tense, the present. Because it appeals to our senses, past events – even if screened in black-and-white or slow motion, or accompanied by a caption specifying the date – are perceived as if they are taking place right now. Hence the audience experiences the horrifying events as if they are taking place while they are witnessing the film. Folman remarks in the film's DVD commentary that this sequence was purposely meant to shock the audience. Actually, it shocks them twice – by making them experience the event and by refuting the premise that animation is simply naïve entertainment. To achieve this rhetorical effect, the film takes the dream as narrated by Boaz back to its visual phase, or its manifest content, to use Freud's terminology.

The rhetorical effect is also enhanced by the fact that the dogs killed by Boaz were common stray dogs, while the ones in the dream are wild beasts. They are grey, reminiscent of wolves with their bared teeth and yellow eyes.[6] Though they run in one direction, they are portrayed from different points of view – moving from right to left, diagonally, etc. – creating the impression of a multi-directional attack. At certain moments they seem to be attacking the audience itself (the 'photographer' runs backwards with his face to the approaching dogs), a technique that draws the spectators into the experience.

The sequence, which takes two minutes forty-eight seconds, is accompanied by a soundtrack comprising the monotonous sound of drums, interspersed with the diegetic sounds of a chair falling down, a car braking, and above all the barking and breathing of the dogs, which combines the sounds made by wild animals such as wolves and jackals.[7]

In the graphic novel, the camera movement and soundtrack are replaced by other rhetorical devices (Folman and Polonsky 2009). Pages 1–4 (in the English version) break down the cinematic sequence into fourteen frames separated by thick black lines, as in a filmstrip. Evoking the filmstrip and the 'full frame' image (a still photo surrounded by a thick black frame with blurred borders) is a nostalgic allusion to the notion of photography as a means of 'authentic' documentation. This naive, nostalgic framing also brings to mind photo albums and their function in shaping emotion and framing memory.

The single picture on page one presents the scenery. Page two consists of three frames, each taking up the entire width of the page. The direction of the viewer's gaze is vertical, from the top down. The dog, which is present in all three strips, progresses steadily towards the viewer. It is first shown in LS (long shot), then in MS (medium shot), and finally in close-up. In this close-up, the dog seems to rip the frame and leap onto the reader's lap. Yet, despite the attempt to create continuity, the movement is fragmentary because of the divided page and the 'leap' of the eye from frame to frame (Kress and van Leeuwen 1998). The items in the three frames contribute to this sense of fragmentation. The viewer can recognize fences, buildings, and walls, but they are seen from different angles and directions. In this way, the graphic novel breaks down the continuous flowing motion of the film (in which music also plays a part) into a succession of frozen moments. Whereas in the film, the flow of motion in time and space creates the impression of moving toward some solution, the fragmentariness of the graphic novel simulates a dream, or a dream recollected in memory (Freud 2006: 527). This feature of the graphic novel adds to the feeling of horror and helplessness, because the world portrayed therein is unreasonable and unstable.

The feeling of fragmentation becomes more intense on page three, which is divided into four horizontal strips. The first and third take up the entire width of the page, while the second and fourth are divided into two; this appears to be a symmetric construction with the 'camera' angle continually changing. Whereas the film creates the illusion that the dogs are running toward the camera, the novel simulates the impressions of someone under extreme stress, who can only perceive fragments of the total picture. In each of the frames, the picture is incomplete; it changes from a long shot to a close-up, and then to a panoramic view of the scene.

The last strip on the page contains a close-up of a dog's head; a very similar but reversed picture appears on page four, but this time it shows the head of a dog shot by Boaz (possibly the same dog who is now coming to take its revenge on him).

Another close-up of a dog's head appears on page seven, a foretaste of disaster, as well as a concise representation of the narrator's distress. According to Caruth (1996), texts that deal with trauma are characterized by the repetition of words and patterns of discourse, giving them a separate literary dimension, which cannot be reduced to a discussion of the text content. In the case under discussion, such a pattern is created by the repetition of pictures. Although Boaz tries to assuage his guilt by claiming that he was commanded to shoot the dogs, the ambiguous ending of the dream and his solitude as he stands in the window leave the question of guilt unresolved.

As an exposition of the overall plot, the dog dream provides the first example of the repetitive structure of the film and the novel. Each level of this structure is a micro-journey intended to return a repressed personal memory through the memories and experiences of others, and at each stage the form serves the content in several intersecting ways. Following Freud, the return of the repressed in Boaz's dream (which precedes the making of the film) is a stage in a process of 'translation', as is the reconstruction of the dream in the discussion with Folman. With its use of pictures, colours, motion, music, sounds, etc., the elaboration of the dream in the film and the novel can be interpreted as a further stage of 'translation', as part of the director/narrator's effort to deal with what has hitherto been repressed. When the dream is illustrated, it takes a concrete form, resembling the 'displacement' described by Freud when he refers to how the latent dream thoughts are translated into the manifest dream content (Freud 2006: 340–44).

Another layer of translation is added when – after the dream has been presented – Boaz and Folman hold a conversation in which they leave the full meaning of the dream unexplained; its meaning is left to be decoded by viewers. According to Mailloux (2001), interpreters adapt the material to their context of interpretation. As members of the Israeli public that has seen the film and/or read the novel, we suggest that the dog dream serves as shock therapy, which forces us to acknowledge a repressed, collective guilt. In the overall construction of the film and the novel, the dog dream is the first stage in the creation of an ideological and political message revolving around the destruction of life, not just of non-humans and not only in the physical sense.

8.4 Carmi's 'Big Woman' Dream

Unlike the dog dream, which began to haunt Boaz twenty years after the war, the big woman dream took place during the war, though it is narrated – and remembered in the present – by Carmi (a friend of Folman's who served in the army with him). Carmi has this dream when he falls asleep on the ship that takes him and some other soldiers to Lebanon. In the dream, a huge naked woman rises up from the sea, boards the ship, envelopes Carmi in her arms (in a position that evokes both the Pietà and a nursing mother) and jumps with him back into the water. She swims on her back with Carmi lying on her belly and having sex for the first time in his life (as he tells Folman). In the distance, he can see the ship exploding and burning with his friends on board. The scene is painted in cold colours – blue and green – aside from two frames (in the novel), which simulate the orange and red of the fire.

This sequence (which lasts two minutes forty seconds in the film and takes up two pages) (Folman and Polonsky 2009: 22–23), functions as a prelude to memories of the war in Lebanon. In both the film and the novel, it appears as a separate unit with unique colours and intertextual references to comics and American television series such as *The Love Boat*. The transition from 'reality' to the dream and back again are clearly marked (Kohen-Raz 2007: 32); as a preface to the dream, Carmi says: 'Then I collapsed on the deck and fell asleep. I always fall asleep when I'm scared. Even now, I escape into sleep and fantasies' (Folman and Polonsky 2009: 21). In the film, Carmi looks out the window as he utters these words. In the novel, the framing of the dream is even more marked because page twenty-two opens with the figure of Carmi at the window and page twenty-three ends with a similar picture. In the first picture, his face is turned to the left, and in the second one – to the right, forming a parenthesis. His gaze marks a passage to an in-between world that serves as a break from the war for Carmi, and offers a temporary respite for Folman and the viewers. Carmi not only commits the dream to memory, but also interprets it as a form of self-criticism, as if he were looking at his past from a great distance: 'I began puking like a pig [. . .] worrying about what the enemy would think if they saw me like this' (21). As in the dog dream, the act of translation takes place on various levels: feelings are translated into their visual expression (in the 'real' dream preceding the film); the dream is verbalized and elaborated by Carmi in the present; and this version is translated into its visual re-incarnation in both film and novel.

The subject-matter of the dream, as well as the stylistic choices made by the artists when translating it into the language of animation, evoke familiar psychological themes: the connection between *eros* and *thanatos*, the desire for life in the face of death, the guilt of the lone survivor, and the desire for a woman who is at the same time a mother, lover, object of passion, and monstrous figure. Freud explains this polysemic meaning thus: suckling is the first sexual experience of a child (Freud 1964a), and since in breast-feeding the mother-lover is seen through the eyes of the infant, she is perceived as huge. While *Waltz with Baṣhir*, in both the film and novel versions, connects to Freud, it also draws from popular culture that has elaborated and recycled his ideas.[8]

The big woman dream can be compared with another sequence in which the Israel commander, who moves into a Beirut villa with his soldiers, watches pornographic films (Folman and Polonsky 2009: 68–9). In the dream, as in such films, the woman is objectified and fragmented. On the face of it, the introduction of pornography is 'justified' by the setting – an innocent young soldier having sex for the first time before entering the battlefield. Yet, the scene is so outrageously banal as to raise the suspicion that the filmmakers have purposefully overstated it. Both the film and novel have a therapeutic function; hence the big woman dream can be interpreted as an attempt to offer a temporary escape into a world of simplistic fantasies while at the same time criticizing such escapism.

Understanding the big woman dream as an intentional cliché is also validated by the references to pornographic, action, and war comics, as well as those depicting the adventures of super- often giant- heroines. Although represented as sex objects, these heroines form a new species of independent women no longer based on male heroes (Daniels 2000; O'Reilly 2005),[9] which enables women to become 'talking subjects' by placing them outside male hegemony (Irigaray 1985). They are active, erotic figures, like the woman in Carmi's dream, whose active role is underscored by the contrast with the male dreamer's passivity as both infant and lover.

The way the scene is designed directs viewers to approach both film and novel as a translation of mental processes. Attention is drawn to the illustrations, the colours, and the allusions, even though the novel differs from the film in this respect. In the film, the feminine figure is softened by the slow swimming movements, the quiet music, and the silencing of the sounds of war, which are heard from a distance. In the novel, on the other hand, each frame stands on its own, and in the absence of motion and music, the association with the bold and sexy comic heroines becomes even stronger. In both cases, however, the implications of using animation and scrutinizing the conventions of the entertainment world in dealing with war, trauma, and guilt are taken to extremes.

The peaceful dream – in Freudian terms, wish fulfilment *par excellence* – is shattered when the ship explodes right in front of Carmi. In this context, his powerlessness and inability to act on his own are given an additional meaning – they make him feel less guilty about abandoning his friends. A feeling of guilt accompanying a memory or a dream, in which the dreamer witnesses a disaster that befalls other people, characterizes the major plotlines in the film and novel of *Waltz with Bashir.* In each of them, attention is drawn to the gaze of the witness (or his victim). We see this in the dog dream, when the dogs fix their eyes on Boaz (Folman and Polonsky 2009: 4) and in the story of Rony Dayag, a friend of Folman's, who stares at his enemies from his hiding place and watches, like Carmi, the disaster that befalls his friends (38–9). The gaze of the Lebanese boy aiming his weapon at the Israeli soldiers a moment before they kill him, mentioned in the story of Frenkel – one of Folman's friends – is another example (55). In all these stories, the viewer's gaze at the horrors taking place in front of them haunts their subsequent memories, which are translated into visual terms in both film and novel.

8.5 The Sea Hallucination

After the meeting with Boaz, the key scene of the film and novel appears for the first time. Pictures from this scene have been included in the film's trailer and appear on the cover of the DVD and the novel, serving as icons by which *Waltz with Bashir* can be easily recognized. In this sequence, which takes place at night, three naked male figures rise out of the sea. Two of them, Folman and Carmi, are familiar to the viewers, while the third is anonymous. On the beach, they put on Israeli army uniforms and begin to walk toward the nearby city, Beirut. In the street, Folman encounters a group of wailing women, which the film's soundtrack and the text in the novel clearly link to the Ṡabra and Shatila massacre, taking place in Beirut between September 16 and 18, 1982, when Palestinian and Lebanese civilians were massacred in camps by Christian Lebanese Phalangists, while the civilian camps were surrounded by the Israel Defence Force. This sequence both anticipates and motivates Folman's quest, because following its first occurrence, he initiates the first meeting with Carmi and sets out to find out what exactly happened that night.

In both the film and the novel, the transition to this sequence is made through a succession of pictures, in which the location changes (Folman and Polonsky 2009: 9). In one picture Folman, who has just taken leave of Boaz, stands – just as Boaz did – on the beach in Tel Aviv gazing at the stormy sea. In the next picture, the landscape hardly changes – same sea, same palm trees and same hotels; however, the signal flares exploding in the sky imply that the past has replaced the present and the city we are seeing is Beirut. In the film, this passage is also marked by changes in rhythm and music (Kohen-Raz 2007: 73). Blurring between different places is typical of dreams and hallucinations, but in *Waltz with Bashir* this technique is used to make a political statement. The city where the horrors took place is not exactly a foreign city, the city of the 'other' that might leave one indifferent; rather, it is Beirut, a Mediterranean twin-city of Tel Aviv. Following Foucault's notion of heterotopia (Foucault 1986), the two cities merge into one, while remaining separate at the same time. The first picture of Beirut is accompanied by the narrator's words: 'That night . . . for the first time in twenty years [. . .] I had a terrible flashback from the Lebanon War' (Folman and Polonsky 2009: 10). The cinematic term 'flashback' becomes synonymous with memory, as if memory has no existence except in cinema. Such a way of expression is not unexpected from a filmmaker, but there is also an essential connection between what happens in cinema and in the human psyche: in both cases, visual images are the ones that capture and retain memory, and enable its restoration (even though what 'really' happened might be drastically transformed in the process).

After this turning point, the sequence itself begins. The first time it is shown in its entirety – one minute eighteen seconds into the film, three pages (Folman and Polonsky 2009, 11–13) into the novel. Though it is referred to as a flashback, it resembles a dream or a hallucination. First of all, the action seems to have no rational explanation; it is neither clear what the soldiers are doing in the water late at night, nor what they are trying to accomplish by going into the city. The elements within the *mise-en-scène* – the slow circular motion of the water, the movements of the three figures drawn like shadows as they put on their clothes, and the monotonous music – combine to create a sort of limbo that exists outside any specific time or place. The isolation and slow rhythm do not produce a calm and peaceful atmosphere; on the contrary, the situation seems troubling, even dangerous. The pictures highlight Folman's vulnerability: he is sunk in water, which makes his movements heavy, and even if the water shelters him, he has to raise his head in order to breathe, exposing himself to danger. His nakedness emphasizes his vulnerability; actually, he is not fully dressed even when he enters the city (he is shown buttoning his shirt).

Later, Folman is seen walking alone in the streets of Beirut, passing by walls hung with posters of Bashir Jumayel, president-elect of Lebanon and head of the Christian Phalange Party that collaborated with the Israeli army. The women who walk past him without observing him are wailing, although they do not utter a sound. The camera moves in a circle around him, illustrating the confusion and disorientation of a person who finds himself in the midst of an event that he does not fully comprehend. Yet, the very act of emerging from the water and going into the city changes his position from a distant observer to an involved witness. At first he is seen from the back and from the side; and then are we shown a close-up of his face witnessing what is taking place in front of him. He no longer turns his back on the troublesome sight.

The sequence of the soldiers rising from the sea, as well as fragments of it, reappear in the film and novel, dividing it into chapters of more or less the same length. It is integrated into the first meeting with Carmi, but ends abruptly before Folman goes to the city and encounters the wailing women. In the novel, this abbreviated sequence is reduced to two frames (Folman and Polonsky 2009: 26–7). Leading up to it, Folman says: 'I have just one image in my mind from then and you're in it, somehow' (26), employing the terminology of cinema. Carmi responds: 'Yes, I remember being in Beirut. The invasion will be with me for the rest of my life' (27). Then he says something that can be considered the key phrase of the whole story: 'The massacre's not in my system' (27). Folman uttered these words for the first time after listening to Boaz: 'to tell you the truth, it's [the massacre] not in my system' (8). It is remarkable that Folman uses the English word 'system' in a Hebrew-language text. This might characterize him as 'a man of the world', who peppers his Hebrew with English. From another perspective, however, it might be a means to create an emotional distance from the topic of the conversation: the foreign language increases (and eases) the distance between talking about the memory of the traumatic event and engaging with it. The scene appears once more during Folman's second meeting with Carmi. In this instance, it is shortened in the film and reduced (again) to two frames in the novel (Folman and Polonsky 2009: 89). For the first time, Folman refers to it as a 'hallucination', a term he also uses in his conversation with his friend Ori Sivan, a filmmaker and psychologist. Hallucinations, according to Freud (2006: 574) resemble dreams in that they transform abstract ideas into concrete sights; they, too, involve translation processes. Moreover, as in dreams, the hallucinatory event is perceived as being real, although it may never have occurred (Freud 2006: 530). In *Waltz with Bashir*, too, Folman needs Carmi to convince him that they could never have entered the sea that night. The meaning, or one of the meanings of this hallucination can be deciphered with the help of Freud, who regards water as symbolizing the womb and links emerging from the water with birth (Freud 2006: 435). In the film and the novel, water functions as a safe, sheltering place; two examples are Carmi's big woman dream and the story of Rony Dayag, who escapes from his enemies by entering the sea and swimming away from them. Ori offers another explanation for the hallucination: the sea symbolizes emotions and fears that impede the memory of the massacre. This explanation is validated by the fact that in its first and third occurrence, the hallucination precedes and delays Folman's encounter with the wailing women. In the novel, the third appearance of the hallucination is reduced to two frames, yet the organization is significant: the background changes from the sea in the first frame to the streets of Beirut in the second frame, which is also distinguished by its darker colours. In line with the observations of Caruth (1996), the hallucination arises from a distance between the actual event and its representation in the mind, and, consequently, in the film and the novel. As mentioned, the repetition itself is a symptom of a post-traumatic condition. According to Caruth, the traumatic event is not processed immediately. The process of grasping its meaning takes a long time and entails moving in circles rather than advancing in a linear direction. LaCapra (2001) calls this repetitiveness 'acting out' and regards it as one way of dealing with post-trauma that can be differentiated from 'working through', in which the traumatic experience is addressed by means of representation such as writing, or animation.

But is the massacre at Sabra and Shatila the traumatic event? Ori, the psychologist, suggests (in Freudian terms) that the trauma in question is something that originates in Folman's childhood, and that his interest in the Sabra and Shatila camps comes from his interest in 'the other camps' (Folman and Polonsky 2009: 91). He specifically refers to the Holocaust experiences of Folman's parents, survivors of Auschwitz. The sea hallucination evokes various aspects of World War II and the Holocaust – for example, when the three soldiers float motionless in the water like dead bodies. As Folman rises out of the sea, the film shows his feet sinking in the water, and for a moment the audience gets the impression that he is drowning. In addition, the soldiers making their way to the seashore look extremely thin, their facial expressions tortured, rather like inmates of a concentration camp. This reference to the Holocaust can decrease the guilt of Israeli soldiers (by turning them into victims) or, conversely, increase it by hinting that the victims have become victimizers. Ori reinforces the first interpretation, as he tries to ease Folman's guilt (Folman and Polonsky 2009: 107). He tells Folman that at nineteen he saw himself in the role of a

Nazi because he did not distinguish between Bashir's Phalanges (who were directly responsible for the massacre) and Israeli soldiers who made it possible but did not perpetrate it.

8.6 The Documentary-Like Ending

In the last sequence of *Waltz with Bashir*, the process of translating the repressed comes to an end. It opens with Folman interviewing the journalist Ron Ben-Yishay (Folman and Polonsky 2009: 108–13). Ben-Yishay's last sentence, 'And then it came over me: what I was looking at was a massacre' (113), is followed by a shot of Folman looking for the last time at the wailing women. The 'camera' rests on his face and then, in an unexpected and shocking metamorphosis, the animated pictures give way to archive photos from the 1982 massacre. For Folman, this exposure to first-hand evidence of the atrocity signifies the end of denial. While photos of the massacre might be familiar to Israeli viewers from other contexts, their placement at the end of the film and the novel imbues them with new meaning. After a long sojourn in the fantasy-world of animation, these photos offer real-world evidence; they are no longer banal 'shock photos' (Barthes 1979) that leave viewers indifferent and disinterested (described by Moeller (1998) as 'compassion fatigue'.) At the same time, the integration of the journalistic photos at the end of the film and the novel sheds new light on animation itself. By moving between the two stylistic poles of animation and real-world evidence, both texts find a powerful form of representation. In the film the photos are sequentially ordered, with solemn music on the soundtrack, thereby creating a coherent whole. In the novel, the documentary-like ending has been reduced to five photos, which take up only two pages (Folman and Polonsky 2009: 116–17); however, they are highly effective because each horrid detail is frozen on them. This technique makes it easier to notice the similarity of the wailing woman in the last photo to one of the women in the animated section. This gives new and surprising coherence to the process of emotional translation that Folman undergoes.

8.7 Conclusion

In discussing *Waltz with Bashir*, we have examined several possible ways of expanding the notion of 'translation'. Applied to one test case, they illustrate our idea of 'multidimensional translation'. We have linked Freud's concept of translation as a move from the unconscious into the conscious and from the abstract into the visual with Jakobson's intersemiotic translation, or transmutation. Following Jakobson, we have included in our discussion both the translation of psychological processes into their cinematic expressions, and the remaking of the animated film as a graphic novel. Based on Mailloux, we have proposed viewing our own interpretation of the film and the novel as an additional layer of translation. In line with Hutcheon (2006: 16), the expanded notion of translation, which is not limited to interlingual transfer, challenges the very distinction between translation and adaptation.

The gradual progress of the plot, which is developed through the use of many details and self-reflection in the process of creating the film, serves as a therapeutic technique in which the filmmaker is both patient *and* therapist; all the more so in the novel, in which the 'freezing' of single frames contributes to the making of a slow, meditative work. An additional aspect of understanding the creation of *Waltz with Bashir* as a therapeutic act is construction of the plot as a psychological detective novel, based on the studious collecting of dreams, hallucinations, memories, and flashbacks that lead step by step to understanding Folman's 'crime'.

As mentioned, Freud regards the transformation of abstract thoughts into visual images as translation. In *Waltz with Bashir*, the aesthetic format in general and the dreams, hallucinations, and flashbacks in particular, can be interpreted as the translation of post-traumatic symptoms into actual visions. In fact, the filmmaker takes viewers back to the sights that triggered the trauma in the first place (though he initially prefers the genre of animation). Although Folman translates the repressed experience into visual images, he also uses words as a major means of expression. He talks to friends and psychologists (Ori is not the only one) creating a web of conversations that refer to the dreams, hallucinations, and flashbacks, and invest them with meaning. The final message is communicated through journalistic photos rather than animation. Each mode of representation highlights, by contrast, the problematic aspect of the other, while at the same time depending on it and reinforcing it. On the one hand, the journalistic photos are an indexical mode of representation, created through a contact with reality; on the other hand, it is the animation that restores the journalistic photos' initial power to shock.

Another aspect of translating psychological processes into visual media to cope with trauma is the frequent appearance of objects and tools used for viewing. These include the television set in the villa in Beirut, used for watching pornographic films; military binoculars; rifle sights; the television camera of the photographer who accompanies the journalist Ron Ben-Yishay; and another camera used to take pictures of the dying horses in the Beirut hippodrome. When the trauma-stricken Folman visits Ori, he is first seen through the door eyepiece, which symbolically distorts his figure. Beyond all these instruments we have the presence of the 'painting camera' (see note 1) that 'shoots' (and hits) the memories and awakens them.

'Repression', Freud said, 'is a failure of translation' (Freud 1985: 208). We have chosen to deal with three sequences that play key roles in the plot. All three create a parallel world of dream and hallucination, and reflect invisible processes in the minds of the characters. Each sequence brings both narrator and audience closer to filling in the gaps in his memory. The question of guilt, however, is not ultimately solved till the end. The tendency to exonerate the soldiers, including the narrator and his friends, and put the blame on the Phalanges or Israel's major politicians instead undermines the act of self-translation – in the Freudian sense – that inspired the creation of both film and novel.

Notes

1 By using oblique angles and playing with light and shadow, the film and the novel pay homage to *film noir* – an homage that has its origins in comics. It is noteworthy that Folman has coined the Hebrew term *matsyera* – 'painting camera' – derived from the root *le-tsayer* (to paint) and similar to *matslema* (meaning camera, based on *le-tsalem* = to take a photograph). The term appears in the leaflet *Mi-Tasrit Le-Seret* (from script to film), which comes with the DVD package. Using cinematic terms such as 'oblique angles' to discuss painting is based on this approach.

2 Unlike the Hebrew-speaking film, the novel was produced in English and translated into Hebrew. Since its focus is on other forms of translation, the present discussion does not deal with the interlingual translation (Jakobson's 'translation proper', 1987).

3 In our discussion, we distinguish between Freud's *Übersetzung* and *Deutung* (interpretation). The latter, which appears in the title of his book *Die Traumdeutung* (English version: *The Interpretation of Dreams*, 2006), is, by implication, the last stage of translation in the sense of moving to a higher level of consciousness.

4 For example: Spiegelman 1986; Satrapi 2003; Engelberg 2006; Satrapi and Paronnaud 2007.

5 Freud was criticized for forcing the idea of wish fulfillment on dreams in which no pleasure is experienced; see Domhoff 2000.

6 The team of illustrators was headed by David Polonsky (art director) and Yoni Goodman (animation director).

7 The soundtrack accompanying the dog dream was created by Aviv Aldema, the film's sound designer.

[8] Two well-known examples from cinema are Fellini's *Amarcord* (1973) and Almodóvar's *All about My Mother* (1999).

[9] See Leland (2007) on superheroines and feminist culture.

Bibliography

Barthes, Roland (1979). 'Shock-Photos'. In *The Eiffel Tower and Other Mythologies*. Richard Howard. trans., 70–2. New York: Hill and Wang.

Bluestone, George (1968/1957). *Novels into Film*. Berkeley and London: University of California Press.

Caruth, Cathy (ed.) (1995). *Trauma: Explorations in Memory*. Baltimore and London: Johns Hopkins University Press.

— (1996). *Unclaimed Experience: Trauma, Narrative, and History*. Baltimore and London: Johns Hopkins University Press.

Chabon, Michael (2003). *The Amazing Adventures of Kavalier and Clay*. New York: Random House.

Daniels, Les (2000). *Wonder Woman: A Complete History*. San Francisco: Chronicle Books.

Dean, Eric T. (1998). *Shook over Hell: Post-Traumatic Stress, Vietnam, and the Civil War*. Cambridge, Mass.: Harvard University Press.

Domhoff, G. William (2000). 'Moving dream theory beyond Freud and Jung'. Unpubl. paper presented to the symposium 'Beyond Freud and Jung?' Graduate Theological Union, Berkeley, CA, September 23, 2000. http://www.all-birds.org/Dreams/dreams029.htm (accessed July 11, 2011).

Eisner, Will (1996). *Graphic Storytelling and Visual Narrative*. Tamarac, FL: Poorhouse Press.

Engelberg, Miriam (2006). *Cancer Made Me a Shallower Person: A Memoir in comics*. New York: HarperCollins.

Ferenczi, Sándor (1916/1910). 'The psychological analysis of dreams'. In *Contributions to Psychology*. Ernest Jones, trans., 80–111. Boston: Richard G. Badger.

Folman, Ari and Polonsky, David (2009). *Waltz with Bashir*. New York: Metropolitan Books.

Foucault, Michel (1986). 'Of Other Spaces', trans. Jay Miskowiec. *Diacritics* 16: 22–7.

Freud, Sigmund (1964a) (1905). 'Three Essays on the Theory of Sexuality'. In *The Standard Edition of the Complete Psychological Works of Sigmund Freud*. James Strachey. trans. Vol. VII, 125–245. London: Hogarth Press.

— (1964b) (1913). 'The Disposition to Obsessional Neurosis'. In *The Standard Edition of the Complete Psychological Works of Sigmund Freud*. James Strachey, trans. Vol. XII, 317–26. London: Hogarth Press.

— (1964c) (1915). 'The Unconscious'. In *The Standard Edition of the Complete Psychological Works of Sigmund Freud*. James Strachey, trans. Vol. XIV, 159–216. London: Hogarth Press.

— (1964d) (1916). 'Dreams'. In *The Standard Edition of the Complete Psychological Works of Sigmund Freud*, trans. James Strachey. Vol. XV, 83–239. London: Hogarth Press.

— (1964e) (1916–17). 'Introductory Lectures on Psychoanalysis'. In *The Standard Edition of the Complete Psychological Works of Sigmund Freud*, trans. James Strachey. Vol. XVI, 45–176. London: Hogarth Press.

— (1964f) (1940). 'An Outline of Psychoanalysis'. In *The Standard Edition of the Complete Psychological Works of Sigmund Freud*. James Strachey, trans. Vol. XXIII, 141–207. tr. James Strachey. London: The Hogarth Press.

— (1985) (1887–1904). *The Complete Letters to Wilhelm Fliess*, trans. Jeffrey Moussaieff Masson. Cambridge, MA: Harvard University Press.

— (2003) (1919). 'The Uncanny'. David McLintock, trans. London and New York: Penguin Books.

— (2006) (1900). *The Interpretation of Dreams*. James Strachey, trans. New York: Avon Books.

Gertz, Nurith and Khleifi, George (2008). *Palestinian Cinema: Landscape, Trauma, and Memory*. Bloomington and Indianapolis: Indiana University Press.

Herrmann, Nathan and Eryavec, Goran (1994). 'Delayed Onset Post-traumatic Stress Disorder in World War II Veterans'. *Canadian Journal of Psychiatry* 39(7): 439–441.

Hutcheon, Linda (2006). *A theory of adaptation*. London and New York: Routledge.

Irigaray, Luce (1985). *This Sex which is not One*, trans. Catherine Porter and Carolyn Burke. Ithaca, NY: Cornell University Press.

Jakobson, Roman (1987) (1959). 'On Linguistic Aspects of Translation'. In *Language in Literature*. Krystina Pomorska and Stephen Rudy (eds), 428–35. Cambridge, Massachusetts: The Belknap Press of Harvard University Press.

Kan, Kat (1994). 'Graphic novels: A Roundup'. *Voice of Youth Advocates* 16: 359–360.

Kohen-Raz, Odeya (2007). 'The Dreaming Character in Film; the Dream as Mise-en-abyme: Reflexivity and Guilt in the Cinematic Dream'. Unpub. Ph.D. thesis, Tel Aviv University.

Kress, Gunther and Van Leeuwen, Theo (1998). 'Front pages: The (Critical) Analysis of Newspaper Layout'. In *Approaches to Media Discourse*. Allan Bell and Peter Garrett (eds), 186–220. London: Blackwell Publishing.

LaCapra, Dominick (2001). *Writing History, Writing Trauma*. Baltimore: Johns Hopkins University Press.

Lee, Stan and Kirby, Jack (1963). *The X-Men*. New York: Marvel Comics Universe.

Leland, Jennie (2007). 'The Phoenix Always Rises: The Evolution of Superheroines in Feminist Culture'. Unpub. MA thesis, University of Maine. http://www.library.umaine.edu/theses/pdf/LelandJ2007.pdf (accessed July 11, 2009).

Lippmann, Paul (1996). 'On dreams and Interpersonal Psychoanalysis'. *Psychoanalytic Dialogues* 6: 831–46.

Mahony, Patrick J. (2001). 'Freud and Translation'. *American Imago* 58(4): 837–40.

Mailloux, Steven (2001) (1998). 'Interpretation and Rhetorical Hermeneutics'. In *Reception Study: From Literary Theory to Cultural Studies*. James L. Machor and Philip Goldstein (eds), 39–60. London and New York: Routledge.

McCloud, Scott (2000). *Reinventing Comics: How Imagination and Technology Are Revolutionizing an Art Form*. New York: HarperCollins.

Metz, Christian (1986). *The Imaginary Signifier: Psychoanalysis and the Cinema*. Annwyl Williams, trans. Bloomington: Indiana University Press.

Moeller, Susan D. (1998). *Compassion Fatigue: How the Media Sell Disease, Famine, War and Death.* London and New York: Routledge.

Mulvey, Laura (2006). *Death 24 X a Second: Stillness and the Moving Image.* London: Reaktion Books.

O'Reilly, Julie D. (2005). 'The Wonder Woman Precedent: (Super)heroism on trial'. *Journal of American Culture* 28(3): 273–83.

Satrapi, Marjane (2003). *Persepolis: The Story of a Childhood.* Mattais Ripa and Blake Ferris, trans. New York: Pantheon Books.

Spiegelman, Art (1986). *Maus: A Survivor's Tale.* New York: Pantheon Books.

Steiner, George (1975). *After Babel: Aspects of Language and Translation.* Oxford and New York: Oxford University Press.

Toury, Gideon (1995). *Descriptive Translation Studies and Beyond.* Amsterdam and Philadelphia: John Benjamins.

Venuti, Lawrence (1998). *The Scandals of Translation: Towards an Ethics of Difference.* London and New York: Routledge.

Walker, Janet (2005). *Trauma Cinema: Documenting Incest and the Holocaust.* Berkeley and Los Angeles: University of California Press.

Weiner, Stephen (2002). 'Beyond Superheroes: Comics Get Serious'. *Library Journal* 127(2): 55–8.

Yosef, Raz (2008). 'Introduction: Visual Evidences: History and Memory in Israeli Cinema'. In *History and Memory in Israeli Cinema.* Raz Yosef (ed.), 1–11. Tel Aviv: Tel Aviv University, The Chaim Weizmann Institute for the Study of Zionism and Israel [*Israel* 14, a special issue, in Hebrew, with an English abstract].

Zadra, Antonio L. (1996). 'Recurring Dreams: Their relation to Life Events'. In *Trauma and Dreams.* Deidra Barrett (ed.), 231–47. Cambridge, MA: Harvard University Press.

Chapter 9

The Paradoxes of Textual Fidelity: Translation and Intertitles in Victor Sjöström's Silent Film Adaptation of Henrik Ibsen's *Terje Vigen*

Eirik Frisvold Hanssen and Anna Sofia Rossholm

9.1 Introduction

Victor Sjöström's film adaptation of Henrik Ibsen's poem *Terje Vigen* (1917) constitutes the starting point of what was eventually characterised as the 'golden age' of Swedish cinema, a period when in particular the production company Svenska Bio's 'quality' film strategy of establishing a notion of Swedish national film art gained critical acknowledgement both in Sweden and abroad (Idestam-Almquist 1952, Florin 1997). The films of this 'golden age' partake in complex intermedial processes, which include the re-appropriation and adaptation of a variety of established art forms: they were adaptations of well-known Scandinavian literary sources, and in addition, the *mise-en-scène* of the filmic images were often modelled on specific paintings or borrowed iconographic stylistic devices from Nordic landscape painting, just as the acting-style was indebted to a Scandinavian naturalist theatre tradition (Florin 1997: 185–96).

In this chapter we aim to demonstrate how such processes of adaptation and media transformation did not only take place through transpositions from the fine arts, as mentioned above, but also in a number of other arenas, for example, the publication of publicity material such as film programmemes or 'exploitation books'. These publications often featured images from the film, sometimes combined with novelised résumés of the story. Other forms of adaptation include the translations of intertitles into other languages, in connection with international distribution.

Terje Vigen is indicative of how 'golden age' films take part in a series of 'versions' within a much broader media context: the film derived from a poem by Ibsen, the images contained motifs and a visual style borrowed from illustrations that were already well-known. Likewise, in film programmemes, résumés of the narrative (in prose), abridged and adapted versions of the poem, as well as still images, were placed side by side. Today, we find DVD releases, and even musical adaptations of the poem integrating a film screen on the stage with images much similar to the silent film.[1] These versions, transformations, and transpositions also exist in different languages and are adapted to different contexts of distribution.

Both translation and adaptation are practices that involve the transformation of meaning from one form of expression into another. It is telling that contemporary theory often understands adaptation and translation as mutually interchangeable or merging terms: the 'cultural turn' in translation theory coincides with the 'translational turn' in cultural theory (Bachmann-Medick 2009). However, there is a significant difference between adaptation and translation. Discourses on adaptation emphasize the media differences between the source text and the adapted version and are preoccupied with new kinds of aesthetic expression and authorship. Translation practices, on the other hand, often ideally shield the process of transformation, and the author remains invisible. Combining these two concepts and practices allows us to examine the equivocal relation to an actual or imagined source text in adaptation practices, a relation that ultimately refracts the concept of 'fidelity' between media and language.

Terje Vigen, much like most of the films of the Swedish 'golden age', represents national or Nordic cultural imaginaries refracted through the prism of Nordic artistic traditions. In an international context, exotic images of the 'Nordic' within a context of 'cinematic tourism' intersect with aesthetic discourses on the relationship between the cinema and other art forms or media (Bruno 2002). The choice of the national romantic Norwegian poem *Terje Vigen* as the starting point of a new cinematic trend in Swedish film production signals both nationalism and transnational Nordic imaginaries, while revealing cultural nostalgia, folklore, and tradition as well as modernity, innovation, and originality.

The purpose of this chapter is to consider one particular aspect of the numerous questions arising from the adaptations and transpositions related to Sjöström's *Terje Vigen* – namely the question of *fidelity* to the source text. This is a key issue debated and problematized in adaptation theory, while relating to media transformations in a broader sense (Leitch

2007: 127–50). Our contribution to this issue is mainly to combine three discourses on fidelity that are often discussed separately:

1. fidelity to the literary precursor,
2. fidelity and 'originality' in discourses on reproducing media,
3. fidelity between languages in translation.

By combining a revised reading of André Bazin's notion of mixed cinema (*cinéma impur*) with a more recent media theoretical discussion on translation, fidelity is here understood as a concept that combines discourses on language, literature, and cinema. The main focus of this chapter centres on the relation between film and literature, but, as we will see, other forms of media transposition (such as the relation between illustrations and film, as well as how the film is presented in film programmes), intersect these questions of literacy and cinematic fidelity.

We begin with a short analysis of the film in terms of adaptation strategies, focusing on the relationship between film images and intertitles. The filmic text is subsequently placed in a broader context through the examination of representations of this relationship in contemporary publicity and reception material, as well as considering the implications of the translation of the film's intertitles into other languages.

9.1.1 Fidelity to the literary precursor: *Terje Vigen* as Ibsen adaptation and 'mixed cinema'

We have chosen a strategy characteristic of the late 1910s – a period that witnessed a discursive shift with regard to adaptation practices, not only in Sweden but worldwide. From the 1890s, novels, theatrical plays (with Shakespeare as the dramatist most often adapted for the screen), poems, as well as paintings and drawings of recognised cultural value were adapted for bourgeois audiences in an attempt to gain cultural recognition.[2] Highbrow culture was often exploited for the 'artistic uplift', and cultural prestige of the cinematic medium. This was part of a more general movement at the outbreak of World War I, described by Rob King as 'a significant reshaping of relations between culture and class, what might be described as the shift from a hierarchical cultural order that once reinforced social divisions to a commercially driven 'mass' culture that has begun to obscure them' (King 2009: 115). In Swedish film discourse *Terje Vigen* was considered an important text in the movement towards cultural prestige, partly because it was enthusiastically reviewed on its premiere by a theatre critic, Bo Bergman, in Sweden's largest daily newspaper, *Dagens Nyheter* (Florin 2003: 63 ff.).[3]

In a global context this period is associated with the evolution of the feature film in classical Hollywood cinema, and a parallel development of the stylistic and narrative functions of intertitles. Claire Dupré la Tour defines intertitles (a term which originated in the 1930s) as 'shots of texts printed on material that does not belong to the diegesis of a film' (thus excluding 'inserts' of diegetic verbal materials such as letters or newspapers) (la Tour 326–31). By 1910, intertitles were commonplace in the vast majority of films, which thereby facilitated a more psychologically based narrative and less self-conscious narration (Thompson 183–9). However the intertitles of *Terje Vigen* constitute a conspicuous example of self-conscious narration through a 'fetishizing' of the source text. Ibsen's poem was written in 1862, and direct quotes from the literary work serve as the basis for the intertitles throughout the film, producing a complex relationship between intertitles and film images. The effect of a 'double narration' (a practice similar to the use of extra-diegetic narrative voice-over in sound film) also has consequences for the film's narrative structure.[4]

Terje Vigen is one example of several Ibsen adaptations for the screen appearing in the 1910s, in Sweden, the United States, Germany, Italy, Great Britain, Spain, and Russia (Hansen 1992). However, Sjöström's film differs significantly from these productions, most of which are adaptations of stage plays.[5] By adapting an epic poem, he not only employed source material transcending the strict unity of space and time associated with Ibsen's naturalist stage plays, but combined expressive, moving images of nature (typical of contemporary Swedish cinema), with a strong emphasis on Ibsen's text. Both poem and film tell the story of an old maritime pilot who was captured and imprisoned by the British during the Napoleonic War in 1814 while trying to rescue his family from starvation, who many years later accidentally re-encounters the British captain responsible for his suffering. As Toril Moi has pointed out, the idealism and nationalism of *Terje Vigen* was never repeated in any of Ibsen's later works, adding that '[r] emarkably for Ibsen, moreover, there is no trace of irony anywhere' (Moi 2006: 177).

André Bazin's concept of adaptation associated with his notion of *cinéma impur* or 'mixed cinema' (Bazin 1967a: 53–75), which is perhaps most clearly set forth in his analysis of Robert Bresson's *Le Journal d'un Curé de Campagne* (1950), an adaptation of Georges Bernanos' novel (Bazin 1967b: 125–43). This film has several similarities with Sjöström's Ibsen adaptation: Bresson declared the intention to rigorously follow the book word-for-word, a strategy that according to Bazin suggests 'the most insidious kind of fidelity, a most pervasive form of creative licence. Of course, one clearly cannot adapt without transposing [. . .] Literal adaptations are not the faithful ones' (Bazin 1967b: 127). Later in the analysis, he explains why:

> Its dialectic between fidelity and creation is reducible [. . .] to a dialectic between cinema and literature. There is no question here of a translation, no matter how faithful or intelligent. Still less is it a question of free inspiration with the intention of making a duplicate. It is a question of building a secondary work with the novel as foundation. In no sense is the film 'comparable' to the novel or 'worthy' of it. It is a new aesthetic creation, the novel so to speak multiplied by the cinema. (Bazin 1967b: 141)

In general, a film cannot quote or encompass an entire other work, it transforms it. What ensues from Bresson's adaptation strategy is according to Bazin 'the paradoxical effect of textual fidelity', in which textual elements (i.e., quotations taken directly from Bernanos' novel) are presented as words being written on a page or as dialogue or voice-over performed in a deliberately monotonous, non-dramatic, non-psychological style. This is in many ways antithetical to the source text, which Bazin describes as 'rich in picturesque evocations, solid, concrete, strikingly visual [. . . .] the film is literary while the novel teems with visual material' (Bazin 1967b: 127). Bazin suggests that Bresson's adaptation almost can be understood as 'a silent film with spoken titles', since the 'spoken word does not enter into the image as a realistic component' (138). The film (as well as Sjöström's Ibsen adaptation) refers to what Bazin suggestively describes as two separate 'realities': the diegetic reality of the fictional world, and a second reality, 'the written reality', of the literary text 'as a cold, hard fact, a reality to be accepted as it stands'. Since the literary text is neither condensed nor edited, but rather fragmented, what is left over must be understood as 'a part of the original [source text]' (136). The whole purpose of the film, according to Bazin, is the fragmentation and spatial disorientation of the source text.

As in Bresson's film, the intertitles in *Terje Vigen* are transposed from the poem in a fragmented form with a couple of instances of subtle alterations: on one occasion the intertitle is formed from fragments from two separate stanzas; while on other occasions the order of the stanzas is disrupted. In general, however, all the film's intertitles represent direct quotations from Ibsen's poem, constituting 'parts' and 'portions' of the source text.

The first intertitles of *Terje Vigen* coincide with the first, well-known stanzas of the poem: *'Der boede en underlig graaspængd en/paa den yderste nøgne ø'* ('There lived a remarkably grizzled man / on the uttermost, barren isle'.) The presence or materialization of the 'reality' of the literary work, presented in fragments, is a strategy that can be found in other contemporary film adaptations, within both the historical contexts of the Swedish 'golden age' and international Ibsen adaptations. For example in the British-made version of *Ghosts* (1915), the adapters take great liberties with the narrative and do not reproduce any of the dialogue, save for the most famous quote from the play – 'Mother, give me the sun!' ['*Gi meg solen, mor*!'] – represented as an intertitle. Here, the reference to the external 'reality' of the source text is undoubtedly more significant than the function of the intertitle within the narrative of the film. The use of direct quotations implies a notion of 'double authorship' underlining Ibsen's authorial presence. Although not included in the completed film *Terje Vigen*, Sjöström's annotated script reveals how the opening originally comprised a prologue showing Ibsen in his study, sitting at his desk, looking in front of him, and then beginning to write.[6] The image would darken, and then be followed by the intertitle, featuring the first verse of the poem and the first image in the film, displaying the old Terje Vigen alone in his cabin. After this presentation of Terje, the script suggests a return to Ibsen at work, writing, followed by an intertitle declaring in the first person: *'Nu skal jeg fortelle, hvad jeg har hørt / om Terje fra først til sidst'* ('And now, all I've heard about Terje / I'll tell you from first to last',) emphasizing Ibsen's status as the film's narrator, while preserving the integrity of the poem. The British version of *Ghosts* follows a similar strategy by beginning with an image of an actor posing as Ibsen, presented with an accompanying intertitle as 'A lifelike representation of the great poet and dramatist'. The emphasis on the visible presence of the author is characteristic of other adaptations of the period: Jack London personally appeared in prologues to several adaptations of his novels during the 1910s, serving, according to Eileen Bowser, as 'a kind of guarantee of authenticity', a visible proof of the famous author's personal approval of the film adaptation (Bowser 1990: 206).

The notion of Ibsen as narrator, and the intertitles as 'reproductions' or fragments of the implied totality that constitutes the film's source text, is further emphasized by the fact that Ibsen's poem in Norwegian was untranslated in the Swedish version of the film, as well as in the Danish and Norwegian copies premiering at the same time. The Swedish copies were in fact bilingual texts, with Swedish titles stating production details at the beginning and end of each reel, while the titles providing fragments of the poem, and consequently narrative content were in Norwegian.[7] The decision not to translate Ibsen's poetic language in the intertitles underlines the mutual, and thus transnational, intelligibility of Scandinavian languages. On the other hand the preservation of Ibsen's language suggests his literary, poetic value – something untranslatable from one language to another, as well as from one medium to another. Some contemporary Swedish reviews praised the decision to retain Ibsen's text, describing the film images as a stately accompaniment to the stanzas; while others criticized both the strategy of 'detaching the skeleton' of the poem and the attempt to visualize the properties of the work. One critic included a direct quotation from the poem in his review to demonstrate the film's lack of success in recreating Ibsen's deep emotions (Liljedahl 1975: 135).

However, the poem of *Terje Vigen* was associated with specific imagery long before the film was made. A widespread book edition published in 1892, with illustrations by the artist Christian Krohg, created similar combinations of text and image as found in the film. Some of the scenes in Sjöström's adaptation actually attempt to recreate motifs, poses, and compositions from Krohg's illustrations, establishing further intertextual links (plate 1). In the 1920s, narrative intertitles were criticized as symptomatic of a narrative form that was often perceived as 'uncinematic'. One critic in 1921 typically described them as 'those deadly inserts, which read 'Little Mary comes home and tells her father that mother has gone away forever', thereby ruining all the action which follows' (qtd. Elliott 2003: 93). Sjöström's film certainly embraces this strategy, but should perhaps be seen as an attempt to create parallels and affinities between word and image, between literature and cinema, as well as displaying various structural and aesthetic differences between the two media. The surtitles are neither simply 'an illustration of a text' nor 'a commentary on an image', but rather an attempt to show, in Bazin's words that 'text and image are saying the same thing, each however in its own way' by way of echoes and multiplications (Bazin 1967: 140). Perhaps the most striking moment in *Terje Vigen* occurs in the famous line '*Anna, mit barn*!' ['Anna, my child!'], which clearly can be read from the lip movements of the actress before being repeated in written form by an intertitle. The interplay between word and image paradoxically can be read as an interaction between the literary work and cinematic diegesis, as well as functioning as form of dialogue.

In *Terje Vigen*, this kind of combination creates a palimpsestic and elliptical narrative; the fragmented nature of the intertitles are paralleled by a similarly fragmented representation of the spatial, temporal, and causal characteristics of the diegetic reality, continually jumping back and forth in time and space. Hence the relationship between word and image does not function in terms of one illustrating or overlapping the other; rather they represent fragments from two separate 'worlds' forming a cohesive whole through their interaction. The description in an intertitle early in the film of Terje not being able to find ease on land is not represented by images that explicitly display Terje's unrest. Instead, we see a single image of the unruly ocean, which functions both as a metaphorical representation of the protagonist's state of mind, as well as a visualization of where he hopes to be. The next image shows him happily working on a ship in a brief narrative vignette not found in the poem.

The relativity of time and space in the narration of the film is a product of this specific word-image relationship, associated with poetry as a specific structuring principle. This is perhaps most clearly reflected in the use of repetition as a poetic mode, both in the intertitles and in the images. Stanzas are repeated in the intertitles, just as they are in the source text; likewise certain images are repeated throughout the film. However, the repetition of words (i.e., fragments of the textual world) and the repetition of images (i.e., fragments of the diegetic world) occur at different points in the narrative. Sometimes the repetition of images is inspired by the contents of the intertitles (i.e., extracts from the poem); an image of Terje suffering in prison is accompanied by an intertitle reading '*Hans nakke bøide sig, graat blev hans haar / av drømmene om hans hjem*' ('His shoulders rounded, his hair it turned grey / from dreaming about his home') followed by a flashback to Terje's playing with his baby daughter the first time he sees her. This is immediately followed by an image of his daughter, now older, in the arms of his wife; hence moving from Terje's (and the spectators') happy memory to a feeling of loss, as he imagines what his family may look like in his absence.

If the extracts from the poem comprise a mixture of first-person narration, pieces of direct dialogue, descriptions of events, and rhetorical figures, the filmic images are equally varied in tone. Several scenes described briefly in the source text are fleshed out in lengthy, wordless sequences: Terje discovering he has become a father, an emotional farewell to his wife, as well as a number of action sequences at sea. The narrative flow and rhythm of the poem is paralleled visually by the constant flow, variation, and mobility of the all-pervading sea.[8]

Sjöström's film ends with the sign of a cross. This parallels the last verse of the source text – particularly in the way the cross has been clearly placed on a graveyard with the setting sun in the background. It seems appropriate to end a film that explores the signifying, structural, and aesthetic affinities and differences between word and image with a scene that clearly draws attention to the image as 'sign'. Such relationships, taking place on a semiotic as well as intertextual level, were further complicated when the intertitles of the film, initially positioned as 'untranslatable' signs, were adapted and translated for international distribution a few years after the Scandinavian premiere.

9.1.2 Fidelity in reproduction media and languages in translation: *Terje Vigen* becomes *A Man There Was*

In this section, translations of Sjöström's *Terje Vigen* will be discussed in terms of how the transference between languages are entangled with media transpositions between published book editions, intertitles, subtitles, and film programmes. Translations of the film *Terje Vigen* must first and foremost be seen in the light of how the untranslated text in the film version functions as a significant aspect of the film. By maintaining Ibsen's Norwegian in the Swedish film version (as well as in the Danish version) the poem is presented, at least to a Swedish audience, as adaptable but untranslatable, a text that can be transposed into other media, into the visual medium of moving images as well as the written form of intertitles. The unusual choice of retaining the foreign language was possible because of the mutual intelligibility between Scandinavian languages. Ibsen's poem was also read and distributed in its Norwegian form in Sweden. Nevertheless, for Swedish spectators, reading intertitles in Norwegian still impedes the understanding of the narrative, and consequently the presence of the foreign language in the film signals that *fidelity to authenticity* foregrounds *intelligibility*. The foreignness of the poem is particularly evident in the Swedish copies of the film, where only the credits were in Swedish. This polyglot assembly marked a difference between the *poem as literary language* on the one hand, and *paratexts as the language of the film production* on the other, and underscored Svenska Bio's attempts to address an educated middle-class audience and foreground the fetishism of the literary text characteristic of 'golden age' films.[9]

Terje Vigen was not distributed outside of Scandinavia until after World War I, and had its first screening in the United States as late as in 1920. The film, however, became Svenska Bio's greatest success abroad to date.[10] When this seemingly 'untranslatable' film was translated into a number of languages for the international market, the explicit display of differences between language and media transpositions was lost.

The mutual exclusion of translation (the retention of the Norwegian text in the intertitles) and adaptation (the transformation of the poem into cinematic form) can be seen in the light of the broader context of the relationship between media and literature. Friedrich Kittler argues that in the discursive networks of media reproduction, language and meaning are replaced by inscriptions of voice and body movements, hearing and sight; such shifts affect our understanding of translation as transference of meaning from one language into another:

> A medium is a medium is a medium. Therefore it cannot be translated. To transfer messages from one medium into another always evolves reshaping them to conform to new standards and materials. In a discourse network that requires an 'awareness of the abysses which divide the one order of sense experience into the other', transposition necessarily takes the place of translation. (Kittler 1990: 265)

Following Kittler's line of reasoning, cinematic translation is, on the level of media inscription, a conspicuous example of how translation 'invents' a new language as the changed conditions of the new media inscription reshape the utterance. In translations of a film, the two languages, one represented through sound, the other through the image, are synchronically or diachronically represented. This is aptly described by Robert Stam as a 'bifurcated' and 'interlingual film experience' (Stam 1989: 60).[11] Compared to the monomedial translation of literature from source text into target text, cinematic translation combines translation with media transposition, and makes the spectator aware of the translation process in the act of viewing.

With respect to the intermedial aspects of silent film, Abé Mark Nornes argues that the intertitle as 'phonocentric' writing (a reproduction of oral speech) allowed relatively free translation practices; this was partly due to 'an alternative phonocentrism in the silence of a silent film', a phonocentricity that connects the written title to the unheard voice of the actor and obstructs the vocal neutrality of the written word and the language equivalence of translation (Nornes 2007: 101). Intertitles thus represent a form of writing where the graphical or visual dimension is accentuated, at the same time as being 'phonocentric', to use Nornes' terminology.

The oratorical dimension of *Terje Vigen* (in Ong's sense of the term as writing reproducing oral speech (Ong 1996: 45)), entails that the voice of the actor/character is overshadowed by the voice of the author/narrator: as mentioned, the film contains relatively few dialogue titles. To understand the processes of translation across media, we must extend the idea of the 'bifurcated' text to include the relationship between the intertitles and the poem. The translated film is bilingual in specific instances of speech representation, translations of moments such as when the intertitle reads the line '*Anna mit barn*!' ('Anna my child!'), as previously mentioned, followed by a close-up of the actress visibly pronouncing these words. This exception of repeated speech representation is, however, significant for a broader understanding of the film's discourse on fidelity: as an often quoted phrase it points back to what can be an assumed shared reading experience for a selected audience, and thus to the literary text as backdrop for the cinematic viewing experience.

9.1.3 International distribution, case 1: translated intertitles

In the 1910s, Ibsen was one of the world's most famous authors, and this was used as a selling point with regard to the marketing of some of the film adaptations of his well-known plays.[12] However, *Terje Vigen*, and Ibsen's poetry in general, was little known to a broader audience outside Scandinavia. A critic of the *New York Times* wrote in a review of the film: 'the original [poem] is not widely known in this country and one who has not read it cannot say how much of it has been preserved in the motion picture' ('On the Screen' 1920). The same review still labelled the English translation a 'travesty' of Ibsen's poem. For an international audience, the awareness of a literary source text as a precursor to the cinematic 'travesty' was more abstract and relied on a general notion of Ibsen's work and adaptations of literary classics; the 'original' was hence more of an idea, something imagined, rather than an actual, recognized text for comparing.

It is significant that the English translation of the intertitles of *Terje Vigen* was carried out exclusively for the film; they were not based on any published English translations of Ibsen's poem (according to the preserved intertitle list, the translator for the film was Edward Adams-Ray, a teacher, writer, and translator).[13] The Norwegian National Library's international Ibsen bibliography lists five translations into English of *Terje Vigen* made before 1920 (Ibsen 2011). The listing, however, does not include Adams-Ray's translation used in the intertitles of English-language copies of Sjöström's film. The absence in the bibliography is perhaps telling of how translations of intertitles, when archiving and organizing cultural heritage, do not fall under the category of 'literature'; they are, of course, unpublished and perceived as integral parts of adaptations into another medium and are therefore unlisted as official translations.

The translated intertitles are also lost in the contemporary DVD editions of the film (published by the Norwegian and Swedish national film institutes), where the Norwegian intertitles have subtitles. The contemporary subtitles rather return to the source text by reproducing an authorized translation of the poem, contrary to the film copies that were screened in the silent period. These two DVD editions have different soundtracks; however, the translated (i.e., subtitled) intertitles from Norwegian in both editions comprise excerpts from the Ibsen scholar and translator John Northam's translation of the poem from the 1980s (Ibsen 1986). At the end of the film in the Norwegian DVD edition we are even told that the subtitles originate from a translation of the poem by Northam published several decades after the film's release. This translation corresponds in no way to the translations in circulation at the time when the film was first screened. Contemporary subtitles consequently return to the poem as an integral part of the film and therefore, on some level, come closer to the intersections between film and poem in the Scandinavian versions of the film. However, Kino Video's U.S release from 2008 actually features English-language intertitles (rather than subtitles) that recreate Adams-Ray's translations of the film. The emphasis on literary versus cinematic traditions and authorship in the different DVD editions is also visible in the film selection: the Norwegian DVD box set is a collection of Ibsen adaptations while the edition from the Swedish Film Institute include other films from the Swedish 'golden age'. The American edition takes an *auteurist* approach, as it also includes *Ingeborg Holm* (1913), another film by Victor Sjöström.

The choice of translating the intertitles of *Terje Vigen* exclusively for the film was not exceptional. The same disregard of published translations pertains to all contemporary translations of the Swedish 'golden age' adaptations. The intertitles of *Körkarlen* (*The Phantom Carriage,* Sjöström, 1921), for instance – to name perhaps the most prominent example of an adaptation from the Swedish silent era – include recognizable, well-known literal citations from the novel by Selma Lagerlöf on which the film was based (just as in the Ibsen adaptation, the novel's first sentence corresponds to the first intertitle of the film). The translation consequently does not allow the potential recognition from a reading experience prior to the film viewing. The deviations from the source text in the translations point towards a more flexible relationship between source and target texts.

9.1.4 International distribution, case 2: media transpositions

The most significant differences between an authorized published translation and the translation from the intertitles appear, seemingly paradoxically, when the poem from the intertitles is transposed into yet another medium, namely the film programme. Under the title 'A Man There Was'. Founded on the famous work, 'Terje Viken' by Henrik Ibsen', a British film programme preserved at the Swedish Film Institute presents the reduced version of the poem (i.e., the parts included in the intertitles) as if it were the whole poem (plate 2).[14] In contrast to Scandinavian programmes, in which prose sections fill in the parts of the poem that are not included in the poem,[15] the English programmes are less respectful to the form of this 'original' and present the shortened text as a poem in itself. The title of the 'poem' in the programme (pointing out that the text is 'founded on the famous work Terje Viken') still indicates that the printed poem is an adaptation; the presentation together with the title constitutes an equivocal notion of the relationship between source text and adaptation.

The most notable difference between the text presented in the programme and the poem is the revision of the length of the stanzas, corresponding to the way the poem is presented in the intertitles. The poem is divided into forty-five stanzas of nine lines each. The intertitles, and the poem in the translated English programme, contain almost the same amount of stanzas (forty-one) but are divided into shorter stanzas of two to five lines each. This means that the poem's stanzas have been (adjusted to the format of the intertitle) separated into two or three parts. As the poem develops, the translation increasingly frees itself from the source text: following the presentation in the intertitles the stanzas are of varying length (two, three, four, or five lines), which of course modifies the rhythm. The rhyming structure, even when the rhymes faithfully correspond to the source text, changes through the fragmented form (for instance, sometimes two lines extracted from the middle of a stanza of the poem stand out for the stanza in the intertitles).

The poem in the programme does not entirely reverse the adaptation process (intertitles transferred into poem). Instead, the programme presents an amalgamated version of the poem as it borrows much of its iconography from the style and form of intertitles: the poem is framed by an ornamental frame decorated with a torch on each side of the frame and decorative stripes forming a rosette on the top of each page. Such framing devices are, as discussed by Kamilla Elliott (Elliott 2003), common in intertitles and are traces of the aesthetic struggle between image and words in intertitles as an intermedial phenomenon; framings, decorations, and images on the intertitle card might be considered as a means to render the written text of the intertitle iconic and cinematographic. The film programme moreover includes other media transpositions as the poem is followed by a prose version of the story illustrated by images of the film and quotes from the intertitles of the poem. The film programme (as both cinematically multimedial and simultaneously literary) negotiates these media borders. These programmes are, in addition, strikingly similar to the illustrated editions of the poem, in which writing is combined with illustrations, and therefore serve as documentation on how the various adaptations of the poem into the new medium of film point back to an inherent multimedial dimension of the literary source text.

The translation, when regarded as a process of media transposition, problematizes and negotiates the notion of fidelity versus infidelity, as well as media specificity and transmediality. Translations of the films and the film programmes are, moreover, entangled with questions of cinematic representation of language, of the 'phonocentric' or 'iconic' aspects of intertitles. There is a chiastic, seemingly paradoxical movement between film and literature: the transference into film amplifies literality by foregrounding the author's words, that is, his 'voice' or writing, and, simultaneously the film interprets the poem as both cinematic, multimedial, oral, or non-literary.

9.2 Conclusion

In this chapter we have examined how Victor Sjöström's film adaptation of Henrik Ibsen's poem *Terje Vigen* actualizes a number of questions of fidelity, both with regard to different forms of textual adaptation, and intermedial and linguistic transformation and translation processes. Sjöström's film shows a very specific and coherent adaptation strategy: there is a faithfulness to the literary and linguistic properties of the source material in combination with double narration and material separation between word and image, between intertitles and film images, and between a textual and a diegetic reality. Just as the use of Ibsen's language creates the impression of untranslatability from one language to another, the film displays an impossibility of translation between word and image, between one medium and another.

However, although any direct, straightforward translation or reproduction between the two material levels of the film do not take place, they nevertheless inform and interact with one another, creating (often non-synchronous) transpositions and transformations with regard to narrative structure (the fragmented, elliptical, non-linear narration, the use of repetition), as well as other expressive aspects of the artwork, demonstrating and exploring not only the differences between different media or textual and material levels, but also their similarities and affinities.

We have examined *Terje Vigen* with regard to the three different notions of *fidelity* (relating to literary precursor, reproduction media, and languages in translation), and demonstrated how these specific notions interact and intersect with each other. The transpositions of adaptation between media (from poem to film, poem to illustration, illustration to film) are entangled with processes of linguistic transposition between languages, since filmic translation functions as a combination or amalgamation of these transpositions. Translation and adaptation might seem to be opposed, but together they rather negotiate and problematize notions of fidelity and 'originality'.

The film programme and the translation of intertitles become conspicuous examples of these different processes of transposition, translation, and negotiation. These types of material are not often discussed as part of an aesthetic reading. However, this analysis has shown how the question of the relation between the arts exposed in adaptation processes is not only related to entities such as a film adaptation and its literary source, but also to various other levels of media inscription.

Notes

1 For a number of examples of recent musical adaptations of Ibsen's poem and Sjöström's film, see 'Terje Vijen is Music'. http://www.ibsen.net/index.gan?id=11159434&subid=0 (accessed May 16, 2011).

2 See Uricchio 1993, Carou 2002, and Buchanan 2009.

3 See also Liljedahl 1975: 254f.

4 For a detailed analysis of the relationship between word and image and the narrative function of intertitles in Sjöström's earlier film, *Trädgårdsmästaren* (1912), see Fullerton 1997.

5 The poem had, however, also been adapted for the screen in 1911, by the German company Deutsche Bioscop-Gesellschaft.

6 Sjöström's annotated script, Swedish Film Institute library collections.

7 Original title cards, Swedish Film Institute library collections.

8 See also Thomas Leitch's analysis of D.W. Griffith's *The Unchanging Sea* (1910), loosely based on the poem 'The Three Fishers' by Charles Kingsley for a discussion of related, but also quite different, strategies for adapting a poem for the screen, including narrativization, repetition, and the use of direct citations in intertitles. (Leitch 2007: 43 ff.)

9 The preserved intertitle cards for the Swedish distribution copies at the Swedish Film Institute include both intertitles with the credits in Swedish and in Norwegian.

10 The company sold 43 copies of the film to foreign markets (including Denmark, Norway, Finland, Belgium, Britain, France, Holland, Italy, Russia, Switzerland, Spain, Germany, Austria, USA, Egypt, India, and Japan.

11 Stam originally writes about subtitling, but the description is adequate also for other forms of translation.

12 Under the rubric 'Advertising Ideas', a review in the *New York Dramatic Mirror* of an adaptation of *A Doll's House* (Maurice Tourneur, 1917) states: 'The fact that Ibsen's 'Doll's House' has been played throughout the country by the most famous stars on the American stage should make the film attraction one of wide popularity', recommending exhibitors to mention Ibsen's name in their marketing ('A Doll's House' 1917: 682).

13 English intertitle text list for *Terje Vigen*, Swedish Film Institute library collections.

14 Exploitation book published by the United Kingdom branch of Nordisk Film Co., Ltd. in London, Swedish Film Institute library collections.

15 See e.g., exploitation book for the Danish market published by Svenska Biografteatern, Swedish Film Institute library collections.

Bibliography

(1917) 'A Doll's House' *New York Dramatic Mirror*, April 28: 682.

Bachmann-Medick, Doris (ed.) (2009). 'The Translational Turn' (Special Issue). *Translation Studies* 2(1). London and New York: Routledge.

Bazin, André (1967a). 'In Defense of Mixed Cinema'. In *What is Cinema? Vol. 1*, Hugh Gray (ed. and trans.) 53–75. Berkeley, Los Angeles and London: University of California Press.

— (1967b). '*Le Journal d'un Curé de Campagne* and the Stylistics of Robert Bresson'. In *What is Cinema? Vol. 1*, ed. and trans. Hugh Gray. 125–43. Berkeley, Los Angeles and London: University of California Press.

Bowser, Eileen (1990). *The Transformation of Cinema, 1907–1915*. Berkeley, Los Angeles and London: University of California Press.

Bruno, Giuliana (2002). *Atlas of Emotion: Journeys in Art, Architecture, and Film*. London and New York: Verso.

Buchanan, Judith (2009). *Shakespeare on Silent Film: An Excellent Dumb Discourse*. Cambridge: Cambridge University Press.

Carou, Alain (2002). *Le Cinéma Français et les Écrivains: Histoire d'une Rencontre, 1906–1914*. Paris: AFRHC/Écoles de Chartres.

Elliott, Kamilla (2003). *Rethinking the Novel/Film Debate*. Cambridge and New York: Cambridge University Press.

Florin, Bo (1997). *Den nationella stilen: studier i den svenska filmens guldålder*. Stockholm: Aura, 1997.

— (2003). *Regi: Victor Sjöström /Directed by Victor Sjöström*. Stockholm: Cinemateket/ Svenska Filminsitutet.

Fullerton, John (1997). 'Relationen Mellan Text och bild i en Förklassisk Svensk Film'. *Aura: Filmvetenskaplig Tidskrift* 3(1–2): 45–87.

Hansen, Karin Synnøve (1992). *Henrik Ibsen 1828–1992: en Filmografi*. Oslo: Norsk Filminstitutt.

Ibsen, Henrik (2011). 'An International Ibsen Bibliography'. http://www.nb.no/baser/ibsen/english.html (accessed March 25, 2011).

— (1986). *Poems*, trans. John Northam. Oslo: Scandinavian University Press.

Idestam-Almquist, Bengt (1952). *Classics of the Swedish Cinema: the Stiller & Sjöström Period*. Stockholm: Svenska Filminstitutet.

King, Rob (2009). '1914: Movies and Cultural Hierarchy'. In *American Cinema of the 1910s: Themes and Variations*. Charlie Keil and Ben Singer (eds), 115–36. New Brunswick and London: Rutgers University Press.

Kittler, Friedrich (1990). *Discourse Networks 1800/1900*. Stanford: Stanford University Press.

La Tour, Claire Dupré (2005). 'Intertitles and Titles'. In *Encyclopedia of Early Cinema*. Richard Abel (ed.), 82–91. London and New York: Routledge.

Leitch, Thomas (2007). *Film Adaptation and its Discontents: From Gone with the Wind to The Passion of the Christ*. Baltimore: The Johns Hopkins University Press.

Liljedahl, Elisabeth (1975). *Stumfilmen i Sverige – Kritik och Debatt: Hur Samtiden Värderade den nya Konstarten*. Stockholm: Proprius förlag.

Moi, Toril (2006). *Henrik Ibsen and the Birth of Modernism: Art, Theatre, Philosophy*. Oxford and New York: Oxford University Press.

Nornes, Abé Mark (2007). *Cinema Babel: Translating Global Cinema*. Minneapolis and London: University of Minnesota Press.

Ong, Walter J. (1996). *Orality and Literacy: The Technologizing of the Word*. New York and London: Routledge.

(1920) 'On the Screen' *New York Times*, April 26: B1.

Stam, Robert (1989). *Subversive Pleasures: Bakhtin, Cultural Criticism, and Film*. Baltimore and London: Johns Hopkins University Press.

'Terje Vijen is Music'. http://www.ibsen.net/index.gan?id=11159434&subid=0 (accessed May 16, 2011).

Thompson, Kristin (1985). 'The Formulations of the Classical Narrative'. In *The Classical Hollywood Cinema: Film Style & Mode of Production to 1960*. David Bordwell, Janet Staiger and Kristin Thompson (eds), 194–213. London: Routledge.

Uricchio, William and Pearson, Roberta E. (1993). *Reframing Culture: The Case of the Vitagraph Quality Films*. Princeton: Princeton University Press.

Chapter 10

Les Liaisons Dangeureuses à l'Anglais: Examining Traces of 'European-ness' in *Cruel Intentions, Dangerous Liaisons* and *Valmont*

Sarah Artt

Choderlos de Laclos's novel *Les Liaisons Dangeureuses*, first published in 1782, has frequently been adapted for the large and small screen. As a book, its epistolary format has a secretive, gossipy quality that has proved consistently appealing to readers; as a story, it continues to fascinate with its portrait of cold-hearted sexual intrigue that seems to translate easily from France's Ancien Régime to New York's Upper East Side. This chapter examines three prominent English-language film adaptations: Stephen Frears's *Dangerous Liaisons* (1988), Milos Forman's *Valmont* (1989), and Roger Kumble's *Cruel Intentions* (1999) and the ways in which they intersect with the epistolary form of the novel. In critical discussion, these three films do not tend to be considered as texts that are both adaptations *and* translations. Frears' *Dangerous Liaisons* is based on the play *Les Liaisons Dangereuses* by Christopher Hampton (who also adapted the screenplay), which was first performed in 1985 by the Royal Shakespeare Company. Hampton's text was itself based on a translation of the Laclos novel from French into English. In *Valmont* the screenplay by Forman and Jean-Claude Carrière was also based on the French novel. Some ten years after the release of the Frears and Forman films, Roger Kumble's screenplay for *Cruel Intentions* re-situates the story of *Les Liaisons Dangeureuses* in the world of over-privileged teenagers on New York's Upper East Side: while the film acknowledges its debt to Choderlos de Laclos's novel in the credits, much of the European references characteristic of Forman's and Frears' films are removed. To understand how all three films work with their source texts, we might usefully begin by examining the relationship between 'translation' and 'adaptation', as expressed in recent theoretical interventions. In his article 'Between the Cat and the Devil: Adaptation Studies and Translation Studies' (2009), John Milton is particularly concerned with texts that undergo 'an interlingual transfer or translation [that] will move it to another language . . . [and] there may also be an intersemiotic transfer, from page to stage or celluloid . . '. (Milton 2009: 58). These films are 'adaptations', in the sense that they are based on a classic novel, but they can also be considered 'translations' of a French source text; in Milton's formulation, they have been subject to an 'interlingual transfer'. This notion of a text being an 'adaptation', as well as a 'translation', challenges many of the notions put forward by other theorists. The *Encyclopedia of Translation Studies* defines an 'adaptation' as 'a text that is *not generally accepted* as a translation but is nevertheless recognized as representing a source text. As such, the term may embrace numerous vague notions such as appropriation, domestication, imitation, rewriting, and so on' (Bastin 2009: 3 emphasis mine). Such terms as 'appropriation', 'rewriting', and 'domestication' have all been employed in adaptation studies to describe the process of textual transformation. While some translation studies scholars are keen to distinguish translations from adaptations, there are others who acknowledge adaptation as 'one type of intervention on the part of translations, among which a distinction must be made between 'deliberate interventions' and deviations from literality' (Bastin 2009: 3). However, Bastin does not acknowledge that texts can be simultaneously identified as adaptations *and* translations. Even Milton is at pains to point out 'the lack of awareness and analysis of the interlingual element in the adaptation of plays, films and novels [. . .] [and how he sees this as largely the result of the fact that] Adaptation Studies are the offshoot of monolingual departments of English Literature, Drama Studies, Film Studies and Music Studies' (2009: 47–8). On this view, a 'translation' only becomes a 'translation' when it incorporates an interlingual element; hence it is fundamentally different from an 'adaptation'. While the focus of this chapter is on the English-language adaptations of *Les Liaisons Dangeureuses*, I will show how the films can also be seen as 'translations' in the sense that they incorporate intralingual transformations that occur alongside adaptations from page to screen.

In his article on Forman's *Valmont* and Frears' *Dangerous Liaisons*, Russell Ganim shows how 'letters in these films represent the sophisticated, if not literary aspects of libertine thought and action. In doing so, they suggest, in a visually discursive way, a certain elegance in a set of relationships characterized by abuse and domination' (Ganim 217). While *Dangerous Liaisons* and *Valmont* preserve the eighteenth century French setting, they follow the majority of adaptations derived from printed texts (particularly those with historic settings in which correspondence constitutes an intrinsic part of the narrative) by having most of the exchanges taking place face-to-face, rather than through an exchange of letters. The Marquise de Merteuil's clipped declaration of war in Letter CLIII is transformed into a chilling verbal and physical performance by Glenn Close and Annette Bening in *Dangerous Liaisons* and *Valmont,* respectively. This (which in Laclos' text is simply written at the bottom of Valmont's letter) is so rapid and terse that it does not even deserve its own separate missive. It marks a departure from Merteuil's normally elaborate, evasive prose; here, she is direct. Both Close and Bening relish the opportunity to deliver a performance that is tinged with gleeful anger that simultaneously evokes the force of the written text and the social implication of the swift response, lacking any conventional greetings or compliments.

To emphasize the historical significance of the letter as a means of communication, Frears' and Forman make substantial use of voice-over accompanying a low angle shot of a character reading a letter. This adaptive technique is very different from Martin Scorsese's film of Edith Wharton's *The Age of Innocence* (1993), which highlights certain phrases in a letter through the use of an iris, and shown in close-up. In Frears' and Forman's films the mere presence of the letter as object, or the voice of the reader or writer is sufficient to create a cinematic representation of Laclos' correspondence.

While *Cruel Intentions* draws on what would appear to be the logical substitute for the letter form in late 1990s America – email – its attitude towards it is somewhat dismissive. When Ronald Clifford (Sean Patrick Thomas) – the transposed Danceny character – is forbidden to communicate with Cécile (Selma Blair), Katherine de Merteuil (Sarah Michelle Gellar) and her stepbrother Sebastian Valmont (Ryan Phillippe) give him the following advice: 'email is for geeks and paedophiles; write her a letter'. In place of Valmont's substantial correspondence with Merteuil, we witness many private exchanges between the two step-siblings that recall the performances of Glenn Close and John Malkovich in *Dangerous Liaisons,* but are reinterpreted for a teenage audience. The fact that Sebastian appears to have his own study in the family apartment recalls the eighteenth century, where 'a place for writing desk and books [. . .] had special social significance for the increasingly leisured middle and upper classes' (Pidduck 2004: 54). His leisurely lifestyle is also evident in the way he writes his leather-bound journal (derided by Katherine as 'queer'). At the film's conclusion, photocopies of the journal are distributed to all the members of Sebastian's social set – that is, the students at the private school which Katherine, Sebastian, Cécile, and Annette (the transposed Madame de Tourvel character) attend. This 'publication' discredits Katherine in a way that recalls the Marquise's public humiliation at the opera in *Dangerous Liaisons,* and her more lurid destruction in Laclos' novel: disfigurement after contracting smallpox.

Dangerous Liaisons engages in a kind of fetishization of the letter as object through its constant deployment of the physical representation of letters – the title itself appears on screen as a letter being opened and then revealed to the camera (paralleling techniques we see used in films where letters are also of paramount importance, such as Max Ophuls' *Letter from an Unknown Woman* (1948), as well as *The Age of Innocence*). However, Frears' film differs in the way it treats the act of letter writing; rather than 'giv[ing] visual expression to retrospective forms of bounded subjectivity [. . .] [and] evok[ing] qualities of interiority, deep feeling and desire' (Vidal 2006: 423), letters constitute a Sadeian narrative of ruthless manipulation, sexual intrigue, and betrayal. Even those moments when the emotions expressed in a letter are read as sincere (as Tourvel (Michelle Pfeiffer) reads Valmont's (John Malkovich's) initial declarations of love and admiration) the reader/viewer is already aware that Valmont's letter is an emotional ruse. Examples of this in the film include the letter Valmont writes to Tourvel, using the courtesan Emilie (Laura Benson) as his desk (Letter XLVII), or the letters Valmont dictates to Cécile (Uma Thurman) (such as letter CXVII) intended for Danceny (Keanu Reeves).

The letters in Laclos' novel, in *Dangerous Liaisons, Valmont,* and *Cruel Intentions* are transgressive in several ways. While the letters are supposedly private, the reader or viewer enjoys the *frisson* of discovering their forbidden contents. This sensation is magnified on the cinema screen, a very public act of display that contrasts with the private act of reading. In all three adaptations the very private act of letter-writing is transformed into something put on show for public display – a strategy very different from the Laclos novel. At the same time the adaptations acknowledge the 'secret' act of writing: while Sebastian in *Cruel Intentions has* a reputation that circulates via the very public act of gossip, he also chronicles his adventures in detail in his diary, which creates a tantalizingly secret text (much like the letters of the novel) that is only revealed at the end of the story. Not only has he written about Cécile and Annette, he has also described Katherine's true character. Katherine, like her eighteenth-century predecessors, knows she must observe social conventions in order to maintain her position of social influence and power, which is why she is at pains to be seen as religiously devout and conscious of sexual reputation. The Marquise de Merteuil in both *Dangerous Liaisons* and *Valmont* is also depicted as carrying out her own clandestine romances; her house is seen to contain a secret bedroom concealed behind mirrored doors in *Dangerous Liaisons*, while the '*petit maison*' we see in *Valmont* functions as a separate establishment exclusively for romantic assignations. In *Cruel Intentions* Katherine is also discovered concealing Ronald under her bed. The Merteuil character's ghoulish joy in attempting to arrange Cécile's defloration in all the texts is therefore understandable – here she is permitted the masculine privilege of watching and chronicling the path of desire – something she cannot do in relation to her own conquests.

So far we have looked at the ways in which the films adapt the Laclos text for the cinema screen, focusing in particular on the ways in which the private act of letter writing is transformed for the very public act of witnessing the film on the screen. However, what renders these adaptations more interesting is the way in which they incorporate intralingual elements; in other words, trying to find 'translations' for a text originally published in French for English-speaking audiences. The recording of the act in some form is therefore the greatest achievement in this text. Certainly video recording is used to great effect in lieu of a letter in *Cruel Intentions*, when Katherine is seen viewing footage from a hidden camera to observe the progress of the illicit romance between Cécile and her music teacher Ronald. This forms a visual parallel with the built-in voyeur masks we see in Forman's *Valmont* in Merteuil's '*petit maison*' where Merteuil and her maid observe Cécile and Danceny; curiously, Katherine never uses this secret footage to reveal the relationship to Cécile's mother. Instead, she simply reveals her suspicion that Cécile and Ronald may be involved in a relationship and the knowledge that Cécile keeps Ronald's letters hidden under her doll's house. Cécile's mother then confronts Cécile and Ronald, ending the relationship on the grounds of her own racial prejudice (Ronald is played by African American actor Sean Patrick Thomas).

One of the other reasons that English language adaptations of foreign works (and *Les Liaisons Dangeureuses* in particular) are infrequently considered as 'cross-cultural' adaptations is because they often tend to be subsumed under the category of the costume film or the heritage film. As Andrew Higson points out in his book *English Heritage, English Cinema*: 'heritage is an attitude towards the legacy of the past [. . .] heritage as a discourse and practice is fascinated by artefacts, ideas, and the like inherited from the past' (Higson 2003: 53). Julianne Pidduck writes that: 'costume suggests the pleasures and possibilities of masquerade – the construction, constraint and display of the body through clothes [. . .] costume is inextricable from historical discourses of the self, and costume drama's play of identity and masquerade retrospectively explores Western subjectivity through the characters of the nineteenth century novel [. . .] if drama suggests the intensification of everyday life, then costume film plays out vivid episodes within the frame of the past' (2004: 4). With so much discourse already circulating about notions of heritage and costume, particularly within British publications on adaptation studies, it is no wonder that the additional context of whose past, whose culture has infrequently come in for examination (unless of course it is the English-speaking past of Britain and America). When we write about costume film, we may then consider a film like *Untold Scandal/Joseon Namnyeo Sangyeoljisa* (Dir. Je-yong Lee, 2003) alongside Frears' or Forman's versions without concerning ourselves with issues of translation. But this issue of translation is an important one in these adaptations, expressed not just at the level of dialogue, but in terms of performance.

In both *Valmont* and *Dangerous Liaisons*, American actors and their accents are set off against the elaborate location and manners of the European setting. In a way, their Americanness sets them apart, particularly John Malkovich who makes his Valmont utterly mercenary – so much so that it is difficult to imagine him as transformed by the love of Tourvel. Forman's *Valmont* is interesting in this respect in its mix of British and American actors – Annette Bening as Merteuil and Colin Firth as Valmont. Bening's American-ness renders her Mertueil decorously observant of social forms, concealing her true brittleness and ruthlessness, while Firth's Englishness renders him plausibly romantic and rakish rather than coldly cruel.

While the story belongs to the past and to a particularly decadent period in European history, even the films that retain the story's historical setting translate it for an Anglo-American sensibility through performance. This is nowhere more in evidence than in the Frears film and the central performances of Glenn Close and John Malkovich as Merteuil and Valmont. While *Cruel Intentions* and *Valmont* signal their European credentials through elaborate *mise-en-scène,* Frears' film transcends its historical setting with two terrifyingly contemporary central performances. This would not of course have been possible without the notoriety that Close achieved with her performance in the controversial *Fatal Attraction* (released in 1987, a year before *Les Liaisons Dangereuses*). Her psychotic man-eater Alex Forrest (the horror version of the independent career woman who threatens the domestic bliss of the man with whom she has a brief affair) mapped perfectly onto the even more ruthless Marquise de Merteuil – an independent woman who fiercely expresses her reasons for never remarrying: '*c'est uniquement pour que personne n'ait le droit de trouver à redire à mes actions*' ['it was solely because I would not allow anyone the right to criticize my actions'] (De Laclos 2002: 345). John Malkovich as Valmont delivered the role as a kind of mercenary of seduction – a performance that would characterize his later work as Gilbert Osmond in Jane Campion's film *The Portrait of a Lady* (1996) or as Tom Ripley in *Ripley's Game* (Dir. Liliana Cavani, 2002).

Sometimes the adaptations deliberately refer to issues of translation in the screenplay. There is an intriguing moment in *Cruel Intentions* where Annette and Sebastian (Tourvel and Valmont) greet one another in French and kiss on the cheek, which immediately prefaces Annette's first moment of surrender to Sebastian as they embrace on a picnic rug. Here the French language and customs are explicitly associated with forceful seduction: *Cruel Intentions* knowingly references the source text, while updating it to a contemporary New York setting. By contrast in *Valmont* and *Dangerous Liaisons*, France and the French language are lightly evoked: the French names and titles (Marquise, Vicomte, even Madame) often appear anachronistic in spite of the period setting. I am reminded of a particularly interesting passage from Edith Wharton's novel *The Age of Innocence* (1920), which describes an experience of the opera: 'an unalterable and unquestioned law of the musical world required that the German text of French operas sung by Swedish artists should be translated into Italian *for the clearer understanding of English-speaking audiences*' (Wharton 2003: 4, emphasis mine). Both *Valmont* and *Dangerous Liaisons* translate Laclos's novel – both in terms of dialogue and performance-styles, into an Anglo-American idiom for a global audience.

To understand how this process of translation works, we might compare these adaptations with one of the few French language film adaptations of Laclos's novel: Roger Vadim's *Les Liaisons Dangeureuses 1960/Dangerous Liaisons 1960* (1959), which is set among the French bourgeoisie in the late 1950s and stars Jeanne Moreau. The familiar source text is evoked in the title, in the placing of a quotation after the title, and in the retention of key character names (Valmont, Cécile de Volanges, Danceny, Merteuil). However, here the Merteuil figure is adapted to become Juliette (Moreau), Valmont's wife who tolerates *and* encourages his infidelities provided he does not fall in love. Juliette is coldly scheming – orchestrating the humiliation of her former lover Jerry Court (Nicolas Vogel), who is set to marry the seemingly pure and ideal French *jeune fille* Cécile (Jeanne Valérie). While letters feature, they are accompanied by telephone conversations, telegrams, and even a reel-to-reel tape recorder which Danceny (Jean-Louis Trintignant) uses to send messages to Cécile. Valmont's correspondence with Juliette most frequently takes the traditional format of a letter accompanied by his voice-over. The fate of Marianne, the Madame de Tourvel figure (Annette Vadim) is Ophelia-esque – she appears to run mad on learning of Valmont's accidental death. Juliette's fate references that of the Marquise de Merteuil in Laclos' novel – in Vadim's film she accidentally burns herself attempting to destroy the incriminating correspondence and must appear in court with half her face scarred where an onlooker comments '*elle porte son âme sur son visage*' ['she wears her soul upon her face'] (my translation). Vadim's film adapts Laclos' book into a contemporary idiom, even to the extent of including an American character. However, the film does not attempt to translate the French dialogue and performances into an American idiom: Jerry speaks accented French and very little English. More recently in 2003, a lavish Franco-Canadian co-production was made for television starring Catherine Deneuve, Rupert Everett, and Leelee Sobieski. In this case all the actors – including those from Britain and America – spoke French. Interestingly no attempt was made to translate the film for an English-speaking audience: the production was (rather unusually) dubbed for English-speaking markets rather than subtitled, and current North American DVDs of the series have only English dubbed dialogue.

The process of translating European texts into an Anglo-American idiom, both in terms of dialogue and performance-style through the vehicle of the remake, has become more widespread in recent years: for example, the current U.S. television series *The Killing* (2011–), which is based on the Danish text *Forbrydelsen* (2007–). The case of *Les Liaisons Dangeureuses* is slightly different – in *Dangerous Liaisons* and *Valmont*, the French setting is maintained, and the shift in cultural context comes from the language and the actors' performances. In *Cruel Intentions*, there are gestures towards the source text's linguistic and cultural origins that remain in the *mise-en-scène* and in limited linguistic examples, such as the exchange in French between Sebastian and Annette.

There is further work to be done here on the ways in which translation works in an adaptation, in linguistic terms as well as in terms of gesture and performance-style. The appeal of Laclos' source text is worthy of further investigation (particularly in terms of the relatively small number of French language screen adaptations, as well as its recent Korean adaptation), as it seems to lend itself to both adaptive and translational strategies, while appearing particularly attractive to a generation rediscovering the epistolary format through email, Twitter, Facebook, and RSS that allows them to read and follow chains of information and comments. *Les Liaisons Dangereuses* is a fascinating text that underlines the importance of considering both adaptational and translational issues in looking at its various journeys from page to screen.

Bibliography

Baker, Mona and Saldanha, Gabriel (eds) (2009). *Routledge Encyclopedia of Translation Studies* (2nd edn). London and New York: Routledge.

Bastin, Georges L. (2009). 'Adaptation'. In *Routledge Encyclopedia of Translation Studies* (2nd edn). Mona Baker and Gabriel Saldanha (eds), 3–6. London and New York: Routledge.

De Laclos, Choderlos (1962). *Les Liaisons Dangeureuses.* Paris: Librarie Générale Française, 2002.

Ganim, Russell (2009). 'Intercourse as Discourse: The Calculus of Objectification and Desire in the Novel and Film Versions of *Les Liaisons Dangeureuses*'. *Neohelicon* 30(1): 209–33.

Higson, Andrew (2003). *English Heritage, English Cinema.* Oxford: Oxford University Press.

Milton, John (2009). 'Between the Cat and the Devil: Adaptation Studies and Translation Studies'. *Journal of Adaptation in Film and Performance* 2(1): 47–64.

Pidduck, Julianne (2004). *Contemporary Costume Film.* London: British Film Institute.

Vidal, Belen (2006). 'Labyrinths of Loss: the Letter as Figure of Desire and Deferral in the Literary Film'. *Journal of European Studies* 36(4): 418–36.

Wharton, Edith (2003). *The Age of Innocence.* Candace Waid (ed.). New York and London: W. W. Norton and Co.

Chapter 11

Turnips or Sweet Potatoes . . .?

Kate Eaton

Las tinieblas de la escena [. . .] Esta frase no es una mera metáfora; por el contrario, quiero expresar con ella que todo autor teatral se mueve en las tinieblas y es que solamente tanteado en ellas que podrá desempeñarse. Ya que el teatro es sinónimo de Magia; hay que adivinar por medio de la percepción mágica esas cuantas verdades que habitan en el cuerpo-teatro [. . .] Es decir que el teatro es nosotros mismos y solo eso. La única diferencia entre nuestro cuerpo de carne y hueso y nuestro cuerpo-teatro es que el primero es un sujeto pasivo y el segundo es un sujeto activo.

(*Piñera 1984: 57*)

[The darkness of the stage [. . .] This phrase isn't merely a metaphor; on the contrary, what I mean by it is that every theatrical writer moves in the shadows and it is only by groping about in them that he can achieve something. Given that theatre is synonymous with magic; then it is only through magical perception that the many truths that inhabit the theatre-body can be foretold [. . .] That is to say that the theatre is our own selves and just that. The only difference between our flesh and blood body and our theatre-body is that the first is a passive subject and the second an active one.][1]

11.1 The Darkness of the Stage

In this chapter (which is part documentation of a translation process and part rumination on the process of translation or adaptation for the stage) I shall chart the evolution of my translations of two absurdist one-act plays by Cuban playwright Virgilio Piñera (1912–79) and the various processes that took them from full first-draft rough translations to pared-down performance versions. The plays in question are *El Flaco y el Gordo* (1959) translated as *Thin Man Fat Man*, and *Siempre se Olvida Algo* (1964), translated as *You Always Forget Something*. I shall give a brief synopsis of each play before moving on to provide some biographical information on Virgilio Piñera and to discuss my own collaborative translation practice. I present some of the strategies that I used to transform the existing translations (in collaboration with the actors and the director) into performance texts. These plays, which were presented as a double bill at the Arcola Theatre, London in March 2010, needed to fit the specific casting and staging requirements of a production using third year students from the Collaborative and Devised Theatre Course at Central School of Speech and Drama in London. The cuts made to the text of *You Always Forget Something* for the Central School production also became the performance text template for the play as performed in both the original Spanish and in English by bilingual students from Hostos Community College in New York in April 2010.

These two translations first emerged from research and development workshops that I had undertaken with professional actors and drama students as part of my practice-led investigation into the plays of Virgilio Piñera and the collaborative processes of translation or adaptation for the stage. The act of transforming the text was in effect my research methodology, and the rehearsal room my laboratory. Although I had to produce translations for my doctorate that were anchored to the page by the heavy ballast of their attendant footnotes, the pre-annotated versions of these translations were designed to eliminate extraneous verbiage and to be as performance-ready as possible. I saw no point in producing 'read-only' academic versions where the mode of transmission was page rather than stage. My previous condition and occupation as actor militated against it. My aim was to craft translated plays, which could (in a ready analogy), like oven-ready chickens cooked instantly to a pitch of performance perfection. From these 'pre-performance' translations the performance versions of the texts emerged as the outcome of a collaborative rehearsal process involving director, actors, and translator. My role as the translator in this process is that of a creator and a curator, retaining a link to the language of the source text. From that template future translations may emerge (and by that I do not mean translations of translations, but future possibilities of translations from the source text) and future performances. In this chapter I shall examine some of the methods by which the map of performance can be plotted and drawn and how, in the visual/aural medium of theatre, words may very well be adapted into movement, music, lighting, and sound. I shall also examine how these 'wordless' moments can be identified. I will also interrogate the comedic/cultural function of root vegetables and other comestibles in relation to these particular translations, and conclude as I began by begging the all-important question: turnips or sweet potatoes?[2]

11.2 One Potato . . .

Thin Man Fat Man might best be described as a grotesque and sinister farce. In the first (and longer) scene of the play a Thin Man and a Fat Man share a hospital room. The entire action of the piece takes place within the single space of this room, and is centred on the binary oppositions of the two hospital beds and their occupants. The hospital itself is a shadowy place of shifting hierarchies, possessed of a fine, restaurant-style kitchen. The doctors and orderlies keep a healthy distance and the patients are left to their own devices. The Fat Man, who has his left arm in plaster, is rich, a glutton, who lives to eat and whose money can afford him a wide variety of succulent dishes from the à la carte hospital menu. The Thin Man, who has his right leg in plaster is poor,[3] a half-starved bag of bones who eats to live, but, having no money must subsist on the meagre, unappetizing rations of watery soup, cornmeal, and sweet potato supplied free-of-charge by the hospital.[4] The Fat Man is verbose and expansive; the Thin Man is sullen and sunken into himself. The Fat Man exploits the Thin Man's desperation and hunger in sado-masochistic style by taunting him with offers of food in exchange for the fulfilment of tasks (such as the inventing of menus to whet the Fat Man's appetite, for example, or the reciting of a complicated recipe for chicken and rice while the Fat Man is eating that very dish) these tasks are always slightly beyond the Thin Man's capabilities and the Fat Man never plays fair. At first the Thin Man, although resentful, is compliant in the Fat Man's game, clinging to the belief that the Fat Man will eventually feed him – but finally he reaches breaking point in spectacular style as he realizes that his hopes are futile and that the Fat Man's food and lifestyle will be eternally beyond his reach:

> THIN MAN: [*Reading*] Cover the pan and simmer for twenty to twenty-five minutes. Uncover the pan, add the drained *petit pois* and mix them in with the rice. Serve the rice up immediately on a dish with the chicken pieces arranged around the outside and garnish with sweet red peppers that have been cooked and well drained.

[*As the Thin Man is reading the final paragraph, the Fat Man shovels the last spoonful of rice into his mouth and then immediately spears the gizzard and eats that too*]

THIN MAN: What are you doing . . . ? What about my gizzard?

FAT MAN: [*Hardly able to articulate for the amount of food he has in his mouth*] The . . . giz . . . The . . . giz . . . [*Laughter*] The gizza . . . [*Renewed laughter*] Ha . . . Ha . . . [*Spurting grains of rice from his mouth*] The gizzard . . . Ha, ha, ha, ha!

THIN MAN: [*Completely losing his cool, he gets up and shouts angrily at the Fat Man*] Son of a bitch! I'm going to rip that gizzard out of your belly. I hope it rots your guts.

FAT MAN: [*Very serious*] And so we descend once more to the level of personal insult. [*Pause*] It's not my fault if you can't read a recipe. We're finished. We're finished. It's my fault for being kind to strangers. [*Pause*] You will never sit at my table again. [*He starts to walk over to the bed*] Now I shall sleep the sleep of the just. Don't let them wake me until six. [*He lies down on the bed face up and closes his eyes*]

THIN MAN: I take far too much shit; that's why this has happened. [*He walks over to the Fat Man's bed and stares at him, then he goes to his own bed and lies down with his hands behind his head, he sighs*] He looks like a fattened pig . . .

At the end of the first scene there is a brief interlude during which the stage is plunged into darkness and the following little ditty is sung three times in quick succession:

As sure as the world is round
And Jack is not called Jim
It is certain that the fat man
Will be eaten by the thin.[5]

The lights come up on a stage strewn with bones and the remnants of a plaster cast. The Thin Man, sitting at the Fat Man's table and wearing the Fat Man's pyjamas has grown preposterously and unaccountably fat; literally, it would seem, overnight. He gnaws contentedly on the remains of a human tibia and pats his by now substantial belly as he regales the audience with details of the Fat Man's death, revelling in his daringly murderous move from iron rations to cannibalism. As the newly fat Thin Man prepares to be discharged from hospital (firmly clutching the dead Fat

Man's wallet), he is told by the Doctor that he cannot go home for another fifteen days. At that moment the Orderly shows a new Thin Man to the Fat Man's empty bed. The old Thin Man starts sobbing and screaming for help as he realizes with horror what fate has in store for him. The play ends as it begins with a Fat Man and a Thin Man sharing a hospital room.

11.3 Two Potatoes . . .

The onstage action of *You Always Forget Something,* like *Thin Man Fat Man,* takes place in the confines of a single room – in this instance the living-room of Lina's apartment in Havana. This space not only represents the departure lounge and arrivals hall for a frenetic whirl of travelling to and from the world outside, but is also the fulcrum for the increasingly manic energy that drives the characters and the play. Lina and her maid Chacha are preparing to fly from Havana to Brighton for an English seaside holiday. Every time that they go away they always forget to pack some item of personal use: for Lina it is always the iodine and for Chacha the aspirins. Indeed as Lina avers: 'You always forget something'. To remedy this forgetfulness Lina manages to convince a sceptical Chacha of the logic of a cunning plan she has devised whereby they will each 'wittingly', that is to say, accidentally on-purpose, leave something behind, thereby allowing them to forget something in the full knowledge that they have forgotten it before returning home to fetch it in order to be able to forget it again. The following excerpt gives something of the flavour of Lina's logic:

> LINA: Yes there is a cure! [*Pause*] Haven't I just told you that from today we will – wittingly – forget to take something? [*Pause*] I will forget the iodine; you will forget the aspirin.
>
> CHACHA: But Madam, how are we going to forget to take something that we always forget to take?
>
> LINA: Because if we know beforehand that we have forgotten to take the iodine and the aspirin, we will know that we won't forget to take the iodine and the aspirin.
>
> CHACHA: Ooh Madam! That's all so complicated!
>
> LINA: Complicated? Simple and . . . safe!

Now this is only half the story. Lina has a rival, the formidable Señora Camacho, a woman whose mania for order leads Lina to describe her as 'anti-forgetfulness personified' and whose personal mantra is 'You never forget anything'. As Lina is hell-bent on proving to Señora Camacho that her own particular mantra of 'You always forget something' is the correct one she intends to provoke a stand-off whereby she can accomplish the difficult task of bending Señora Camacho to her will. Part of the 'complicated' logic of Lina's plan involves returning home post-haste from Brighton to Havana to retrieve the forgotten items in time to receive a pre-arranged telephone call from Señora Camacho:

> LINA: Now I shall explain my plan to you: next Monday the twenty-seventh, that's to say a week today, as we are taking our morning dip on a beach in Brighton, I shall suddenly say to you: 'Chacha, I forgot to put the iodine in the suitcase!' [*Pause*] And you will say to me . . .
>
> CHACHA: [*Interrupting her*] And I forgot the aspirins, Madam!
>
> LINA: Perfect! Then – dishevelled and hysterical – we will catch the plane and enter through that door [*She points to it*] at the precise moment that Señora Camacho is calling this number.
>
> CHACHA: To be perfectly honest, I don't see the point of that call.
>
> LINA:You don't? Then wait until you hear Señora Camacho's screams of rage.
>
> CHACHA: I don't know Señora Camacho but I can't imagine she's going to scream just because you've told her to call you on Monday the 27th.
>
> LINA: She's going to scream when she hears me. Señora Camacho is anti-forgetfulness personified. As she never forgets anything, she can't stand forgetfulness in others. [*Pause*] When I tell her, over this telephone [*She points to it*] that, in light of my perennial forgetfulness, I have wittingly forgotten to take the iodine and the aspirins, she will scream with rage [*She roars with laughter*]

Once Señora Camacho has made the call and is apprized of Lina's plot, she rushes round to Lina's apartment in high dudgeon, armed with lists, luggage, and her hapless maid Tota ready to do battle and to convince Lina of the error of her ways. Señora Camacho who has literally packed everything for any eventuality (including, it turns out, the mummified body of her dead husband), into her rather capacious suitcase, seems to be winning the war when much to Lina's glee, she is felled by the discovery of an un-itemized sweet potato among her toiletries. Battle lines are redrawn with the sweet potato coming to symbolize all that is ridiculous about the entrenched viewpoint of each of the women. The play then spins off into a tongue-twisting lexical listing of ever more preposterous items that must be included in the luggage, before being brought to a hysterical and fevered finale through the timely discovery of an eavesdropping intruder (in the form of a fleeing lover), who conveniently adjudicates the argument and brings matters to their illogically logical conclusion.

Both plays are short, but deceptively so. They are portmanteau plays which, like Señora Camacho's suitcase, open out to reveal that they contain far more than a cursory viewing might indicate. There is a compression of thought and action upon first reading that starts to expand exponentially once the plays begin to be translated onto the stage. Both plays are extremely wordy, full of puns and set phrases, and other translational conundrums. In *Thin Man Fat Man* (abbreviated henceforth to *TMFM*) in particular, as Matías Montes Huidobro (1973: 225) has observed, Piñera uses a whole variety of sayings and expressions throughout the course of the play that make reference to food, the act of eating, or the body parts engaged in eating; a strategy that I have tried to recreate as far as possible in the translation. The title of *You Always Forget Something* (abbreviated henceforth to *YAFS*) is in itself a cliché of everyday speech of the kind that Piñera was extremely fond of parodying. At the end of that play as both Ricardo Lobato Morchón (2002: 198) and William Ruiz Morales have observed, the words cease to be moored to their meaning and are linked only by their phonetic similarity to each other. As Ruiz Morales states:

> *El texto trata de alejarse del sentido para acercarse a su forma [. . .] Las palabras no siguen aquí un orden determinado por su significado sino por el significante y su fonética: el absurdo solo adquiere lógica en el plano puramente textual.* (2005: 88)
>
> [The text tries to distance itself from sense in order to get closer to its form [. . .] The words don't follow here an order determined by their meaning but by their phonetic signifier: the absurd only attains logic on a purely textual level.]

In the same article Ruiz Morales goes on to describe *YAFS* as being almost a workout for actors,[6] while *TMFM* is no less demanding of its players. The stage-directions for both plays provide a musical counterpoint and a secondary rhythm of movement and repetition that mirrors the spoken word, and cannot therefore be completely ignored without upsetting the balance of either play. Both possess what Cuban theatre critic and historian Rine

Leal has perceived to be the salient characteristics of Piñera's dramatic works:

> *Sus personajes entran y salen de sí mismos, se ramifican, se transforman frente al espectador, dialogan entre sí, y crean un ritual acogido a las leyes del teatro. Las mejores obras de Piñera ofrecen esta estructura en la que se producen analogías, repeticiones, interrupciones temporales, claves ocultas, vueltas en redondo, exorcismos y ceremonias, convenciones y novedades. El juego puede ser anulado y recomenzado cuantas veces sea necesario, siempre y cuando el espectador participe en él, es decir lo acepte como teatro.* (2002: xiv)
>
> [His characters *enter* and *exit* from themselves, they branch out and transform themselves in front of the spectator, they talk among themselves and they create a ritual according to the laws of theatre. Piñera's best plays have a structure to them in which there are analogies, repetitions, temporal interruptions, hidden codes, about turns, exorcisms and ceremonies, conventions and innovations. The game can be stopped and begun again as many times as necessary, as long as the spectator participates in it, that is, accepts it as theatre.]

Virgilio Piñera was not only a prolific playwright, but also a poet, short-story writer, novelist, and essayist. Famed for a sharp wit and an acid tongue, he was a polemicist who charted the extremes of human nature. His style of writing defies exact categorization, but might best (especially in the case of his plays, novels, and short stories) be described as darkly humorous, absurdist, or grotesque.[7] Piñerian characters usually inhabit a hostile, topsy-turvy world, where the natural order of things has been inverted, and their options have become severely restricted. The characters in his plays inhabit enclosed spaces; the outside world is there; it impinges and it threatens, but it is never brought directly onto the stage. Cuban theatre director Humberto Arenal has described the fate of Piñera's characters thus:

> *Sus personajes no aspiran ni a la gloria ni a la felicidad. Están condenados a vivir al margen, sin salida. No hay escapatoria posible. Están condenados a existir en un universo sombrío y encerrado. Les esta negada toda posibilidad de ser felices. Están acorralados en un pasadizo tenebroso, en el cual apenas les es posible respirar en paz. Y todo esto recurriendo con frecuencia al humor, a la sátira y al vituperio.* (2005: 154)
>
> [His characters aspire neither to glory nor happiness. They are condemned to live on the margins, with no way out. There is no escape

possible. They are condemned to live in a dark enclosed universe. All possibility of being happy is denied to them. They are cornered in a gloomy passageway in which it is scarcely possible for them to breathe in peace; and all this with frequent recurrence to humour, censure, and satire].

Between 1946 and 1958 Piñera lived mainly in Argentina in self-imposed semi-exile returning to Havana just before the triumph of the Revolution. He counted the Polish exile Witold Gombrowicz among his friends in Buenos Aires, and headed the committee of writers who helped translate Gombrowicz's novel *Ferdydurke* into Spanish. Although an enthusiastic supporter of the new Cuba, Piñera's homosexuality and intellectual non-conformism led to his marginalization during a well-documented period of recent Cuban history, when state-sponsored homophobia and petty bureaucracy stifled creative freedom. During the mid-1960s when Piñera was beginning to be more widely known internationally, he was prevented from travelling abroad by the Cuban authorities, and was therefore unable to fulfil translation and publishing deals that he had made during previous visits to Europe. He spent the last ten years of his life pushed to the margins of society. A living literary ghost who nonetheless continued to scribble away frantically on the sidelines, as well as making a living as a translator of secondary texts from French to Spanish.[8] After his death in 1979, the slow process of posthumous rehabilitation began and his status in Cuba shifted from that of literary ghost to literary giant. The process of reclamation continues.

11.4 Word Soup

What role does the theatre translator play in this process? Should the theatre translator be a visible participant in what David Johnston has called the business of 'stage-craft [. . .] an integral strand of that multi-layered process of making a play work on stage' (1996: 7), or a hidden hand scribbling in the background, transcribing texts from the limits of one language/culture to the limits of another? Can a translator of theatre texts be both liberator and performer, a miracle-worker raising dusty scripts and forgotten 'foreign' playwrights from the dead? As I have already stated, the act of translation and adaptation for the theatre is also my research methodology for my doctorate, and in collaboration with different groups of actors (both professional and student) led by Gráinne Byrne, the artistic director of London-based contemporary theatre company Scarlet theatre, and her Polish-based associate Katarzyna Deszcz, I have been investigating Piñera's theatre through the medium of translation, adaptation, and performance. Scarlet Theatre evolved out of the women's theatre collective Scarlet Harlets, which started in 1981 as a company devoted to new writing.[9] In the past I have worked for Scarlet as an actor as well as a translator, and I decided that it might prove fruitful to apply some of the collaborative techniques for the devising and creating of new works for the Theatre to the process of developing the Piñera translations for performance. In my first act as a theatre translator (2003), I translated Piñera's 1957 absurdist comedy *La Boda* [*The Wedding*] for a Scarlet theatre production. I enjoyed the collaborative process and appreciated the actors' ability to literally think on their feet. I began to develop ideas of how the practice of an active and 'stage-oriented', rather than a passive 'page-oriented' approach to theatre, translation might be developed. My reason for choosing the Piñera piece derived from a production of *La Boda* I had seen at the Havana theatre Festival in 1997, performed by a company called Teatro de la Luna [theatre of the Moon] led by Raúl Martín (a young director who had acquired a reputation in Cuba for life into the Piñera canon). Something about the production reminded me of Scarlet Theatre's recent production of *Princess Sharon*, itself a reworking of one of Witold Gombrowicz's absurdist plays, *Ivona, Princess of Burgundy* (1938).[10] It was only later that I discovered the link between Gombrowicz and Piñera, which inspired me to pursue a collaborative translation project.

The original Scarlet rehearsal process involved actors, director, and writer working together during a research and development week on the basics of the play.[11] The actors would improvise freely and create characters and possible scenarios; the writer would then shape the resultant material into a script ready for the beginning of rehearsals a few months later. This process was later also applied to adapting existing scripts and translations, and from there it was a short step to commissioning new translations, with the translator forming part of the collaborative creative team. In this model of performance, translators and actors alike engage in a process of translation and adaptation; not only working with a target text based on the foreign source text, but adapting that target text to the requirements of the stage. This adaptive process might include exercises such as liberating the target text by playing the action of the scene rather than the word; finding the physical space of that text through the relationships of the characters; converting stage directions into the actions they describe; and using music, movement, games, mask work, and other improvizational techniques. Piñera's stage directions, as Amado del Pino has observed

(2004: 52), exist at an almost 'choreographic level', and possess rhythms that mirror the rhythms of the spoken text. They provide important clues as to the performance-language of the play, and how that might be translated into action.

The preliminary work of translation, which produces the first draft, is a lonely act that involves the translator-as-wordsmith working alone. This process represents the first reading of the text, but also establishes the limits of where the translator can take a translation destined for performance. The research and development workshop is the halfway house between page and stage. It tests what the translation is made of, but also – and very importantly – focuses attention on the source text. Actors are the adapters par excellence of a translated text and of finding a way to make it work, because in the end they are the ones exposed on the stage.

11.5 Two Comedies of Erroneous Root Vegetables

Rehearsals for the Piñera Project (as the enterprise was dubbed) began at Central School of Speech and Drama in January 2010. The six student actors (four women and two men) were all aged in their early to mid-twenties. The stage managers, lighting, sound, set, and costume designers were also students, who were overseen by the tutors from their respective courses. Both cast and crew were self-disciplined and motivated as they approached the task of commuting off-site; heading east from north-west London for final rehearsals and performances in the very much less spacious Studio 2 at the Arcola Theatre in east London.[12] The production would need to be adapted to the limitations of a space in which everything would be explicit and there could be no hiding backstage. Hence the cast had to work quickly and efficiently and try to make a virtue or a feature of any restrictions they encountered.

The students had not previously heard of Piñera, which was not surprising since his plays are a fairly unknown quantity outside of Cuba. Gráinne and I were keen to transfer the knowledge that we had accumulated through our Piñera research, workshops, and experimental performances. I remained in the rehearsal room, not only in my capacity as translator, but as the cultural reference point for all things Piñerian. My function as a translator in the rehearsal room was not to over-interpret where meaning was obscure, but to act as a subsidiary director responsible for creating the aural landscape of the plays. As primary director, Gráinne was responsible for the overarching concept and the visual realization of the word upon the stage. Both Gráinne and I worked in tandem to decipher Piñera and discover the performance language of his plays.

Rehearsals began with a full read-through. *TMFM* existed in a revised second draft based on earlier research; consequently I had a fair idea of which parts of the play could be omitted for performance. An excerpt from *YAFS* had previously been presented as part of an Arts Council-funded initiative *Pieces of Piñera*, produced by Scarlet Theatre and directed by Kasia Deszcz and Gráinne Byrne at the Arcola Theatre in October 2009.[13] As a result *YAFS* needed less work to be done to it than *TMFM*.

During the early stages of rehearsals, the actors created pictorial storyboards in which each play was broken down into units describing each segment of the story. For example on the *TMFM* wall there were photos of well-known comedy double acts such as Morecambe and Wise and Laurel and Hardy.[14] The actor playing the Thin Man created a poster-size collage of photos of different foods, recipes, and dishes entitled '[The] Thin Man's Wish List'. All the actors also wrote character-sketches for the parts they were playing.

The process of adapting my translation began immediately. If I was unable to attend rehearsals Gráinne and I would communicate by email, with a typical exchange going something like this:

> GRÁINNE: Hi Kate, I'm cutting a lot of the expositional stuff at the beginning. A lot of the information comes out later through the dialogue with the Fat Man.
>
> KATE: Hi Gráinne, I'm fine with most of that. The only thing I'd question is cutting the line: 'That fat guy is murderous and how he eats!' as like the skeleton reference it hints at what fate has in store (i.e. he will be murdered and he will be eaten). Likewise I wonder about cutting the Thin Man imitating the Fat Man (unless you are doing it visually) because he starts out by imitating him and ends up impersonating him so this speech in fact mirrors the speech at the beginning of scene 2 when the Thin Man is polishing off the Fat Man and inhabiting his pyjamas – something to think about anyway.
>
> GRÁINNE: Yes good points. We are doing a lot visually but I will look again.

One of the main decisions that we made at the beginning of rehearsals was to make a turnip rather than a sweet potato the vegetable *leitmotif* that traveled between the plays. The first play of the evening to be performed was to be *YAFS*: as mentioned in the synopsis Señora Camacho is floored by the discovery of an errant sweet potato in her suitcase. The sweet potato [*boniato*] is a commonly eaten root vegetable in Cuba, and it also has indubitably phallic connotations. We were certainly not wishing to lose layers of innuendo, but we decided to include a vegetable more familiar to British audiences:

> TOTA: [*She stands up, she takes a piece of paper from one of the pockets in her dress and reads slowly*] Detailed inventory of the items that Señora Juana Camacho Widow of Pérez will take with her on her trip. [*Pause*] Garments: two morning dresses, two afternoon dresses, two evening dresses; three petticoats, three pairs of knickers, three pairs of long johns, three brassieres, five pairs of stockings. [*Pause*] Toiletries: a bottle of eau de cologne, one of lavender water, one of mouthwash, a pot of face cream, a tin of talcum powder, one of face powder, and a . . . a . . . [*She clears her throat, coughs and looks confused*] and a . . . a tu . . . tu . . . tu . . .
>
> SEÑORA CAMACHO: [*Surprised*] What's the matter, Tota? Can't you read your own writing?
>
> TOTA: [*Stammering*] Madam, it's just that . . . here . . . I don't understand . . . [*She bursts into tears*]
>
> SEÑORA CAMACHO: Come on! Pull yourself together! Keep reading.
>
> TOTA: [*Fearful*] Madam, it says here a . . . turnip . . .!
>
> SEÑORA CAMACHO: [*Astonished*] A turnip? But that's not a toiletry; anyway, I never take a turnip with me on my travels. [*Pause*] Let's see, let's see! [*She rummages feverishly in the suitcase. Finally she pulls out a turnip*] Here it is! And what a turnip! [*To Tota*] Since when have we taken turnips on our travels? What were you thinking of, putting it in?
>
> TOTA: [*Wringing her hands*] I'm sorry, Madam, it won't happen again.
>
> LINA: [*Laughing heartily*] Perhaps she was reading the shopping list as well and the turnip slipped in amongst the toiletries.

For reasons that resist exact definition, the single word 'turnip' in English, (like the single word '*boniato*' in Spanish) seems to have more comedic value than the two words 'sweet potato'. It also allows the possibility of compensatory word play, as there is a useful alliteration between the words 'turnip', 'Tota', 'travels', and 'toiletries', which replicates the rhythmic and alliterative way Piñera plays with the word '*boniato*' in the Spanish. We wanted to provoke a sense of the comedic, clownish, silliness that is prevalent in Piñera alongside the darker shades of the grotesque, so the fact of a turnip turning up in a suitcase was played for laughs. In our production the turnip resembled an incendiary device that was passed between the women at the end of the play before the final exorcism:

STRANGER: [*Sarcastically*] I hate to contradict you, Madam, but I would say that you forget almost nothing.

SEÑORA CAMACHO: [*Shouting*] No, not almost nothing; absolutely nothing.

STRANGER: And the turnip, Señora Camacho?

LINA: [*Imitating the Stranger*] And the turnip, Señora Camacho?

CHACHA: [*The same*] And the turnip, Señora Camacho?

TOTA: [*The same*] And the turnip, Madam?

SEÑORA CAMACHO: [*Reproachfully*] Et tu, Tota?[15]

TOTA: [*Shrugs her shoulders*] Sorry, Madam. But there it is large as life. We can't bury it!

The turnip then migrated into *TMFM* where it was fed to the unfortunate Thin Man. Our Thin Man was also fed on boiled cabbage rather than the Spanish '*yuca hervida*' [boiled cassava] – a plain dish often served as an accompaniment to meat, but rather tasteless if served on its own. Actual food was not served in our production; the actors ate using sense-memory techniques, while the plates had ostentatious labels declaring their contents.

The dishes were served in a highly stylized way by a succession of white-coated orderlies (played by the four female actors), who moved to a sinuous tango beat while making eye-contact with the audience. These same orderlies adjusted the positions of the two hospital beds and the screens to denote temporal shifts and changing perspectives at different points in the play. Rhythm and movement were also important to the playing of *YAFS*. Both Lina and Señora developed a way of moving that was dictated by their opposing inner mantras (always forgetting versus never forgetting), while Chacha and Tota counter-balanced each other in the way they moved and spoke. Sound effects for *YAFS* were provided by the two male actors wearing white coats and sitting in the front row of the audience.

11.6 She Sat Among the Audience Inexplicably Mimicking . . .

I watched all six performances of the Piñera double bill to gauge audience reaction. Antón Arrufat has said of these plays in particular:

Poseen lo que constituye una constante en su obra: producen en el lector o el espectador un desconcierto, una especie de duda sobre los supuestos y valoraciones morales de su vida o conducta. Son obras esencialmente provocadoras. (Espinosa 2003: 196)

[They possess something that is a constant in his work: they produce an uncertainty in the reader or the spectator, a sort of doubt about the moral suppositions or values of their life and or their conduct. They are essentially provocative works.]

If the plays have the power to disconcert a home-grown (i.e., Cuban) audience, then they doubly disconcerted British playgoers, who were unsure what it was they were watching. The first-night audience listened carefully and tried to take on board the intellectual arguments but seemed uncertain as to whether they were 'allowed' to laugh or not. After the first night we further adapted the beginning of *YAFS* to the demands of performance by signposting the comedy; as a result the second-night audience laughed uproariously, as did the third-night audience. By this stage the actors were also settling into the complicated choreography of performance. The turnip translated well in its function as a sweet potato and the comedy was finally understood.

There is often a faint suspicion among those witnessing a newly translated and adapted play by an unheard-of-foreign-playwright that the texts cannot be any good, otherwise they would have been translated before. The only way to persuade people otherwise is to continue translating and adapting, both in the study and in rehearsal, so as to create delicious theatrical fare and re-calibrating culturally specific root vegetables. If it is out there and being performed then the audience should not fear it.

Notes

[1] Unless otherwise stated all Spanish to English translations in this chapter are my own. The excerpts from the plays are taken from my existing English translations. The full Spanish text of each play can be found in the 2002 Cuban edition of Piñera's collected plays as listed in the bibliography.

[2] It will be noted that in this introduction I use the terms adaptation and translation interchangeably. This is because I believe that, during the process of transforming a source text into a performance text, the distinction ceases to assume much significance.

[3] He broke his leg trying to steal a chicken. We do not learn how the Fat Man broke his arm. Eating perhaps?

[4] These obviously constituted iron rations in Piñera's universe - something akin to Dickensian workhouse gruel. For the purposes of the London production this became 'Watery soup, lumpy porridge and a turnip'. I shall return to the vegetable theme later.

[6] Morales 2005: 86–8.

[7] Piñera's early absurdist piece *Falsa alarma* (1947) [*False Alarm*] pre-dates Ionesco's *La Cantatrice Chauve* by a couple of years.

[8] As Piñera's friend, fellow Cuban writer Antón Arrufat, has commented:

Como su puesto de traductor era modesto, de escasa relevancia o influencia social, Piñera no fue removido. Cambió el contenido de su labor: si antes tradujo a Madach, Foucault o el Marat-Sade, ahora le entregaron autores africanos y vietnamitas vertidas al francés. (2002: 13)

[As his post as a translator was a modest one, of little social influence or relevance, Piñera was not removed. The content of his work changed: where before he had translated Madach, Foucault or the Marat-Sade, now he was given African and Vietnamese authors translated into French.]

[9] See 'About Scarlet' (2011).

[10] Kasia Deszcz directed this production for Scarlet Theatre in 1997. The version called *Princess Sharon* was recomposed from an existing English translation of *Ivona* by Krystyna Griffiths-Jones and Catherine Robins (1969). This translation was reconfigured by Kasia and her husband Andrej Sadowski who returned to the Polish original and then took it back into English in conjunction with the company. Kasia Deszcz later used the template of the English adaptation to create a new Polish production of *Ivona* which was extremely successful and subsequently won a prestigious Polish theatre award.

[11] See Cousin (2000: 4–53) for documentation of the processes involved in creating two Scarlet productions: *The Sisters* (an adaptation of Chekhov's *The Three Sisters*) and *Paper Walls* (a piece of devised theatre).

[12] The Arcola Theatre moved premises in January 2011 to its current site in Ashwin Street, Hackney, London, E8.

[13] The other plays presented as semi-staged excerpts were: *Dos Viejos Pánicos* (1967) [*Two Old People in a Panic*], *Falsa Alarma* (1948) [*False Alarm*], and *Jesús* (1948) [*Jesus*]. The purpose of the showcase was to gain audience feedback and to decide which play to take to full production.

[14] The title of the play in Spanish, *El Flaco y el Gordo* is a deliberate inversion of *El Gordo y el Flaco* the name given in Spanish to the legendary slapstick comedy duo Laurel and Hardy.

[15] In the original this is simply '*¿Tú también, Tota?*' [You too, Tota?] But I could not resist the delicious symbolism and forlorn grandeur of '*Et tu, Tota?*' as a translational gambit of which Piñera might have approved.

Bibliography

'About Scarlet' (2011). http://www.scarletTheatre.co.uk/about/ (accessed July 29, 2011).

Arenal, Humberto (2005). *Seis Dramaturgos Ejemplares*. Havana: Unión.

Arrufat, Anton (2002). *Virgilio Piñera: Entre él y yo*. Havana: Unión.

Cousin, Geraldine (2000). *Recording Women*. London and New York: Routledge.

Espinosa, Carlos (ed.) (2003). *Virgilio Piñera en Persona*. Havana: Unión.

Gombrowicz, Witold (1969). *Princess Ivona*, trans. Krystyna Griffiths-Jones and Catherine Robins. London: Marion Boyars.

Johnston, David (ed.) (1996). *Stages of Translation.* Bath: Absolute Classics.

Lobato Morchón, Ricardo (2002). *El Teatro del Absurdo en Cuba (1948–1968).* Madrid: Verbum.

Montes Huidobro, Matías (1973). *Persona, Viday Máscara en el Teatro Cubano,* Miami: Ediciones Universal.

Piñera, Virgilio (2002). *Teatro Completo: Compilación, Ordenamiento y Prólogo de Rine Leal.* Havana: Letras Cubanas.

del Pino, Amado (2004). *Sueños del Mago.* Havana: Ediciones Alarcos.

Ruiz Morales, William (2004). 'Memorandum: Siempre se Olvida Algo'. *tablas* LXXX(3/05): 86–8.

Chapter 12

The Mind's Ear: Imagination, Emotions and Ideas in the Intersemiotic Transposition of Housman's Poetry to Song

Mike Ingham

12.1 Rationale

The present chapter will explore an intertextual, interdisciplinary phenomenon that has not been very closely studied by those who work in the field of adaptation studies, namely the setting of secular poetry for vocal musical performance in the form of art song. Given that the musical and poetic ideas that go into the creative mix are rarely synchronic, and that the poem is, except in highly unusual conditions of production, invariably the source text inspiring the musical creation, it seems appropriate to consider the practice as a legitimate area of adaptation studies. This approach naturally recognizes the relevance of established scholarly perspectives in the disciplines of musicology and intermediality (Wolf 1999). However, in the present study the relationship between source and target texts (terms which inevitably imply kinship with translation studies) will be explored with special focus on how the poem texts are transformed by vocalization in terms of repetition, variation, expansion, contraction, dilution, accentuation, and colouring of words – and the utterance and performance of written verse as sound vocalization within the tempo-rhythm of performance (all significant aspects of the intersemiotic transfer process.)

Instead of a musicological approach privileging musical form, harmony, and compositional technique, I intend to employ the rubrics of *intermedial* adaptation (i.e., creative transposition from one artistic medium to another) as my critical tool of enquiry. Here the critical interface with translation studies is certainly relevant to discussion. Lawrence Venuti's notion of formal interpretants (structural correspondences to and deviations from source to target text) and thematic interpretants (ideological, value-related ones) in his 2007 article 'Adaptation, Translation, Critique' clarifies in a more global sense by drawing attention to what seems to be fast becoming a 'tradaptation' field in which boundaries are increasingly blurred. However, given that translation tends to be written and interlingual, whereas adaptation is often intermedial and frequently, though not always, intralingual, there remains considerable daylight yet between the two scholarly domains. Venuti's emphasis on what he refers to as 'the hermeneutic relation' between source and target texts is instructive, in that he invites the adapter to both interpret and interrogate the material for adaptation (Venuti 2007: 25–43).

Adaptation, appropriation, transformation, and transposition are all terms that have often been applied somewhat loosely and interchangeably in adaptation discourse, but adaptation tends to be the umbrella term. Appropriation – as for example in radical Brechtian treatment of classic source plays or in musical 'variations' on another composer's theme – tends to connote a thoroughgoing recontextualization of source material in which textual elements may be placed in a different form, juxtaposed with new elements, or subject to considerable variation, even to an unrecognizable degree. According to Julie Sanders: 'adaptation signals a relationship with an informing source text or [. . .] On the other hand appropriation frequently effects a more decisive journey away from the informing source into a wholly new cultural product or domain' (Sanders 2006: 26). She also refers to adaptation as 'a transpositional practice, casting a specific genre into another generic mode, an act of re-vision in itself' (2006: 18).

The term 'transposition' is very pertinent to musical adaptation, but re-visioning is only partially applicable to the practice; indeed re-auditing might be a more viable way of exploring the poem-to-song adaptation. The addition of poem adaptation into art song to the broader adaptation discourse is timely and of critical importance, because of its performativity and its unusual combination of literal fidelity and radical transformation. This distinctive generic characteristic tends to place song setting adaptation roughly halfway along a theoretical continuum between the more literal textual affinities of the respectful adaptation or translation and the more independent qualities of the free appropriation or analogy. As a result in most cases it is neither a true adaptation nor a true appropriation, even if it does inhabit a separate though parallel 'cultural domain'. As in other genres of adaptation, song setting is a hybrid praxis. But only in song setting adaptation does the integral song source text remain present. Unlike other genres of adaptation/translation it is not superseded by a replacive target text version in any literal definition. To that extent song setting is an additive praxis rather than a replacive one.

Exploring the interdependent roles of the imagination, the intellect, and the emotions in the act of intersemiotic translation, adaptation, and performance seem highly pertinent, if intersemiotic studies are to continue growing away from their structuralist, linguistics-oriented roots. This chapter will review critical precedents, present possible theoretical models, and examine specific strategies for expressing and transforming thought and idea and retaining and infusing the ideational and emotional world of the poem text with the expressive-affective dimension of musical-vocal performance. The major case study source will be A. E. Housman's collection *A Shropshire Lad* and the various recorded adaptations/settings of it by Somervell, Butterworth, Ireland, Gurney, Vaughan Williams, and others. The rationale for my choice is that settings of Housman's poetry have played a vital role in propagating the work and a major factor in promoting what Benjamin famously referred to as the 'after-life' (Benjamin 1973: 72) of a text. Tenor singer and author Stephen Varcoe refers to the publication of *A Shropshire Lad* as 'one of the most important poetic events in the story of English song' (Varcoe 2000: 78). Of the more than 400 settings of Housman's poems, some cycles such as Vaughan Williams' 'On Wenlock Edge' have, after initial controversy, been truly transformative in the development of English song (cf. Evans 1918; Hold 2002). A further reason for exploring the subject through the prism of Housman settings is that in his characteristically self-deprecating way, Housman himself, almost in passing, synthesizes some of the key arguments related to the whole question of emotion and intellect in poetry – and by extension, poetry settings – in his one and only critical discourse on the subject, his 1933 Cambridge lecture, 'On the Name and Nature of Poetry' (Housman 2010: 230–56).

12.2 Song Settings as Translation/Adaptation: Intermediality, Melopoetics, and Tippett's 'Destruction Theory'

In her 2006 book *A Theory of Adaptation,* Linda Hutcheon makes a strong case for the spirit of pluralism engendered by cultural recycling, replication, and transmission, with a significant nod of acknowledgment in the direction of meme theory (which could be usefully applied to determine which texts are most popular for setting and why – a question that I have insufficient space to explore in the present chapter). Her study only touches very lightly on song settings within the wider range of cultural cocktails concocted by multifaceted varieties of adaptation, but her observation is relevant to the present discussion: 'Poems simply set to music are also adaptations from the telling to the showing mode when they are performed' (Hutcheon 2006: 44). She goes on to discuss the live performance implications of William Bolcom's ambitious song settings of Blake's *Songs of Innocence and Experience* as a good example of showing work that was originally conceived as a 'told' creation, as well as multimedia performances of Schubert's *Lieder* cycles, involving the aesthetics of dance. This is all well and good, and we must naturally acknowledge the vital importance of ekphrastic relations between works of literary art and visual experience in the field of adaptation studies. However, the oral–aural dimension of experience seems to be neglected in such an appraisal of poetry-to-song adaptation. Operatic adaptation, which tends to predominate in the now well established field of word and music studies, also tends to be treated by Hutcheon and other theorists much more from a perspective of visuality rather than orality/aurality:

> Knowing or unknowing, we experience adaptations across media differently than we do within the same medium. But even in the latter case, adaptation as *adaptation* involves for its knowing audience, an interpretive doubling, a conceptual flipping back and forth between the work we know and the work we are experiencing. (Hutcheon 2006: 139)

These questions of doubling and of live experience are of course crucial to any study of the song setting, but to do justice to the doubleness of the correspondences between poem and song, we have to depend less on the eye and much more on the ear. 'The mind's eye' is a far more familiar locution than 'the mind's ear', but without relying on the close rapport between the aural faculty and mental processes, it is impossible to attempt a worthwhile evaluation of song as adaptation of poetry. Without going down the admittedly valuable path of a more scientific psycho-acoustic emphasis on the interplay between sound and form and emotion and intellect, it is nonetheless possible to elicit insights gleaned from theories and theorists, from practice and performance, and from intertextual and intermedial correspondences. Essentially the study relies much less on what might have been gained or lost in the intersemiotic translation process, than on the interdependence, intersubjectivity, and reciprocity of the creative partnership.

As Peter Newmark has pointed out: 'the music of a great song is, in outline, interpreted or translated by its text, but a full interpretation then takes into account the depths and subtleties in the music, which goes far beyond the words' (Newmark 2006: 6). He stresses that the symbiosis between the [usually] two composers and two or more performers [singer and instrumentalist(s)] is finely balanced between creation and interpretation, and that herein lies the magic which is only fully realized in live performance. This experience can to an extent also be experienced through a different medium, namely that of electronic audio recording (CD/DVD), which may or may not exclude the visual component of the experience. Referring to recitals and performances of song settings he reflects that: 'the words may escape them. Sometimes this hardly matters. But in the case of Schubert and Schumann (who both set Goethe and Heine) or of Britten and Finzi (who both set Hardy) and others, much is lost if the music and poem, the singer and pianist [or instrumental group] are not heard and understood together. It is not easy for a listener to achieve this 'fusion'' (Newmark 2006: 7).

Writing of Gerald Finzi's 'care, consideration and almost aristocratic sensitivity toward his texts, not only in interpreting them faithfully but in setting them in music which follows just note and accent' in his great treatise on modern English song, *Parry to Finzi – Twenty English Song Composers*, Trevor Hold admires 'the way he magically transforms the contours and rhythms of the poetry into the contours and rhythms of music' (Hold 2002: 420). Hold's valuable insight into the poetry–music dichotomy is that the composer's poetic sensibility is paramount if the poetry is to be an aesthetically independent and integral creation, more than simply a vehicle for an exercise in songwriting. Thus, insofar as song settings are considered successfully adapted works, a fine sense of auditory and interpretative balance between the poem set and the song produced is required. This is unlike the situation of many works of adaptation, in which the target text/performance needs are generally felt to outweigh any perceived imperatives for representing a source text with some degree of accuracy, fidelity, or subtlety.

Newmark's *apercu* (2006: 6) that 'the music (the setting) and the poem of a serious song are analogous to a text and its translation' is also useful in this context, because the two cultural products co-exist in parallel and for different, though sometimes overlapping, audiences. However, the idea of text as something written, and usually interlingual, rather detracts from the dynamic creative synergy afforded by performance and enunciation/declamation of words where meaning is created to some extent visually but primarily orally and aurally. Newmark's categorization of the music as 'the feeling, the emotions, the tone, analogous both to colour and to the sound of the vowels', while 'the poem is the intelligence, the thinking,' the nuance, analogous both to design and to the sound of the consonants' (Newmark 2006: 6) is very insightful, instructive, and relevant to the theme of this chapter. His idea that one can differentiate between the semantics (word meaning, pitch, tonality) and the pragmatics (volume, rhythm, pauses) may be perhaps reductively structuralist; however, his emphasis on diction seems to me of critical relevance. The meaning of the song, and thus its cognitive and affective response, is likely to be enhanced and illuminated by distinct and crisp diction and phrasing. We will look more closely at the relationship between poetic prosody and diction and musical/vocal prosody and diction in the latter part of the chapter.

T. S. Eliot's influential essay (based on a 1942 speech given at Glasgow University) 'The Music of Poetry' argues for a close affinity between poetic and musical sensibilities in the poet (composer-poet Ivor Gurney being one of the few examples after Thomas Campion, whose poetic and musical sensibilities were genuinely in tandem with one another, although many composers have shown fine poetic sensibility). At the end of his piece Eliot reiterates his idea of a strong connection between music and poetry arguing that:

> a poet may gain from the study of music [. . .] I believe that the properties in which music concerns the poet most nearly are the sense of rhythm and the sense of structure [. . .] I know that a poem, or passage of a poem, may tend to realize itself first as a particular rhythm before it reaches expression in words, and that this rhythm may bring to birth the idea and the image [. . .] The use of recurrent themes is as natural to poetry as to music. There are possibilities for verse which bear some analogy to the development of a theme by a different group of instruments. (Eliot 1957: 38)

Eliot's insights are to a considerable extent shaped by his development of a poetic musicality in his *Four Quartets*, on which he was hard at work at the time of this speech. It is clear from the generalities of his ideas on the music of poetry that Eliot was not referring to the systematic formalist approaches of many musicological or linguistic-stylistic methods of analysis, but to something more intuitive and ineffable. Well before Eliot, French symbolists, such as Rimbaud, Mallarmé, and above all Verlaine, (and later Valéry, who exercised considerable influence on Eliot's poetic development) had explored this musico-poetic correlation in their work and sought to promote rhythmic patterns to equal or even superior status as the semantic component of their poetic language.

A number of other commentaries on the interaction of music and poetry are pertinent to this discussion, and none more so than Eliot's sometime friend and associate, Ezra Pound, whose oft-quoted dictum that 'music begins to atrophy when it departs too far from the dance [. . .] poetry begins to atrophy when it gets too far from music' (Pound 2000: xii) relates closely to his belief that poetry was not so much a mode of literature but of performance art. Even more pertinent to the present discussion is his observation on poetry and song from his essay on translating Cavalcanti, entitled 'Guido's Relations': 'there is a distinction between poetic lyricism, the emotional force of the verbal movement, and melopoeic lyricism, the letting the words flow on a melodic current' – a comment referring to the song-speech renditions of Italian sonnets (Pound, 2000, 89). From Pound's coinage of the term 'melopoetics', a useful designation for his own intermedial experiments with songs and opera based on the poems of Villon and Catullus, a new field of melopoetic study as a separate branch of musicology has emerged. This has been characterized by the creative-critical work of Lawrence Kramer (himself a setter of Pound's poetry), and especially in his groundbreaking study, *Music and Poetry: The Nineteenth Century and After* (1984). In the article 'Dangerous Liaisons: The Literary Text in Musical Criticism', Kramer posits the viability of a melopoetic approach as opposed to a structuralist one:

> In contrast [to the narrative aspect] to study a composition in its lyric aspect – perhaps in relation to a lyric poem, perhaps not – is to think about conceptual and emotional rhythms [. . .] Assuming that an effective melopoetics can be practiced on something like the model suggested here, what is it good for? [. . .] The preceding paragraph already hints at one answer: the literary categories of lyric and narrative offer new and productive terms for thinking about music even in the absence of specific comparisons. The need for such innovations would seem to be clear, even urgent, as formalist models of musical criticism and analysis fall into increasing disfavour [. . .] The melopoetic methods we have been outlining are particularly useful because they evolve away from an initial separation of semantics and structure. (Kramer 1989: 165)

Another significant and more contemporary commentator on melopoetics is Richard Kurth, whose article 'Music and Poetry: A Wilderness of Doubles' discusses the 'confrontational double-encounter between music and poetry that is the *Lied*' (Kurth 1997: 7). Kurth reviews the Nietzschean refutation of the mimetic fallacy in music and explains why 'the mimetic view' is a conceptually inadequate way of perceiving the art song adaptation: 'When depiction or embodiment are involved, and perhaps even in the case of representation or symbolization, music is conceived more as a *graphic* or *plastic* medium than as an *aural* [his italics] one' (Kurth 1997: 7). Kurth's argument turns on the notion of doubling and, following Nietszche, counterfeiture, deploying the poststructuralist notion of simulacra to analyse the narrative and aesthetic double-encounter of Heine's poem (*Der Doppelgänger*) and Schubert's setting of the poem. Here the idea of the simulacrum is useful, particularly in relation to the voice or persona of narration, which expresses the words of the song setting, and is a relevant model for exploration of the narrative double world of *A Shropshire Lad*.

Before elucidating and illustrating specific arguments from the Housman settings, it is advisable to consider the authoritative opinion of a sceptical voice, constituting a rebuttal of the more positivist views summarized above. In his essay that serves as a conclusion to Denis Stevens' compendious *A History of Song*, the composer Michael Tippett dampens the ardour of those who argue for the idea of a creative symbiosis between poem and song setting:

> The moment the composer begins to create the musical verses of his song he destroys our appreciation of the poem as poetry and substitutes an appreciation of his music as song [. . .] As soon as we sing any poetry to a recognizable melody we have at that instant left the art of poetry for the art of music [. . .] I am inclined to think that a composer responds less to a poem's verbal sound when he chooses that poem as a vehicle for his dramatic art, than to the poem's situation, lyrical or dramatic. (Qtd. in Stevens 1970: 462–3)

Any attempt to synthesize these antithetical positions is likely to be extremely challenging but also meaningful for any relationships between poetry and music. We will need to consider not so much the musicality of poetry (which has long been postulated and discussed), but the musicalization of poetry in song adaptation and the poetics of song. It might be possible to find those qualities of balance and reciprocity that tend to be the properties of adaptation, as opposed to appropriation which constitutes 'a more decisive journey away from the informing source into a wholly new cultural product and domain' (Sanders 2006: 26). If Tippett's view holds, then we are talking more about appropriation and virtual effacement of the source text's ethos than we are of adaptation or of any notion of 'doubling'.

12.2.1 *A Shropshire Lad* and its sung adaptations: Housman's intellect–emotion dichotomy

Housman anticipated the arguments surrounding not only settings of his poems, but also song settings in general in his Leslie Stephen Cambridge lecture of May 1933:

> When I examine my mind and try to discern clearly in the matter, I cannot satisfy myself that there are any such things as poetical ideas [. . .] Poetry is not the thing said, but a way of saying it. Can it then be isolated and studied by itself? For the combination of a language with its intellectual content, its meaning, is as close a union as can well be imagined [. . .] Meaning is of the intellect, poetry is not. (Housman 2010: 248)

The fusion of the thing said and the way of saying it parallels the union of poetical and musical expression in the ideal song setting; not only of melodic contour approximating to prosodic contours in the written text, but also of musical accentuation, bringing out the semantic and phonetic qualities of the poetic accentuation. In declaring that in his view and his creative experience, 'poetry indeed seems to me more physical than intellectual' (Housman 2010: 254), one might mistakenly assume that Housman was in some way anticipating the more physically engaged and performative poetry of a later generation. This reference to the physical aspect of poetry, as against its ideational, intellectual elements, is famously reputed to have antagonized F. R. Leavis' followers. However, the physical experience was associated, as Housman indicated in his talk, with a genuine sickness in the pit of his stomach when attempting to purge himself of – or to use another somatic metaphor, give birth to – the poetic creation.

Housman's laudably holistic view of poetry probably reflects too a combination of resistance to the over-intellectualized literary criticism of his academic surroundings and diffidence and/or evasion regarding thematic interpretation on account of his repressed homosexuality. He had no wish to share the spotlight generated by the Oscar Wilde trial that took place a year before publication of his book of poems. Put simply, Housman didn't welcome close analysis of his texts, preferring to let them speak for themselves. This is a further reason why they lend themselves so remarkably well to song adaptation. The emotion, or attitude, and the movement is on the surface, while all else is implicit and subtextual in *A Shropshire Lad*, though the ideas are more explicitly expressed in some of his later poems. A good song setting captures this mood and emotion and clarifies rather than obscures the thoughts and ideas that preceded or accompanied the creation of the verse, in other words achieving the melopoeic felicity that Pound invoked in his Cavalcant essay.

Not only was Housman sceptical about his own poetry and its appeal to a reading public, he was slow in recognizing the value of musical treatment of his verse. However, after initially poor sales of the book and also prompted by his natural generosity, he tended to grant permission for the adaptation of his poems into songs and song cycles. Hearing that the composer had cut out two stanzas from his poem (XXVII) for his song setting adaptation, Housman asked how Vaughan Williams would like it if he had two bars cut from his music. With a pert reference to the unsuitable quality of the offending stanzas Vaughan Williams responded, asserting the right of the song setter to 'set any portion of a poem he chooses provided he does not alter the sense' (Grant Richards, qtd. in Hold 2002: 12). There is a possible explanation for the apparent illogicality of an author, who almost invariably refused permission for inclusion of his poetry to appear in anthologies or be broadcast on the radio, granting permission for musical settings.[1] While not a devotee of art songs, Housman appreciated the pastoralist movement of old English folk song collections associated with Cecil Sharp and with compositional settings by Vaughan Williams, Butterworth, Gurney, and others. Perhaps because they appeared to share his nostalgia for a simple English arcadia of the 'blue-remembered hills' variety, the part-time poet sensed kindred spirits at work. This was all the more reason to chide Vaughan Williams for his seeming and probably unanticipated 'disrespect'.

However, it should be noted that Housman had a similarly jaundiced view of book illustrators and their embellishments of the published version of *A Shropshire Lad*: 'The trouble with book illustrators, as with composers who set poems to music, is that they are wrapped up in their own art and their precious selves, and regard the author merely as a peg to hang things on' (Housman 2009: 3). His comment unintentionally but felicitously crystallizes the familiar tension between fidelity and 'originality' in adaptation discourse. Appropriators of texts, as both Sanders' and Hutcheon's studies note, can be said to be more 'wrapped up in their own art' and consequently less interested in preserving elements of the texts they have used for their own artistic ends.

Nonetheless, it is clear that *A Shropshire Lad* proved a rich source for potential adapters. One reason for its popularity with English song composers is its quality of 'Arcadian elegy', as Piers Browne has pointed out (Browne 1990), reflecting Housman's feeling for the Latin classics, but not, felicitously, the poet's own remarkable erudition on that subject. What was unprecedented and remarkably modern about the formally old-fashioned verse of the collection was its underlying and coded homoeroticism and its brooding intimation of class *ressentiment*. Most remarkable of all, the collection presciently foreshadowed the anthems of doomed youth yet to be written by a younger generation who went to the First World War with copies of Housman in their backpacks. Three composers who set Housman's poems – Ivor Gurney, E. J. Moeran, and George Butterworth – were among that number, and the last of the three didn't come back. The song settings of the early twentieth century helped to transform Housman into a war poet *avant la lettre*, one who seemed to be writing about the futility and oblivion of that 'war to end all wars', but who was in fact referring to the First Boer War (1880–81), in which his brother Herbert had been among the fallen. From the very opening poem, *1887*, ambivalence and distanced irony is discernible and is juxtaposed with the more obvious voice of elegiac melancholy and fatalism for which the collection is renowned.

The musicality of Housman's verse is in part derived from its ballad-style versification, its predilection for rhyming couplets or regular alternating rhymes, and general avoidance of enjambment and its consequently strong end-rhymes. Iambic and trochaic rhythmic patterns are effectively used – with a predilection for skilful and telling inversion and intermittent but powerful spondaic variation – with occasional deployment of anapaestic meter. Its diction is also relatively straightforward and throughout Germanic–English words are consciously preferred to words of Latin–Italic etymology. As Housman himself noted in a letter to a friend: 'its chief sources are Shakespeare's songs, the Scottish Border Ballads and Heine' (qtd. Browne 1990: 53). Certainly Heine (the wistful, elegiac tone and rhythmic pulse) is a discernible influence, but there are also remarkable echoes of Blake (the seemingly simple versification and almost mesmeric rhyme schemes). Some of the poems are arranged in quatrains or in a few cases cinquains, while others consist of a long single stanza in which the rhyme and rhythm rests on a rhyming couplet device, as in Blake (e.g., XXXVII 'As through the wild green hills of Wyre'). The musicality of the verse is also perceptible in its driving momentum contrasted with its reflective end-of-stanza cadences, in its ballad-like rhythms, and sonorities.

In 1995 all sixty-three A *Shropshire Lad* poems were issued on CD (Hyperion CDA66471/2, reissued in 2002 as CDD22044), half of them in settings by various composers, the others read. Those poems read by Alan Bates have a distinctly musical vocal quality, especially when heard together with settings by Butterworth, Ireland, and others. In Bates' beautifully modulated readings the mood and feeling are conveyed within a regular tempo and some interesting variations of pitch and timbre indicating shifts of voice from the putative poet Terence to his friends (other 'lads') and a few other 'characters'. Bates uses his wide vocal repertoire to bring out the timbre of the different unnamed characters/personae in the poems designated for speech performance. A notable feature of his delivery is in his expressive range of dynamics with fine gradations between loud to soft, a phenomenon that one associates more with the marked score of the sung adaptation than with a spoken performance. For the most part the persona is either this poem-writing lad, but other lads' voices are featured. The Butterworth setting (which according to Peter Pirie is 'a masterpiece [. . .] a *Lied* that challenges comparison with Schubert's "Der Doppelgänger"' (qtd. Butterworth 1974: n.p.)), sits well alongside Bates' multi-accented spoken performance of other poems. The latter inflects his voice evocatively, affecting a slight but effective west-country burr for some of the implied soldiers and farm lads who narrate.

This mixed-mode recording by Hyperion illustrates Roland Barthes' idea of 'the grain of the voice', which he defines thus: 'the very precise space (genre) of *the encounter between a language and a voice* [. . .] the *grain*, the grain of the voice when the latter is in a dual posture, a dual production – of language and music' (Barthes 1977: 181). One of Barthes' objectives is 'to displace the fringe of contact between music and language' (181), and this insight is most valuable in the context of the present discussion. The grains of Bates' voice and that of tenor Antony Rolfe Johnson on the Hyperion recording, as well as those of outstanding British baritones Roderick Williams and Stephen Varcoe and tenor Adrian Thompson on their recordings for Hyperion and for Naxos in the English song series, contribute to this encounter between language and voice. However, we need to assess the extent to which the song composition enhances the encounter between language and music to ascertain whether or not the song cycle adaptation 'destroys the poetry' (to invoke Tippett's dictum).

In *Sing English Song: A Practical Approach to the Language and the Repertoire,* Stephen Varcoe devotes considerable attention to the dynamics of performing songs from A *Shropshire Lad* cycles. For Varcoe 'there is a succession of 'carriers' of the message in a song: poet, poem, composer, song, performers and listener' (Varcoe 2000: 60), thus emphasizing the ideas of reciprocity, creative interfacing, and symbiosis. He encourages the would-be interpreter of poetic songs to explore all of these factors:

> Does his or her life story have a bearing on the subject of the poem? [. . .] If the poem under consideration is one of a set, how does it stand in

> relation to its companions, even if those companions have not been set to music? The composer may have been aware of all of these elements or possibly some of them, or even none at all, and it can be fascinating to try figuring out whether any of them entered his or her mind, or whether the composition was a spontaneous response to a naked set of verses. (Varcoe 2000: 61)

As Varcoe points out in his analysis of the first poem of the poignantly lyrical Butterworth cycle 'Loveliest of Trees': 'the beauty of a musical setting [. . .] is that music itself largely appeals to the irrational, feeling mind, and thus we have a musical 'explanation' of the poem in terms which complement its non-intellectual side. Our perception of the meaning is sharpened by the music' (Varcoe 2000: 64).

However, the degree to which the musical side predominates to the virtual exclusion of the semantic component of the words of the poem set depends to a large extent on the composer's understanding of and empathy with the poet's voice. The notion of musical structure takes several forms: strophic (all verses/stanzas set to the same melodic and harmonic template); strophic, with slight variations; or non-strophic (i.e., through-set with varied and developing colouration in accompaniment and vocal line). However, this is not the most important factor in adaptation: more emphasis is placed on melodic contour, vocal range, and vowel–consonant relation in the vocal line. With excessive vowel sound setting and vocal delivery the text setting tends to approximate more closely to vocalization or operatic expressivity, and the words themselves are relegated to the background of production and reception. Settings by C. W. Orr, Samuel Barber, Lennox Berkeley, and Mervyn Horder typify this target-oriented approach to poem-to-song adaptation. In addition, in their settings there is often considerable chromaticism in the melodic contours and tonality and wide-ranging note intervals in the vocal score. By contrast, Arthur Somervell's simple strophic settings and folk-melody-like vocal lines based on diatonic harmonies that are underscored by lighter piano accompaniment place considerable stress on key consonantal sounds, and hint at the verse prosody in a parallel musical prosody. The ten settings of the cycle also succeed in evoking a sense of narrative continuity, albeit an unsophisticated one.

Finally we can consider the settings that achieve a fine balance between more prosodically imitative treatments of the verse, and more interpretatively free and idiosyncratic settings. These include the sensitive and virtuosic works of Butterworth, Gurney, and Vaughan Williams. Their cycles project an approach to text transformation that respects the phonological contours of the source text, but also introduces dramatic effects and mood-enhancing devices in the musical expression in both vocal line and accompaniment. Obviously time signature values and shifts (of which there are many, especially in Butterworth) necessarily impose a different rhythmic structure, but in the case of these song cycles, as with Somervell, musical rhythm and accent permits poetic rhythm and accent to be recognizable. This is definitely not the case with the free adaptation-cum-appropriation-oriented composers, including Orr, Berkeley, and Barber, where the grain of the voice is purely musical. In the cases of the better-known setters/adapters, however, the grain of the voice, and thus the beauty of the songs, is predicated on the encounter between Housman's language, the composer's ear, and the singer's voice.

Somervell's 1904 cycle (the first Housman settings) is primarily strophic and ternary (ABA structure with melodic/harmonic variation in the second verse), and it has been highly praised for following Housman's verse prosody more closely than any other setters. As Hold points out, Somervell's verson is a true song-cycle in the Germanic *Liederkreis* tradition, with its cross-thematization between some songs (notably 'Loveliest of Trees') and his restrained musical setting, which reflects the restrained and understated tone of the poems.[2] Unlike some other setters, especially Ireland, who assign their own titles to both cycles and individual songs, Somervell employs Housman's first lines in lieu of titles. Hold refers to the surface nature of Somervell's setting style, which doesn't attempt to convey any notion of the Housman subtext: 'one would never understand from Somervell's cycle that the Lad's problem was 'the love that dare not speak its name'' (Hold 2002: 93), but his synchronic critique seems somewhat harsh.

Vaughan Williams, by contrast, in his 1909 version of six poems for tenor, piano, and string quartet takes more liberties with the setting of Housman's verse, and in the final song ('Clun') adapts Housman's text by omitting the humorous doggerel prelude. Arthur Jacobs is one critic who found his settings 'over-emotional' (qtd. in Stevens 1970: 158) and preferred Somervell's for their restraint. However, the evocative sweep of the cycle is palpable. It is this cumulative effect with songs of greatly varying length that enables the standout settings – 'On Wenlock Edge', 'Bredon Hill', and the dialogic 'Is My Team Ploughing?' – to work their magic on the listener.[3] Two pictorial effects (mimetic, one might say, despite the controversial nature of the term) enhance the grain of the language, and go some way to associating the cycle with the musical tone-poem form. They are the resourceful use of strings to create the gale in 'On Wenlock Edge', and the interplay between piano and strings in 'Bredon Hill' to evoke the ringing of church bells – not just as a single dramatic effect, but a carefully interwoven motif. All of the songs articulate the text well, but, unlike Somervell, the background music is complex and evocative, acting as a counterpoint or commentary on the sung text. The near eight-minute setting is abnormally long and points forward to the canticle-type text settings of later composers such as Britten. Given the work's important position in the present-day English song repertoire, it is surprising to find that it was the cause of a vitriolic and barely gentlemanly conflict in the columns of *The Musical Times* in 1918. One critic, Ernest Newman, a strong supporter of Butterworth and Somervell, dismissed what he saw as the work's excesses and liberties with the source texts. Respondent Edwin Evans caustically rebutted Newman and praised Vaughan Williams' transpositions for 'realising the inner qualities of the poems'. Evans perceives the link between this song cycle and a tendency to react against over-intellectualized music: 'This is a return to the natural functions of music and reassertion of its independence, which had become compromised by purely intellectual considerations [. . .] 'On Wenlock Edge' derives some of its power from a similarly [emotional/sensorial] direct appeal that, for want of a better word, one may designate as *physical*' (Evans 1918: 249, emphasis mine).

Butterworth's two cycles were published as two groups of six songs, despite being conceived as a song cycle. The simplicity and directness of the settings belie their compositional skill 'art concealing art' (Hold 2002: 241). The limpid beauty of the opening song 'Loveliest of Trees' sets the tone for what follows. The song, one of the best loved of all, begins memorably with a falling cascade of notes to evoke imprecisely, and therefore appropriately, both the cherry blossom hanging and the Lad's prescient feeling of decline and mortality.[4] The shifting tonality and key progressions of the final verse are very subtly scored, conveying a sense of restlessness.

E. J. Moeran's adaptations vary in clarity and quality, but his mature set of songs contains two of the most beautifully articulated settings of Housman. 'Oh Fair Enough Are Sky and Plain', and 'Loveliest of Trees' are both wistful; like Butterworth's songs they are a perfect fusion of text and vocal line, with an unintrusive yet subtly suggestive piano accompaniment. The mood changes in the middle verse and the piano accompaniment becomes spare and tonally indeterminate. In all of these songs the phrasing and subtle modulations of voice and music match the mood of the respective poems, marking the development of emotion and idea in the poem.[5] They are excellent paradigms of empathic and sensitive transposition, faithful to the poem's inner truth and yet at the same time to their own distinctive sound world and aesthetic.

More than any other setter Ivor Gurney understood the different rhythms of modulations of poetry and music, being both a gifted poet and a prolific songwriter. His two cycles, 'The Western Playland' (for baritone, piano, and string quartet) and 'Ludlow and Teme' (for tenor, piano, and string quartet) were both published and performed after he returned from the War, and both express the spontaneity of joy in nature, admixed with nostalgia and melancholy. Trevor Hold refers to the 'lyrical intensity and sensitivity of word-setting' (Hurd 2002: 293), of the best of the songs in either collection, and points out insightfully that Gurney is not afraid of inserting silences into the score. On reflection it is generally true to say that Housman's words are better served in 'Ludlow and Teme' than in the other cycle. Gurney's lush, evocative, and imaginative scoring for tenor, piano, and string quartet in 'Ludlow and Teme' tends to make the settings at the same time rich and also busy, but in the songs 'When Smoke Stood Up from Ludlow', 'Ludlow Fair', and 'When I Was One-and-Twenty' Housman's phrasing and sensibility are perfectly articulated.[6] By contrast in 'The Lent Lily' there is a fragile beauty that goes beyond Housman's simplicity, 'filling in the spaces between the poet's text with musical commentary' (Hold 2002: 293), which tends toward appropriation, and, as with many other songs in the two cycles, represents a very independent creation far removed from Housman's rhythmic pulse. Above all, in the slower-tempo songs he employs very melismatic word settings that accentuate and attenuate vowels to the detriment, at least in some places, of crisp consonantal clarity.[7] Gurney, like Vaughan Williams, was keen to assert his adapter's right to serve his own inspiration, but he indubitably succeeds in evoking the bucolic side as well as the more introspective aspects of the Housman texts.

John Ireland's versions in his 'The Land of Lost Content' cycle are musically accomplished, but many of them are excessively dark in terms of emotional expression of the text; it is difficult to make out the words distinctly. Melismatic treatment of the text is less of a problem than extended vowel sounds, which confer a somewhat gushing and almost sententious quality to some of the songs, if one juxtaposes them with the simplicity of the poems. A notable exception is 'Hawthorn Time', his moving adaptation of ''Tis Time I Think By Wenlock Edge', which expresses the feeling of the poem with more romantic pathos than Housman probably intended, including a repeat of the final couplet which he certainly would have hated.[8] Orr, Berkeley (who adapted later Housman poems), and Melvyn Horder all lack the directness and clarity in diction of the earlier setters of Housman; their more modern settings reflect a move away from folk-song style as the century progressed. Many of these transpositions also convey the emotional/spiritual anguish, but not, crucially, Housman's spirit of stoical endurance. Samuel Barber's setting of 'With Rue My Heart Is Laden', is different in this respect. It invests the words with heartfelt pathos juxtaposed with a winsome and sinuous melodic contour and tinged with deft chromaticism and delicately suggestive piano figures. It is without doubt a small gem of transpositional clarity, musically speaking. That said, the musical diction tends to usurp the source poem's poetic diction and eschew its prosody,[9] partly because the text is short, a perennial problem for song setters.

12.3 Conclusion

In his irascible reaction to works from other media that interpreted or adapted his poems from *A Shropshire Lad,* Housman asks the rhetorical question 'is the author merely a peg to hang things on?' (Housman 2009: 3), implying a deep mistrust of creative transformations of his texts. Given the death wish frequently expressed in the collection by various personae, including the simulacrum of a putative authorial voice, we might say somewhat flippantly that Housman prefigured the 'death of the author' conceit. Housman's diffidence toward his own creative powers and the anonymity of his personae – only their low social status and youthfulness being relevant, together with the fact that they are ascribed a voice and yet only the sketchiest of characteristics, insufficient to constitute a sense of identity – contributes to this depersonalization process. The popularity of his poems as transpositions into song cycles, and as accompaniments to coffee table books of glossy and artistic photographs of the Shropshire countryside, tends to reinforce this view.

The answer from the present study may well be: 'Yes, the poet is simply a peg to hang the new things on', but more importantly: 'No, the poems themselves are not merely pegs'. Rather, they serve as inspirational sources for adaptation (as well as appropriation) by artists who, on account of the poetry's special qualities of transferability, utilize them for a range of expressive purposes. One major target text adaptation feature is that by common understanding of succeeding generations, including that of the song setters, the context of the poems has been irrevocably transferred to World War I instead of the Boer War. Another is that lyrical delight in the evocation of 'The Western Brookland' for Vaughan Williams and Gurney came from a native love and appreciation of the West country and not out of an imaginary nostalgia for a 'land of lost content', which for Housman existed merely more as mental figment than intimate experience. Ireland's own homosexuality adds a more poignant flavour to his versions, as do Butterworth's premature demise, and Gurney's incarceration in a London mental hospital. More importantly though, the musical transposition of Housman's poems results in many of the individual songs and even whole cycles employing a vocal colouration and range that has much more to do with the English song tradition, derived from British folk music and the German *Lieder* tradition, and little to do with Housman's world.

Thus, while not conclusively agreeing with Tippett's strictures on the nature of poem-to-song transposition, we must acknowledge the intelligence of his viewpoint. Some musical settings appropriate more than simply adapt – 'substituting the music of music' for the hypotext or source text. Others, by contrast, allow the rhythm and rhyme pattern of the poem and its intrinsic speech prosody to be felt by the listener, and in contradistinction to Tippett's claim, preserve the verbal feel of the poetry in the vocal line. After his experience with earlier settings of poetry, including 'On Wenlock Edge', Vaughan Williams adopted a different approach with settings of 'Three Rondels' by Chaucer which he entitles 'Merciless Beauty': 'Instead of 'destroying' the poetic form, he matches the music with it' (Hold 2002: 117). If the song score is compared to a palimpsest, we can say that the poetry can be perceived underneath and that it is essentially the same text but reconfigured and embellished. In the case of the appropriated version the poem source has become more or less completely obscured by the rewriting.

At the same time, a distinction needs to be made between those composers like Somervell, Gurney (in his second cycle), Butterworth, and Moeran who approximate more closely to the qualities of intersemiotic translation outlined by Newmark; that is, the consonant sounds are clearly articulated and the vowels are not excessively elongated; also there is a syllabic style of musical setting of the poetry that generally predominates over more neumatic or melismatic strategies, and thus promotes the flow of meaning and rhythmic continuity. Having said that, the Gurney and Vaughan Williams settings display strong tendencies for accelerating and retarding the sung line in accordance with the dramatic atmosphere of the poem. Vocal vibrato and the predilection of both composers for assigning long note values to the last word of a given line may be seen as exemplary of Tippett's argument. But, that said, there is certainly greater reciprocity and musico-poetic integration in their settings than in those of some of the other compositions by other setters. Prosody, diction, melodic contour, vocal expressiveness – in all of these aspects of composition and performance the poem text and the song lyric are closely conjoined. The themes and ideas, as well as the juxtaposition of thought and emotion, in the source text tend to be retained, though communicated to the listener through different devices and nuanced by the different emphases of poems chosen for the respective cycles. Last, but by no means least, the sense of rhythm and versification that is to a great degree the life-pulse of Housman's poems can be perceived in many of these song adaptations. *Contra* Tippett, I would argue that the sophisticated poetically sensitive mind's ear of these composer-adapters has facilitated a genuine dialogue between source and target versions. The ideas and underlying themes of the source text poetry tend to recede into a distant subtext, as the expression of powerful lyric emotion and of dramatic mood take precedence. Melismatic word and phrase settings, extended vowel sounds, and a generally wider range of Debussy-like impressionistic effects predominate. The vocal tessitura tends to be broader in order to enhance dramatic expressivity. In consequence, source poem ideas, themes, narrative, character/persona, and attitude are all subordinate to the musical appropriation.

Contrary to Housman's own view, intellect and idea in the reception of poetry and song cannot be discounted. Perhaps the most obvious reason is that they are a vital element of the composition process, both source work and target adaptation. It is evident that existing paradigms for translation and even adaptation need to recalibrated if they are to incorporate the genre of song settings of poetic texts. One fundamental principle for such analysis is that live or recorded performance transforms the context of both the poem and the subsequent compositional setting utterly. It doesn't 'destroy' the poetics of the source text, but it does transmute that text into an emotionally and cognitively 'other' experience and expand its semiotic frame of reference. A wider application of the intersemiotic, adaptation-oriented approach to song settings, whether for accompanying piano, vocal group, chamber ensemble, or full orchestra and, crucially for different types of voices, and naturally different types of source texts, can be considered. Naturally insights can be gleaned from more formalist, musicological approaches; but from the perspective of adaptation, musicology alone is not the answer to understanding the strange alchemy of music and poetry, or to grasping the 'arch of meaning' that according to Stephen Varcoe 'stretches over a whole song, because a unified poetic and musical idea is unfolding' (Varcoe 2000: 69). Only such a unified approach to the study of song adaptation allows our mind's ear to enjoy both the ideational and the emotional content – the duality and the synthesis of the poem and its sung interpretations.

Notes

1 I am indebted to an anonymous reviewer of the present chapter, who pointed out this seeming paradox in Housman's attitude to re-presentations of his poetry, and surmised the reason for it, most plausibly I believe.

2 The subtle vocal/ piano melodies and harmonies, e.g. the bell-like chime figure in 'In summer-time on Bredon', foreground the words, but are also inventive; the syllabic setting of 'the street sounds to the soldier's tread', each note signifying one rhythmic step, are examples of Somervell's euphonious sense of prosody. The use of a single note for the first stanza of 'Into my heart an air that kills' enhances the song's effectiveness as does the subtle reprise of the lovely melody of 'Loveliest of trees'.

3 The wider melodic contours of these songs are consistent with the dramatic style and word painting of the strings and piano; 'On Bredon hill' is dramatic recitative with impressionistic soundscape; by contrast the two short interlude songs 'From far, from eve and morning' and 'oh, when I was in love with you', are pithy and simply set;

4 Butterworth's evocative ascending melody for the pastorale 'When some stood up from Ludlow' is suppressed by the darker tones that are introduced in the bird's refrain, 'What use to rise and rise', and in the last stanzas the jaunty melody fades; however the words continue to stand out; the pause before 'and that will be the best' is brilliantly poignant.

5 In No XX',Oh fair enough are sky and plain', Moeran's mellifluous melodic line in the setting of the words and exquisite *cantabile* piano serve the folk-like verses 1, 2, and 4, whilst his brief allusion in verse 3 to the cloudy, negative thoughts of the lad, contemplating drowning, provide a slightly dissonant and tonally and rhythmically alien counterpoint to the dominant melody and harmony. This mood change gives the song great character. The gentle irony of the final line as the gazer beholds his own image in the water and sees, 'a silly lad that longs and looks and wishes her were I', is enhanced by the return to the earlier wistful melody and the judicious use of *rallentando.*

6 Gurney's evocative ascending melody for the pastorale: 'When some stood up from Ludlow', is suppressed by the darker tones that are introduced in the bird's refrain, 'What use to rise and rise', and in the last stanzas the jaunty melody fades; however the words continue to stand out; the long pause before 'and that will be the best', is brilliantly poignant; the melody and driving rhythm in 'Ludlow fair', – 'there's chaps from the town and the field and the hill and the cart' (all monosyllabic utterances) are equally memorable and compelling; the lyricism of the second set of songs actually matches any of the other cycles in inventiveness, but a much of the lyricism lies in the instrumental accompaniment, rather more than the vocal lines.

[7] E.g. the attenuated phrasing of the drawn-out melodic lines of 'here I lie down in London and turn to rest alone', and 'the poplars stand and tremble by pools I used to know', in 'Far in a western brookland', and 'bear from hill and valley the daffodil away that dies on Easter day', in 'The Lent lily' efface their respective source poems' diction and rhyme scheme through the almost operatic length of vowel sounds; Gurney's long note values for many simple words in these songs enhances musical mood but detracts from the words' recognizable speech contours.

[8] The final line, 'Lie long high snowdrifts in the hedge that will not shower on me', has a plaintively nostalgic quality and in the repetition that brings the closing cadences this quality of pathos is attenuated by the use of *rallentando* in the phrasing. Housman disapproved of repetition, but the perfectly balanced musical accent and prosody justify Ireland's poetic license aesthetically, as any non-partisan hearing will attest.

[9] In 'With rue my heart is laden', the poem's iambic rhythm is brisker than the song version's slower dreamy mood; the 'leaping of lightfoot lads', is achieved by the lilting ballad rhythm of the poem, while the leaping in Barber's song is evoked by a broader diction involving longer vowel sounds and wide note intervals in a pleasantly crafted melodic line. The fading of the roses is expressed by the falling figure and fading of the piano notes, together with the haunting vocal cadence of: 'in fields where roses fade'.

Bibliography

Barthes, Roland (1977). *Image, Music, Text.* Stephen Heath, trans. London: Fontana Press.

Benjamin, Walter (1973). 'The Task of the Translator'. In *Illuminations.* Harry Zohn, trans. Hannah Arendt (ed.), 55–82. London: Fontana Press.

Browne, Piers (1990). *Elegy in Arcady – An Artist's View of Housman's Poetry.* 2nd edn. Southampton; Ashford.

Butterworth, George (1974). *A Shropshire Lad and Other Songs.* London: Stainer & Bell.

Eliot, T. S. (1957). 'The Music of Poetry'. In *On Poetry and Poets.* London: Faber & Faber: 28–42.

Evans, Edwin (1918). 'English Song and 'On Wenlock Edge'.' *The Musical Times* 59(904): 247–49.

Hold, Trevor (2002). *Parry to Finzi: Twenty English Song Composers.* Woodbridge, Suffolk: Boydell Press.

Housman, A. E. (2010). *A Shropshire Lad.* Archie Burnett (ed.), Rev. edn. Harmondsworth: Penguin Books.

Housman, A. E. (2009). *A Shropshire Lad with Photographs.* London: Merlin-Unwin Books.

Hutcheon, Linda (2006). *A Theory of Adaptation.* New York and London: Routledge.

Kramer, Lawrence (1989). 'Dangerous Liaisons: The Literary Text in Music Criticism'. *Nineteenth Century Music* 13(2): 159–67.

Kurth, Richard (1997). 'Music and Poetry: A Wilderness of Doubles'. *Nineteenth Century Music* 21(1): 3–37.

Newmark, Peter (2006). 'Serious Songs: Their Texts as Approximate Translations of their Music'. *Translation Quarterly* 41: 1–9.

Pound, Ezra (2000). 'Guido's Relations'. In *The Translation Studies Reader.* Lawrence Venuti (ed.), 2nd edn, 81–93. London and New York: Routledge.

Pound, Ezra (1960). *ABC of Reading.* New York: New Directions (orig. edn. 1934).

Prawer, S. S. (1964). *The Penguin Book of Lieder.* Harmondsworth: Penguin Reference Books.

Sanders, Julie (2006). *Adaptation and Appropriation.* London and New York: Routledge.

Stevens, Denis (ed.) (1970). *A History of Song.* Rev. edn. New York: W. W. Norton & Co.

Varcoe, Stephen (2000). *Sing English Song: A Practical Approach to the Language and the Repertoire.* London: Thames Publishing.

Venuti, Lawrence (2007). 'Adaptation, Translation, Critique'. *Journal of Visual Culture* 6(1): 25–43.

Wolf, Werner (1999). *A Study in the Theory and History of Intermediality.* Amsterdam: Rodopi.

Chapter 13

Cultural Adaptation and Translation: Some Thoughts about Chinese Students Studying in a British University

Ruth Cherrington

13.1 Introduction

When considering adaptation and translation, the focus is often on the role of the paid professional whose job it is to reproduce a text not only into another language but possibly into another textual form such as from literature to film. But most translations and adaptations are carried out by non-professionals; those who visit, or live, work, or study in another country or another culture. They may even be in their own country, but work for a foreign multinational, an increasingly common experience in the era of globalization.

In terms of analysis, we see simultaneous complex and challenging processes, part conscious, part unconscious, at work. This is certainly the case with overseas students studying anywhere in the world; not just in Britain. This chapter focuses on Chinese students studying at a British university, as an illustrative case study of wider issues and questions about what will be termed here *self-adaptation* and *self-translation.* By *self-adaptation* I refer to what might be described as an acclimatizing process; *self-translation*, on the other hand, describes how students might cope with that process. It is hoped that this short discussion-piece might provoke more in-depth comparative studies from different academic contexts. Students from China coming to live in another country face their own challenges in the process of self-adaptation and self-translation. What they may learn about the formal aspects of translation (involving source and target texts) in the classroom might be of limited use outside of it, just as the textbook English they learned in China may be too formal to help them when talking with university cleaning staff, canteen assistants, and other students in the foreign academic context. They will have to adapt what they have previously learned to different linguistic and cultural situations. This short discussion is very much a think-piece, including proposals for widening our understanding of 'adaptation' and 'translation' from purely formalistic concerns to encompass individual experiences of day-to-day existence. I base my ideas on many years of teaching Chinese students in Great Britain as well as in China, as well as teaching students of other nationalities elsewhere in the world. I intend to highlight some neglected areas – notably the difficulties, emotional as well as academic, faced by students while adapting to the new realities abroad that might be at odds with those they are more accustomed to in their native cultures.

13.2 Some Conceptual Background

It has long been recognized that possessing an extensive vocabulary and understanding the grammar of a foreign language are not enough to be able to survive in another language and culture. The concept of communicative competence, formulated in the early 1970s (Hymes 1971) was meant to bridge that gap, to go beyond grammar and to include the socio-linguistic appropriateness of utterances. However, experience has shown that the processes of self-adaptation and self-translation go far beyond the socio-linguistic sphere. Educators have not only to consider their students' capabilities, they have to evaluate the appropriateness of different educational resources and materials, as well as determine their classroom pedagogy. Such issues are frequently discussed with regard to the students and the desired outcomes in terms of their attitudes and abilities. In a document published by the Council of Europe in 1995, it was recommended that 'great importance [should be attached] to helping young people in its member countries to understand and respect other peoples' ways of thinking and acting, based on other beliefs and traditions' (Byram and Zarate 1995: 5). Exactly how that process of understanding should take place is left unexplained. I propose that non-native speakers have to undergo a process of *self-adaptation*, in which they try to adapt their existing cultural knowledge to the realities of living in another culture; and subsequently performing *self-translation* – in other words, learning how to respect other people's beliefs and traditions by drawing on the knowledge gained from the process of self-adaptation. Byram and Kramsch (1993, 1997) have highlighted the complexities of this process in their beliefs that teaching language also means teaching cultures. Kramsch wrote that: 'an intercultural approach to the teaching of culture is radically different from a transfer of information between cultures. It includes a reflection both on the target and on the native culture' (1993: 205). Through a process of self-translation and self-adaptation, the students can create their own personal realms of interculturality, enabling them to move between source and target cultures. To negotiate the processes of self-adaptation and self-translation, students need to reflect critically on where they come from, and how that knowledge can be used to make sense of the target culture. Without such self-reflexivity, the intercultural ideal is probably doomed.

13.3 Self-Adaptation and Self-Translation

Foreign students do not just 'translate' the texts on their academic curricula: they have to adapt and translate everyday encounters and activities as well. This means not only drawing upon language and translation skills, but also upon social, political, and, indeed, psychological resources in order to make sense of specific phenomena. Adapting to a target culture not only involves getting used to different ways of doing things, but also involves the continual adaptation to what students see and hear around them in terms of their own cultural perspective, in order to make sense of what is going on in a way. The subsequent process of self-translation is used to ensure that the experience of the target culture doesn't threaten or overwhelm their understanding of their own cultural identity. Depending on the distance between their home, or source culture (HC), and their lived-in, or target culture (LiC), there will be greater or lesser degrees of challenge involved.

We can view this as a process of filtering information and experiences, as well as language, for self-adaptation and self-translation. They will have to 'read' and make sense of what they are experiencing in terms of their own experience. This *process* is continual and the desired aim is to produce a liminal space where they can move between their own culture and the target culture, not only in terms of linguistic performance, but also of cultural understanding – Kramsch's so called 'third space.' When starting out on their life in Britain, problems can be posed, not only for Chinese students themselves, but also for those interacting with them, such as their educators. Such problems are not just linguistic but cultural as well. On this view, perhaps those members of the target culture who encounter Chinese students have to undergo their own processes of self-translation and self-adaptation, so as to promote cultural understanding. We are all living texts, who have to translate and adapt ourselves to shifting realities. To achieve this, both the Chinese students and those around them adopt numerous strategies that can have both positive and negative outcomes.

13.4 The Strategies

At one end of this scale would be the strategy of *minimum contact* and interaction with the target culture, choosing to spend instead as much time as possible with members of one's own culture or language group. While complete withdrawal is impossible, contact is sporadic enough so that the experience of living in the target culture does not call into question the Chinese students' existing beliefs and thought processes. This strategy entails little effort in terms of self-adaptation and self-translation: students seldom question their own sense of self-identity, as their contact with the target culture is largely restricted to enduring lectures, writing assignments, or attending formal social events such as departmental gatherings or graduation ceremonies.

I use the verb 'endure' deliberately here because for some students the tasks of self-adaptation and self-translation can seem very trying, almost painful. They look forward to returning home in the holidays, not having to speak in English and attempting to engage with the target culture. Not all students based in Great Britain are attending university out of personal desire or ambition: some are simply fulfilling the wishes and ambitions of their parents, which they feel duty-bound to respect. They may understand the advantages of obtaining a degree from a British university, but the obstacles that have to be overcome to reach that goal are sometimes quite considerable.

At the other extreme is a strategy of *immersion*, a process of self-adaptation and self-translation that involves breaking free from one's Chinese peers, and interacting as much as possible with the target culture (the educational environment, local people.) Students pursuing this option might take up voluntary work organized by the university in order to become more involved in the local community, while rejecting aspects of their source culture by adopting the target culture's fashions, hair styles, or languages. This can be considered a form of rebellion linked to youth culture, but it indicates a preference for the target above the source culture. The danger of this process of self-adaptation and self-translation is that students might become alienated from their peers, as well as upsetting parents and families back home by appearing 'too Western.' More significantly, it might prompt the students to question the value of whether they should return to their home culture once their degree course has concluded. There are various points between these two extremes occupied by the majority of Chinese students. Perhaps the members of the target culture – students, educators, and other people involved in the life of a university – need to do more in terms of their own personal self-adaptation and self-translation; in other words, understanding the process of filtering that occurs, as Chinese (or other students not from the home culture) try to determine how to adapt and translate to the foreign culture, and thereby learn how to survive and succeed in an environment different from their own.

13.5 Some Consequences and Illustrative Examples

It is said that the past is another country, but for some Chinese students it takes coming to another country such as Great Britain to understand more about their own cultures. This might not be an easy process, but can prove rather disturbing, as they understand through self-adaptation and self-translation that there are multiple histories and multiple ways of representing countries, cultures, and peoples. When I taught in China in the 1980s, the country was only just beginning to open up to the outside world and change was tentative, uncertain, and ambiguous. The younger generation of students then was dealing with the contradictory aspects of the 'reform and open door policy' – *gaige kaifang*. I termed them 'Deng's Generation' after the then leader, Deng Xiaoping (Cherrington 1997a and 1997b).

The 'noughties' generation of Chinese students I taught in Britain grew up only knowing reform and was familiar with Western phenomena. They took for granted many things that their counterparts in the 1980s would have only dreamed about, and many of which were off-limits, still considered too 'bourgeois' by many families, such as dancing, listening to pop music, and shopping (Cherrington 1991). Some things, however, have not altered so much as China's urban landscapes and skylines, with some issues persisting – especially in the sphere of politics such as censorship, human rights, and attempts to control the media. As I was teaching cultural and media studies in Great Britain, such issues presented problems for students attempting to adapt and translate in the target culture. These were always students who would come into my office to discuss not only their essay plans and reading, but the wider cultural challenges they were facing. Sometimes their anxiety was very tangible and it was not unusual to have tears shed.

They were preoccupied with political issues and the consequences for them if they began to question more deeply not only what the British government was doing both at home and abroad, but what their own government were doing back home. They faced the hitherto unforeseen problem of questioning the truths, values, and ideologies that had formed such a significant part of their education in the source culture. They were asked to critically analyse texts – not only written texts but people, spaces, and other aspects of daily life – that exposed them to more than one version of 'the truth.' They had unprecedented access to information, different viewpoints, and a variety of cross-cultural experiences, which could sometimes seem overwhelming, and hence impede the process of self-adaptation and self-translation. This might not have been the case in their home cultures: whereas in contemporary China, there is much more freedom of the media than previously existed, there are still attempts to control the Internet with varying degrees of success and failure (Cherrington 2008).

One student told me: 'Here [in Britain] I can access websites that I am not allowed to in China. I can read different accounts [. . .] I feel confused, upset [. . .] My parents warn me, tell me not to believe lies, but it's not that [. . .] it's a way of thinking.' She was upset and unsure how to deal with the experience of self-adaptation and self-translation in the target culture. For those who tried to deal with this issue through the immersion strategy, they were often prompted to question what they were brought up to believe, as they came to understand how cultures constructed different phenomena in different ways. This proved equally traumatic.

For those who veered more to the minimum contact strategy, there was less cognitive dissonance perhaps, but they were faced with the prospect of failing academically, as they found it difficult to adapt and translate to the processes of critical analysis and weigh up different points of view that are part and parcel of a British academic education. I could sometimes see the look on anxious faces, the desire in their eyes for the 'right' answer, the one correct way of thinking that would get them the good marks they and their parents wanted. When told there was no one 'correct' way, they looked downhearted and perplexed. These were not just educational issues, though they are part of it: there were political and psychological layers involved. What were they to do? And what was I as an educator meant to do when they became anxious about what they were learning and how they were learning? Having a sympathetic approach and an open mind went a long way, but I still felt inadequate because I knew that many students would return home after their course and have to undergo another painful experience of self-adaptation and self-translation.

This issue is one that should preoccupy anyone involved in teaching students from other cultures; by encouraging them to open their minds, we might simultaneously prompt confusion and even fear of the consequences of thinking in different ways. Some students didn't go home; they preferred to stay in the target culture and try and look for further opportunities. Others returned to their home culture with low grades. Sometimes these grades were not simply due to low academic standards; some students found it so difficult to become involved in the processes of self-adaptation and self-translation that it affected their performance both inside and outside the classroom.

While this chapter has focused specifically on Chinese students in Britain, the ideas it raises apply to educational experiences in any cultural context. Those faced with the ordeal of adapting and translating the experiences of a target culture can often feel intimidated or insecure – especially when they are prompted to question the values, attitudes, and belief of their home culture. To overcome this difficulty, everyone in the home culture who encounters these students – educators, support staff members, and other students – needs to participate in the same processes of self-adaptation and self-translation. Only through a process of acquiring *mutual* understanding can that 'third space' be established. More importantly, what this chapter has tried to suggest is that both 'adaptation' and 'translation' are not just formal processes – involving the transformation of texts – but experiences encountered by everyone as they try to adjust to different cultural mores.

Bibliography

Byram, Michael, Morgan, Carol et al. (1994). *Teaching and Learning Language and Culture*, Clevedon: Multilingual Matters.

—, and Zarate, Genevieve (1995). *Young People Facing Difference: Some Proposals for Teachers*. Strasbourg: Council of Europe Publishing.

Cherrington, Ruth (1991). *China's Students: The Struggle for Democracy*. London: Routledge.

— (1997a). *Deng's Generation: Young Intellectuals in 1980s China*. Basingstoke: Macmillan Publishing.

— (1997b). 'Generational Issues in China: A Case Study of the 1980s Generation of Young Intellectuals.' *British Journal of Sociology* 48 (2): 302–20.

— (2008). 'The Internet in China: A Liberating Force?' Review of *Chinese Cyberspaces: Technological Changes and Political Effects*. Jens Damm and Simona Thomas (eds) (2006). *International Institute for Asian Scholars (IIAS) Newsletter* 48 (Summer): 36.

Hymes, Dell. (1971) *On Communicative Competence.* New York: Harper & Row.

Kramsch, Claire (1993). *Context and Culture in Language Teaching.* Oxford: Oxford University Press.

Kramsch, Claire (1997). 'The Cultural Component of Language Teaching.' *British Studies Now,* 8: 4–7.

Index

adaptation,
  definitions 22–6, 62–3, 97, 146, 163
  novel into film 126–41, 162–70
  novels 67–78
  poetry 188–209
  theatre 45–51, 81–98, 100–9, 170–85
advertising 21–41
Atatürk, Mustafa Kemal 6

Bachman-Medick, Doris 56–7
Barnstone, Willis 9
Barthes, Roland 199
Bassnett, Susan 1–2, 14, 42, 50, 55
Bates, Alan 198–9
Bazin, André 147–9, 151–2
Belinky, Tatiana 66–9
Benjamin, Walter viii, 47
Blake, William 191
Bresson, Robert 148–9
bricolage 84–7
Brisset, Annie 113–15, 118
Butterworth, George 199–200, 202, 205
Byrne, Gráinne 179–84

Charron, Marc 26–7
Chesterman, Andrew 23, 39, 99–100, 108
Chong, Ping 81–98

De Laclos, Choderlos 162–70
Delabastita, Dirk 12–14
Delisle, Jean 22, 26

Eliot, T. S. 193
Even-Zohar, Itamar 63–5

fidelity 8–9, 51, 66–7, 77–8, 147, 153–5, 159
Folman, Ari 123–41
Frears, Stephen 162–3, 166–7
Freud, Sigmund 3, 8–11, 13, 123–6, 128–30, 137–41

Gambier, Yves 23–6
Garneau, Michel 5, 16, 112, 114–19
Genette, Gérard 22–3
Gentzler, Edwin 2
Gurney, Ivor 197, 202–3, 205

Hampton, Christopher 4, 46, 162
Hartmann, Heinz 10–11
Hermans, Theo 12, 37–8, 43–4, 47, 63–4
Hong, Zhang Qi 102–9
Housman, A. E. 188–209
Hutcheon, Linda 1, 49, 55–6, 99, 123, 190–1, 197

Ibsen, Henrik 145–59
interdisciplinarity 12–14, 42–3, 210–16
intermediality 188–91
intersections 87–90
intertextuality 96–7, 182–3, 188–90

Jakobson, Roman 17, 123–4, 127–8, 139–40

Kramsch, Claire 211–12
Kurth, Richard 194–5

LaCapra, Dominick 126–7
Lefevere, André 2, 7, 14, 30, 42, 50, 56
Leitch, Thomas 6, 13–14, 42, 146–7, 159
Lepage, Robert 16, 112–13, 115, 119
Lévi-Strauss, Claude 82, 84
localisation 27–8

Milton, John 2–3, 7, 45, 99–100, 109, 163

music 188–209

Newmark, Peter 191–3, 205
Nord, Christiane 26, 38, 63, 68, 78

Oittenen, Rita 43–4, 47–8, 70
O'Reilly, Kaite 46–7
O'Thomas, Mark 1

Pelletier, Lucien 116–18
Piaget, Jean 3, 9–14
Piñera, Virgilio 170–85
Pound, Ezra 194
Pym, Anthony 28

Reiss, Katharina 62–3
Riordan, Tim 13

Salter, Denis 5, 112–13, 114–16
Sanders, Julie 22–3, 35, 44–5, 47–8, 49, 55–6, 58–9, 99, 189, 195, 197
Shakespeare, William 6, 14, 16, 20, 100–9, 110, 111, 112–13, 115, 120–2, 147, 198
  The Merchant of Venice 101–9
Shropshire Lad, A 190–1, 195, 196–207
Sjöström, Victor 145–59
Snell-Hornby, Mary 64
Somervell, Arthur 200–1
Stam, Robert 1, 11, 42, 54–5, 58–9, 108, 154

Tippett, Michael 195, 205–6
Toury, Gideon 8, 63–5, 127
tradaptation 5, 16, 18, 112–20, 189
translation,
  causal model 99–103
  definitions 44–5, 57–8, 62, 97, 146, 158–9
  documentary 68
  novels 67–78
  theatre 45–51, 81–98, 100–9, 170–85
Turkish Republic 3–8, 11–12
Tymoczko, Maria 3–5, 56

Van Gorp, Hendrik 1–2
Varcoe, Stephen 199–200, 206
Vaughan Williams, Ralph 190, 197, 200, 201–2, 203, 205
Venuti, Lawrence 1–2, 21, 43, 45, 51, 56, 99–100, 108, 127, 188–9
Vermeer, Hans 26, 38, 41, 62–3